"*Beyond Crisis* is the new bible for managers wanting to make sense of the changing force fields within and without our organizations."
Bill Liao, Co-Founder of XING.com and Founder of WeForest.com

"In *Beyond Crisis,* Gill Ringland, Oliver Sparrow and Patricia Lustig have given us a simple and powerful look at the kind of organizations that will thrive in the 'new normal'."
Chris Worley, Center for Effective Organizations, Pepperdine University

"A real wake up call. The real world and the financial world are in flux. Organisations and their managements must be self-renewing, alert, adaptable and ready to prosper in the new circumstances and uncertainties."
John Grout, Policy and Technical Director, The Association of Corporate Treasurers

"If you want to know how countries, companies and individuals can master the winds and the waves that will dominate the next decade, this is the book for you."
Rupert Pennant-Rea, former editor of the Economist, Deputy Governor of the Bank of England

"If leading your organisation sometimes feels like changing the front wheel of a bicycle whilst you are still pedalling it as fast as you can, this is a book you should read."
Sir David Brown, former Chairman, Motorola UK

"Beyond Crisis is full of compelling reasons, clear advice and practical models to help almost any enterprise remain viable beyond the deeply unsettling systemic failures that characterise today's business environment."
Professor Richard David Hames, Dhurakij Pundit University, Founding Director Asian Foresight Institute

"We are in uncharted territory. There are few people who any longer think that the world post-crisis will be anything like the world before. Ringland, Sparrow and Lustig provide a clear description of the way that leaders need to think in this new reality. In doing so, they give us hope."
Estelle Clark, Business Assurance Director, Lloyd's Register

"This book really gets to the heart of how to turn crises to your advantage. In this next decade organisations must face and overcome new challenges and if you read this book then you will see a clear path to take to emerge as a winner."
Peter Blampied, Country Manager, Navigon AG

"The authors' deep and broad experience is transformed into essential material for companies wishing to face today's challenges of volatility, unpredictability, complexity and accelerating change. Here is a book which every leader must not only read, but also buy for everyone on the management team."
Prabhu Guptara, Distinguished Professor of Global Business, Management and Public Policy, William Carey University, India, and Executive Director, Organisation Development, Wolfsberg, Switzerland

Beyond Crisis

Beyond Crisis

Achieving Renewal in a Turbulent World

Gill Ringland, Patricia Lustig and Oliver Sparrow

A John Wiley & Sons, Ltd., Publication

This edition first published in 2010
Copyright © 2010 John Wiley & Sons

Registered office
John Wiley & Sons Ltd, The Atrium, Southern Gate, Chichester, West Sussex,
PO19 8SQ, United Kingdom

For details of our global editorial offices, for customer services and for information
about how to apply for permission to reuse the copyright material in this book please
see our website at www.wiley.com

Library of Congress Cataloging-in-Publication Data

Ringland, Gill.
    Beyond crisis : achieving renewal in a turbulent world / Gill Ringland, Patricia
Lustig and Oliver Sparrow.
        p. cm.
    Includes bibliographical references.
    ISBN 978-0-470-68577-8
    1. Financial crises–United States.   2. Finance–Government policy–United
States.   3. Bank failures–United States.   4. Intervention (Federal government)–
United States.   I. Lustig, Patricia.   II. Sparrow, Oliver.   III. Title.
    HB3722.R56   2010
    658.4'01–dc22
                                                                            2009054376

A catalogue record for this book is available from the British Library.

Typeset in 10.5/15 Monotype Janson by Toppan Best-set Premedia Limited
Printed in Great Britain by TJ International Ltd, Padstow, Cornwall

Contents

Preface   xiii

Acknowledgements   xvii

Introduction   1

Part I   What Happened?   13

Chapter 1:   A Short History of the Crisis   15
               The roots of the financial crisis   15
               The role of the financial sector   18
               Personal, corporate and government debt   23
               Executive Summary   28

Chapter 2:   The New Operating Environment   29
               Demographics   29
               Economic development and social interactions   32
               Communications, science and technology   39
               Resource and other systemic challenges   40
               Executive Summary   42

Chapter 3:   What Lies Ahead?   43
               The short term   43
               The medium term   45

Longer-term scenarios   51
Executive Summary   57

Part II   What Organisations Can Do   59

Chapter 4:   Organisational Design   61

Aligned to the previous environment   61
Dealing with the next decades   67
Successful organisations in very
   challenging environments   69
Executive Summary   74

Chapter 5:   Renewal   77

Measuring renewal   77
Firms' self-perceived weaknesses   80
Hurdles to innovation   82
Foxes and Hedgehogs: their roles in renewal   86
The double-cone: a framework for Foxes
   and Hedgehogs   90
Executive Summary   93

Chapter 6:   The Importance of Purpose   95

Clarity of purpose   95
Senior management and the Board   96
Leadership   98
Competence   101
Setting a purpose   103
Executive Summary   106

Chapter 7:   Five Qualities for Renewal   107

The journey and destination   107
Values   108

	Narrative	111
	Insight	115
	Generating Options	117
	Machinery	119
	Executive Summary	121
Chapter 8:	The Structure of Renewal	123
	Organisational change	123
	The Three Ring Circus	124
	Linking the Three Ring Circus	128
	Executive Summary	132
Chapter 9:	Managing Renewal	133
	Getting going	133
	Evolution of a PS-RO	137
	Managing a PS-RO system	139
	What about the workers?	141
	The diagnostic tool	144
	Executive Summary	145
Part III	A Toolkit for Purposeful Renewal	147
Chapter 10:	Values	149
	Core Values	150
	The origins of Values	155
	Aligning your Values with a PS-RO	157
	Unlocking extraordinary competence	162
	Measuring behaviours	166
	Legacy	173
	Executive Summary	173
Chapter 11:	Insight	175
	Scenarios as a source of Insight	176

Relationship of Insight to the other
   PS-RO qualities   177
Methods for developing Insight   178
Horizon scanning   179
Forecasting as part of Insight   182
The scenario process   186
Describing the organisation   190
Audit of exposure to risks   193
Practical aspects of gathering Insight   202
Quantifying scenarios   208
Insight and the Three Ring Circus   209
Executive Summary   212

Chapter 12: Generating Options   213

   The Options journey   215
Innovation   218
Changing the portfolio   228
Executive Summary   235

Chapter 13: Narrative   237

   What is a Narrative?   239
The individual Narrative   245
The organisational Narrative   249
Developing organisational Narrative   255
Executive Summary   261

Chapter 14: Machinery   263

   Renewal   264
The formal planning system:
   the role of the Three Ring Circus   265
Five interlocking parts in the Machinery   273
The '95' organisation   287
The '99' organisation   289

	Groups	292
	Executive Summary	298
Conclusion:	A Purposeful Self-Renewing Organisation	299
Endnotes		305
Index		317

Preface: Why You Should Read this Book

It is a universally acknowledged fact that the financial crisis of 2006–2009 highlighted massive faults in the banking and credit systems and precipitated a rapid slide into panic and a grudging bailing out at governmental level. In the ensuing months many political and economic experts voiced different views of why the monetary systems went wrong, and how they may be better arranged in the future. Some observers have taken the discussion further and looked at the implications for major organisations from the position of the bottom line.

But we believe the days when you could expect 'Business as Usual' are gone for good; organisations must now adapt and change or they will fail. They have become toxic; people, at all levels, are unsure about what to do, what the rules are, what's expected of them and of the organisation. Staff have become increasingly risk averse and lack confidence. We have devised the antidote to toxic organisations, and have designed a blueprint for success in the twenty-first century.

What's our authority to do this? Why listen to us?

Between us we have over 100 years of experience working as senior managers in multinationals, and as consultants to major corporates, governmental departments and third-sector organisations. Our expertise, in common with our colleagues in SAMI Consulting, is futures, strategy planning, organisational change and development; we work constantly with uncertainty. That said, we are pragmatic – we want to know what works and why. We've worked with hundreds of organisations across the world, enabling them, by applying aspects of what is now included in this book, to become more effective and successful. You will see that we use many examples and case studies; most of them come from our direct experience.

There's no question that, in order to change successfully, you need to be clear where you have come from and why. For some time now, we have been analysing what has been happening in organisations over the last decades. The financial crash of 2006–2009 provided the spur for us to co-ordinate our analysis and our thinking, and formalise our ideas for a successful twenty-first-century organisation.

In this book we lay out the hugely complicated situation which is the current operating environment for many organisations and make sense of it. We help you to recognise not only the patterns which are now emerging globally, but also your place – and your organisation's place – within them.

We have identified what the organisation of the future needs to be like. We believe organisations will need to follow the Darwinian imperative and evolve. We've called this evolving organisation the Purposeful Self-Renewing Organisation or PS-RO.

It is a relatively simple remedy; but it requires senior managers to accept that they will need to continually take stock of the environment in which they find themselves and adapt and respond to what they find; they will need to be continually renewing. This evolution will require them to identify and adapt their best 'genes': procedures, processes, thinking, innovation and creativity. They will also need to reject 'bad' genes. The good news is that it is not costly to build a Purposeful, Self-Renewing Organisation. However, it does take time to analyse what is needed, and it takes a different style of leadership to make use of the structure that results from this. It requires training, chiefly for doing tasks which nobody undertook before.

In this book we demonstrate HOW the future organisation will work and WHY this will be successful. We hasten to add that we recognise every organisation is different and that there is no one-size-fits-all solution. But we do know that to be successful, a PS-RO will need to have five qualities: Values, Insight, Options, Narrative and Machinery. To that end, we supply a toolkit which provides you with the necessary tools to create your own PS-RO.

We believe that the future need not be overwhelmingly daunting; 'getting the job done' can be challenging, stimulating, inspiring, rewarding and enjoyable. PS-RO staff are respected and responsible, informed and insightful, exhibiting qualities of confidence and leadership that lead to long-term success – and, crucially, profitability.

Finally, to create your own PS-RO we do not ask you to establish planning groups or other cost centres because we believe that the wisdom of the organisation must be tapped directly. What are needed are long, purposeful conversations, backed by insight into which everyone with something to say has their voice. Then you will see renewal: establishing clarity, hunting out useful ideas and capabilities, creating options for the future and exploiting new abilities for the present. As you can see, this goes beyond traditional strategic planning; what we envision is the desire – and the will – to create an environment which encourages and enables a whole organisation to take charge of its destiny.

We hope that you enjoy reading *Beyond Crisis*.

Patricia Lustig   patricia.lustig@samiconsulting.co.uk

Gill Ringland   gill.ringland@samiconsulting.co.uk

Oliver Sparrow oliver.sparrow@samiconsulting.co.uk

Acknowledgements

First we have to thank our families for putting up with the gestation of this book, as we neglected them and most other things during various stages of writing and as a final disruption moved editorial meetings around our houses.

The ideas in this book have, as the Preface makes clear, been developed over a number of years. This has involved discussion with a number of SAMI colleagues: Mike Atack, Andrew Black, Adrian Davies, Cathy Dunn, Colin Fletcher, Ilaria Frau-Hipps, Jane Langford, Lynda McGill, Michael Owen, David Pearce, Andreas Priestland, Nic Pulford, John Reynolds, Gordon Ringland, Richard Walsh and Molly van der Weij.

We were encouraged as we developed the ideas into a book by comments and positive encouragement from many people – Sir David Brown, Jeremy Brown, Estelle Clark, Louis Cooper, Miles Cowdry, John Grout, Prabhu Guptara, Richard David Hames, Gwyn Jones, Bruce Lloyd, Laura Mazur, Martin O'Donovan, Bernado Sichel, Martin Thomas and Chris Worley. Some of these have kindly let their names and comments be used on the cover.

Nic Pulford provided technical support as we wrestled with the text, endnotes and figures, and Lynda McGill provided a logical brain, a sounding board and editing skills to vastly improve the manuscript. Oliver Sparrow produced the figures from the amateurish input of his co-authors.

Ellen Hallsworth at John Wiley provided guidance on early versions of the book and provided skilful editorial advice throughout, and Nick Mannion of John Wiley patiently iterated with us to arrive at the cover you see today.

Introduction

The uncertainty of the future offers us some near-certainties. Life in large organisations will become ever more complex, time and resource constrained. Competition will be more intense, and scrutiny will be unrelenting. At the same time, the world has seen a financial crisis and faces ongoing changes in the world balance and global systemic challenges. We seem to have reached a number of tipping points. How can organisations thrive in this environment?

This book provides a clear and coherent model for senior managers to use in responding to these challenges.

If you're reading this book, you're likely to know about strategy and to have a track record of success within established organisations. Recently, however, you may have begun to feel that the tools and systems that used to work are inadequate to the challenge of the world that is unfolding. These same structural issues confront state, private sector and non-profit organisations in equal measure.

How will the world be different over the next decades?

The last decades have had some disruptive events – the stock market crash of 1987, the Asian collapse of 1997, the dot.com boom and bust. However, consistent growth and low interest rates provided a benign umbrella. The industrial countries showed steady growth and low inflation, commodity and wage costs remained stable and the populous countries of Asia were content to grow rapidly whilst taking in the low-skilled work of the wealthy world. Energy price inflation and concerns about environmental and security issues, food price increases and related trends suggested that all was not well with this model before the financial crisis. Central bankers appeared to have inflation in hand, but their expansionist policies allowed exceptional levels of debt to develop. The resulting housing and share price boom led to an unsustainable expansion of consumer debt. This, together with the monetary slackening after the dot.com collapse, was one deep root from which the financial crisis grew.

The collapse of a short-term bubble – banking – has revealed the far larger bubble that needs to be pricked: debt. This will take time to purge from the system. So, the financial crisis which started with sub-prime mortgages in 2006 has revealed something very different beneath that tranquil surface of the last two decades.

The world ahead of us will be very different. It will be fast-moving and innately challenging. Demographic change and education mean a shift in the patterns of labour skill and cost. The ageing industrial nations – and China – are not well placed as their workforce ages and retires. Further, skills that were once restricted to the industrialised nations are now widely available, further enhancing the shift in international competitiveness towards new entrants. Much the same can be said for technology, which continues its relentless expansion in depth and range. The debt burden of the wealthy nations means that their recovery from the crisis will be slower than the new competitor nations. Competition will be intense, and on new terms. Global systems issues – such as environmental change, but also international law and finance, access to raw materials and the management of intellectual property – all require the rich nations to sacrifice some of their power. This combination of power rebalancing and an institutional vacuum implies that the next decade will be a turbulent one.

To make sense of the emerging world order, we have developed some frameworks for thinking about the short, medium and long term. The short term is, essentially, concerned with the way out of the financial overhang, debt and unemployment situation in the West. The medium term depends on how the wealthy world comes to terms with the new economic and political conditions, with new competitors. The longer term is constrained by the events to date and in the short and medium term, and by the capability of the world to tackle global systemic challenges.

This leads us to develop three scenarios which fundamentally inform our thinking in this book: a *Low Road* scenario, in which the crisis extends beyond the financial sector, unemployment remains high and growth low; a *My Road* scenario, in which, while the industrialised countries continue to suffer, the billion new consumers in the cities in Asia, Africa and Latin America create a new style; a *High Road* scenario, in which the international mechanisms that have been successful in gaining emergence from the financial crisis are quickly able to develop, to start to tackle some of the global systemic challenges, in some places.

In all three scenarios, the next decade will be turbulent for the economies and organisations of industrialised countries.

Organisations in a challenging world

Economies are not, of course, much concerned with individual organisations. Markets are supposed to allocate assets to flow from mature or dying organisations to labour and capital markets where they can be allocated to new activities that require them. Though the mechanisms for this are often sticky, especially inside organisations, the key question for organisations in the industrialised countries is: how can we avoid becoming mature and, eventually, dying?

Meanwhile, many large organisations have been managed with a common set of management systems and tools: the orthodoxy was everything that could be delegated beyond the bounds of an organisation should be; and what remained when this was complete should focus on uniformity, predictability and reducing costs. At best, this leads to optimisation around what used to be appropriate. At worst, organisations lose the ability to renew themselves. Today's world requires combining the ability to operate under a regime of increasing competition, with the ability to adapt quickly.

The use of a common set of tools and technologies has made organisations increasingly similar, intensifying competition. Product life cycles have accelerated. Profits are squeezed by this, a process called 'commoditisation'. Actions which organisations take to evade this often use the same measures that caused it, accelerating the race. Yet this is a race which cannot be avoided.

This cycle can be broken by renewal, by changing how things are done and what is to be done. Such renewal needs to be purposeful, taking the organisation to a new, unique situation from which it can evade the forces of commoditisation. Defining and carrying out that purpose requires a number of qualities.

The Machinery – the dynamic infrastructure – to generate purposeful renewal is different from that used in the day-to-day aspects of the organisation. It takes unspecified potential, ideas and more ideas, and makes them concrete. It does this against changing criteria, often based on 'what might be' in the turbulent environment. This potential, evolved into project proposals, is then able to compete for the organisation's resources.

We symbolise this with a double cone, Figure 0.1. In the lower cone, direct and indirect procedures formalise insights that directly and indirectly develop this 'unspecified' potential. Where

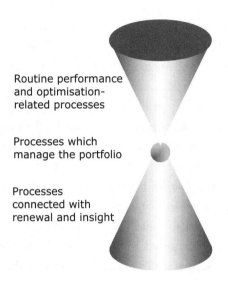

Routine performance
and optimisation-
related processes

Processes which
manage the portfolio

Processes
connected with
renewal and insight

Figure 0.1 The double cone

the cones meet, assets are allocated and projects are approved. In the upper cone, radiating out from this, the now-specified activities are subject to normal commercial disciplines.

What is needed?

The knowledge which purposeful, self-renewing organisations need to tap is scattered widely throughout the organisation, and amongst customers, suppliers and other stakeholders. Renewal is not often these people's first priority. The psychological types who tend to inhabit the upper cone are often impatient with open-ended debate. Machinery is, therefore, required to generate useful conversations across these divides. The result is something which is easy to sense but often difficult to define: a sense of collective competence.

Psychologists use the term 'competence' to mean a situation in which an individual or group has a clear grasp of the situation and has access to the tools with which to respond to it. Groups with competence can operate at much higher levels of potential stress

– in much faster and more complex environments – than groups which lack this quality. The world that we face will be complex, very fast moving and open to all manner of mistakes. Groups that are able to focus quickly on issues through sharing common insight have a particular strength.

Renewal needs to match both the current situation and the changing environment. To do this, the organisation needs analytical Insight. It also needs a clear sense of its Values, the choices which it has made around often intangible issues such as brand positioning, staff relationships and the like. Third, it needs to relate its current activity and asset base to practical ways forward, its Options. These are joined by the organisational Narrative. The Narrative is the shared set of reflexes that knit the organisation together. The first four qualities of Insight, Values, Narrative and Options generation are held together through the operation of the fifth quality, that of Machinery – used here in the sense of active and dynamic infrastructure, covering people and processes. All five qualities need to be in place if purposeful renewal is to be achieved.

Figure 0.2 shows the Machinery holding the other four qualities together and managing their interactions. An organisation which is using these five qualities for renewal is what we call a 'Purposeful Self-Renewing Organisation', or PS-RO.

The need for and creation of a PS-RO is the focus of this book.

The Machinery that connects Insight and Values so as to generate and interact with Options generation and the Narrative will be unique to the needs of any one organisation. However, there are some generally applicable ways in which these processes can be clustered.

One of these has already been discussed: asset allocation and project approval, which sits on the point where the two cones meet in Figure 0.1. The process for asset allocation is likely to be integrated with divisional plans, both in respect of their demand for resource and also their contributions to overall activity. The

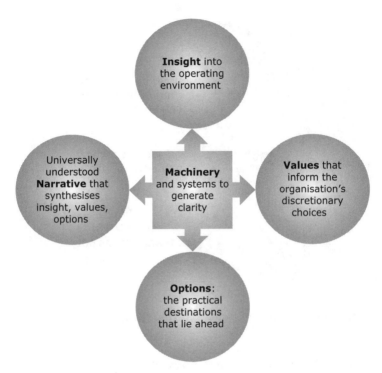

Figure 0.2 Five qualities of a PS-RO

required performance for each, the overall resource flow during the next few years and the expected overall balance of the portfolio are important outcomes from this part of the Machinery.

Two other loops will be general to all organisations: one of these relates to the performance of established activities in the upper cone, the other applies to the slower activities, which clarify Insight, Values and which generate the discussions that result in renewal. These occur in the lower cone.

These three sets of activity are symbolised by the arrows wrapping Figure 0.3. Seen from above, these create three concentric loops, activities which must, of course, inter-communicate. We term this the Three Ring Circus.

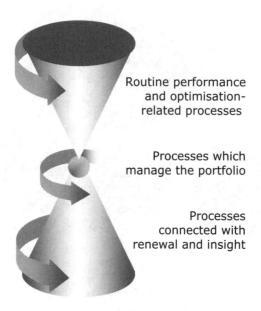

Routine performance
and optimisation-
related processes

Processes which
manage the portfolio

Processes
connected with
renewal and insight

Figure 0.3 Three process loops – the Three Ring Circus

A Purposeful Self-Renewing Organisation

The PS-RO model defines the broad shape of the organisation that is fit to succeed in the turbulent, fast-flowing river of change. Readers should note that almost by definition there can be no single correct form for a PS-RO. A PS-RO permanently strives to adapt itself to its particular changing circumstances.

A PS-RO has all five qualities in place, and is actively changing its nature to meet anticipated situations ahead. It is aware that such anticipation can be mistaken, so it works hard to manage its *Insight*. It makes sure that everyone is aware of its *Narrative*, sure in the sense of testing that people have heard and are acting on this. It is clear about its *Values* and has ensured that these are uniformly applied across its expanse. It has considered its *Options* and has not only defined the broad nature of the journey that it wants to undertake, but has set in place processes to filter proposals so as to ensure that they meet the necessary criteria. Finally, it has in place the *Machinery* and flows needed to maintain all of the above – this consists of two essential components: formal processes, some long lasting, some of them ephemeral and structured to meet passing needs; and a social structure that displays extraordinary competence.

Organisations which exhibit competence have worked hard and long to instil a sense of common purpose throughout the organisation. It is embedded in the Narrative, and built from Insight, Values and Options by way of Machinery. Narrative and competence come together to create new solutions. Sources of renewal begin life completely unspecified. They are vague possibilities that have a long way to go; without a supportive process of developing the ideas, most will be lost.

The ability to detect new ideas is not universal. The people who detect ideas are often young and close to their training or engaged with suppliers and others outside the organisation. They need to recognise potential when they see it. The general nature of the kind of ideas and renewal that is welcome needs to be clear to all involved.

Isaiah Berlin suggested that the way people prefer to think about abstract problems could be classed as the way of the Fox and/or the way of the Hedgehog: 'The Fox knows many things but the Hedgehog knows one big thing'.[1] Foxes are sceptical of big ideas and grand schemes, and are always looking for pragmatic solutions to immediate problems. Hedgehogs enjoy sweeping ideas and systematisation. They are articulate simplifiers, people who can easily brush aside or overlook ideas that do not fit into their current template. Such templates can be ideas such as shareholder value, customer focus or a belief in perfect markets. Activity in the upper cone tends to reward Hedgehog-like thinking and working styles. Fox-like skills are needed if the lower cone processes are to work.

Both styles are needed. Renewal depends on the attributes of both Foxes and Hedgehogs.

How is all of this to be put in place?

Curiously, implementation is relatively easy once the understanding is in place as to what needs to be done. Lou Gerstner wrote about his time at IBM in his book *Who Said Elephants Can't Dance?*:[2] he concluded that even large and complex organisations like IBM could change – and change quickly – when shown how.

We can offer you a blueprint to build your PS-RO, but all organisations are different. It is a key contention here that there is no one 'right' design. For any given organisation, within the context of its current and particular circumstances, there *will* be a 'right' design, but matters never stand still. There will be times, for example, when technology changes rapidly or perhaps when stakeholders are particularly demanding. Your Machinery will need to shift its focus in order to accommodate such changes. The strength of a PS-RO is that it evolves to meet the emerging challenges.

Chapter 9 provides a guide to handling the issues that you may face as you create a PS-RO; and a web link to an online diagnostic tool which we provide to help you tackle some of the practical issues you face as you design your PS-RO.

Part III of this book changes tone and pace: it is about the nuts and bolts of how to create a PS-RO, combining practical advice with briefing on tools and sources of help.

Chapter 10 focuses on Values: both personal and organisational, and their alignment in a PS-RO. It will help you to see how you can implement agreed, aligned Values in your organisation. A successful, sustainable organisation needs employees who are aligned with its core Values. They give people a sense of stability when they are in an organisation undergoing course correction and operating in uncertainty.

Chapter 11 is about the Insight processes. Insight is the ability to make sense of the external world and its future, integrate it with the internal world and harness that understanding to assess the organisation's strengths, and to provide a basis for generating options for taking the organisation forward. It fits with the other four qualities to help the organisation move from pure ambiguity and uncertainty at the bottom end of the lower cone to a place where it can use the information for its own survival, success and advantage.

Chapter 12 discusses how to develop Options generation processes for a PS-RO. Options take the information generated by Insight and, using innovation, core Values and organisational Narrative, identify the choices that are open to an organisation.

Chapter 13 covers Narrative, the glue that holds the organisation together – it connects the core Values, Insight and Options. It helps to begin to specify what was unspecified so that people can work with what was uncertain and ambiguous, and encourages innovation aligned to the organisation's direction and strategy, facilitating renewal. It saves the time of senior managers by ensuring that projects presented to them for investment are aligned to the organisation's direction, and allows for effective communication between senior managers and with shareholders.

Chapter 14 describes the Machinery needed. Machinery – as in 'machinery of government' – places a central role in a PS-RO. It supports and integrates the other four qualities to enable an organisation to be a PS-RO.

Finally, we suggest further sources of help in creating a PS-RO.

Executive Summary

- Life in large organisations will become ever more complex, time and resource-constrained, organisations will be forced to adapt quickly.
- The world ahead of us will be fast moving, turbulent and challenging. Demographic change and increased education mean a shift in the patterns of labour skill and cost. Competition will be intense and on new terms.

- Global systems issues will require the rich nations to cede some of their power. Additionally, the rich nations will take time to recover from the debt crisis. We develop three global scenarios to provide a framework for thinking about this turbulence.
- The kind of renewal needed will require the attributes of both cunning Foxes and focused Hedgehogs: most organisations have tuned themselves to the previous business environment and have lost the capability to adapt.
- The qualities of Insight, Values, Narrative and Options generation are held together through the operation of Machinery. These are the qualities needed to create a Purposeful Self-Renewing Organisation, or PS-RO.
- Implementation of a PS-RO is relatively easy once it is understood what is needed.

Part I

What Happened?

Chapter 1

A Short History of the Crisis

With the financial crisis still bubbling as we write in late 2009, we will first consider its roots and its potential impact in order to set a context for the later chapters.[3] We show that some of the factors leading to the events of 2006–9 were anomalous, others will continue, but that the effects will be felt well into the next decade. Governments and consumers in the West will be particularly constrained as they tackle paying off their debt. In the meantime, the newly industrialising economies enjoy many advantages: their savings are high, their labour cheap and skilful, their access to technology is rapidly approaching that of the Western economies and many have large internal markets. All of this presents a competitive threat to established industrial powers.

The roots of the financial crisis

The financial crisis that began in 2006–7 with defaults on 'subprime' mortgages in some parts of the USA serves as a decisive punctuation mark. It marked the end of a period of 'fake' stability, one in which all the indicators seemed to support a mode of operation and a set of assumptions that we now have to question. We

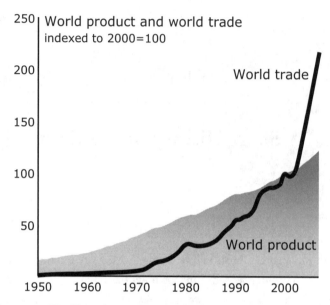

Figure 1.1 World product and world trade

begin this chapter with a review of the roots of the crisis, in the view that to fully understand where we're going, we need first to mark where we are.

We have been through a period of asset price inflation. Figure 1.1 shows a simple plot of world trade against world product, both in money of the day, from 1950 to the present.[4] There is a lengthy period in which the two maintained a 1 : 1 relationship[5]. The relationship began to change in the early 1980s, with world trade increasing at a much faster rate than world product. The Asian crisis, the dot.com collapse and the massive failure of financial management in 2006 provided a series of challenges which initially appeared to be accommodated without disrupting the growth of world trade.

The growth of world trade was a symptom; the cause was a mixture of real, external factors and a belief which persisted for a generation and beyond in the financial industries that credit was uncapped. The key drivers included the following eight factors:

1. Steady or falling (in real terms) commodity and energy prices which drove up consumption.
2. The doubling of the global work force, and the much more than doubling of their intellectual capacity through education and training, which led in its turn to mobility of labour to where it could be used effectively.
3. Near universal productivity growth was based on the use of increasingly cheap information technology. Between 1960 and 1999, manufacturing's share in US GDP and total employment both halved, to about 15%. Over the same period, its physical output increased 2–3 times and prices decreased in real terms by 75%.[6]
4. Labour costs for low-skilled workers in the industrial world were nearly static in real terms.
5. Connectivity and new institutions offered access to the global work force and to world savings.
6. The end of the Cold War led to the apparent supremacy of the Western model of governance. There was near universal and immediate economic response to a standard economic model that comprised sound finance, unimpeded market forces, rational and predictable regulation and taxation, open borders to trade in manufactured goods, all making up the so-called International Monetary Fund (IMF) model.
7. There was a wave of privatisation and deregulation in the industrial world. This spread to the former Comecon countries in Eastern Europe, and in China and India.
8. Finally, financial deregulation had a series of important impacts, as discussed below.

The immediate responses to this growth of world trade were the extension of consumerism in the West and the beginnings of fast growth and liberalisation in the developing economies, most notably in Asia and the ex-Comecon countries in Eastern Europe.

The response of the financial sector was that the world had found a way to manage complexity – through bottom-up choice in markets and democracy, all integrated by sound governance – and that things would find their own equilibrium through benign neglect.

This model has much to commend it. However, 'benign' is a word laden with values: whose benignity? For whose advantage? In the short term it suited US and other political leaders to allow central banks to maintain historically low real interest rates, to permit a housing boom that went off the scale, with consumers taking on a vast burden of debt.

Asian savings funded some of this expansion, while demographics in the wealthy world meant that many had accumulated savings and pension funds that needed to be invested. A glut of capital forced down price/earnings ratios on securities. Increasing shareholder activism was driven by this and other factors, such as the boom in mergers and hostile acquisitions, and consumerism applied to securities markets expanded by low trading costs. Companies could not compete with the high returns from the financial sector and were squeezed for cash for organic investment. Boards were ejected by shareholders if they were not content with the company's performance.

The role of the financial sector

The financial sector had been hugely important in the early twentieth-century stock markets, but had since declined to a small share of the market. Retail banking was famously parodied in *Liar's Poker* as 3/6/3: borrow at 3%, lend at 6%, be on the golf course at 3pm. Merchant banks did esoteric things on a small scale and had no great significance. Few banks engaged in asset trading, in the sense of playing zero-sum games with other people's money.

Changing regulation

In the early 1990s, banks discovered the joys of corporate finance and expanded rapidly into new areas. This was accelerated by the repeal of the depression-era US Glass-Steagall Act in 1999. This had separated commercial from investment banking, and its repeal opened the door to new monolithic firms.

All manner of new products were on offer. Mergers and acquisitions were studied and actively promoted to corporate chieftains with ready finance. Methods of borrowing to please shareholders with a short time horizon – such as to buy back shares, or to pay dividends – were parts of the package. The chief offer that had unambiguous positive sum value associated with it was, however, the wide range of packages that claimed to manage risk exposure.

Hedging of risk

Portfolios that are constructed from many unrelated risks that are small in comparison to the total are proportionately less exposed to volatility than the constituent components. That is how insurance works: if your house burns down, that is a catastrophe for you, but it is not such a proportional disaster for an insurance company that holds tens of thousands of such risks. You are, therefore, happy to pay a small sum to remove the financial – if not practical – risk; and the company can accept it knowing that the likelihood of all of the houses that it insures burning down in the same time period is very low.

It is, however, a crucial caveat for insurance that the risks must be 'uncorrelated', must not respond to a common precipitating factor, such as war.

Offers claiming to manage risk exposure allowed companies to 'hedge' risk; buying what was sold as insurance against currency movements, inflation, commodity price changes and supply chain defaults. This was a powerful gain and the corporate treasury function became closely linked to – or outsourced to – banks.

Borrowing

This closeness also encouraged borrowing on a vast scale, often for financial transactions – such as acquisitions – rather than for investment in plant and equipment. The new monoliths sent teams of people to visit corporate CEOs in order to suggest projects that they would then finance: acquire this, strip out that – it seemed that you could create hundreds of millions of dollars out of absolutely nothing.

Figure 1.2 shows the mergers and acquisitions value in the USA as a percentage of the GDP.[7] It emphasises the amazingly large peaks of activity in the decade 2000–2008.

Own-account trading by banks and CDOs

Banks found another interesting area: own-account trading. That is, they could use their current assets to borrow, and use that

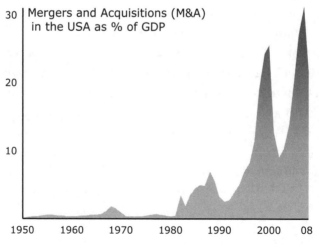

Figure 1.2 Mergers and acquisitions as a percentage of US GDP

money to speculate in markets. At first controlled by regulatory limits, this soon went 'off the balance sheet', being handled by entities to which the regulatory control did not apply. More and more complex instruments were devised, including the now-notorious collateralised debt obligations, or CDOs. As they illustrate the abstract nature of what was being done, these are worth a general description.

A bank creates a new legal entity, usually called an SPE or special purpose entity. It places a collection of assets into this, which are divided into various classes of risk exposure, here meaning chiefly proneness to volatility. Each CDO or group of assets has a class.

Ratings agencies validated these structures, and had to compete against each other for the privilege. Over-strict assessors were less likely to be selected, all things being equal.

CDOs were purchased by other institutions. The high-risk ones offered a high return, and low-risk ones provided supposedly quality assets against which further money could be borrowed, so repeating the cycle. This is called 'securitisation', and allowed banks to take on dizzy levels of debt that was certified to be triple-A. As we have now seen, they in practice often contained toxic assets or assets which all moved in the same direction when times got hard.

Some figures may serve to put this in context:[8]

Table 1.1 World values

World added value, 2007 approximately	$35 trillion
World value of equities, 2007	$40 trillion
World value of derivatives, inc. CDOs	$1000 trillion
World values of credit default swaps	$70–90 trillion

Boom and bust in financial services

The upshot was that the banking sector boomed, paid out very high salaries and bonuses, and lost control of its fundamentals. Senior staff had very little idea what their subordinates were doing, as the instruments were technical and changed very rapidly. Accounting structures that worked on a mark-to-market basis – that is, booked (marked) assets at what they were worth 'in the market' at the moment of booking – had to work within an extremely ill-defined framework: what, ultimately, was the market value of a derivative built on a dozen CDOs that were themselves spires above huge, mixed bunches of assets that included the now notorious sub-prime property portfolio?

Banks also found one more area in which to expand their activities. This was the churning of assets. Brokerage fees are charged when a trade is made, but not otherwise. Thus, portfolios that are extremely active – perhaps through automated ('quant') trading or solely through the 'need' to access ever-more complex instruments – were portfolios that made money for traders.

Once again, some figures put matters in perspective. Brokers' fees in 2007 were assessed as being around $500bn, which is 1½% of gross world product. The typical costs of such management fees are 2% of a portfolio's worth per annum, which accumulates to half of what a pension fund is worth over 25 years.[9]

The consequence of all this is that financial services represented about 10% of world profit in 1965 and 35% in 2005.[10] Huge fortunes were made and high salaries paid to people who did not understand – and were not in control of – their organisations. They were cruising on the success of the underlying structural features. As long as expansion continued, the bubble would continue to grow.

The bursting of the bubble placed pressure on states to bail out the banks, which in many cases they did. Figure 1.3[11] shows the scale of the US commitment set against other major projects from history. Some of the money spent will be recuperated by the state

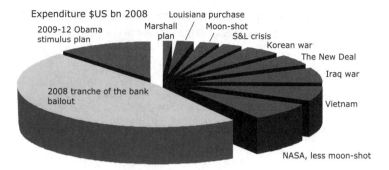

Figure 1.3 The scale of the US bank bailout

– ultimately from shareholders and consumers, of course – and this implies a long, slow process during which government expenditure will be severely constrained.

Personal, corporate and government debt

The unprecedented scale of personal and corporate debt in the USA from 1952 to 2009 is shown in Figure 1.4.[12] During this time, the Western economies have changed from being mostly saving economies to being mostly debt-ridden economies. At its peak in 2009, the personal debt averaged 139% of income (versus, say, 62% in 1960 or 101% in 2000). Debt services took an all-time high of 14.4% of personal disposable income in 2007, from which peak it has fallen only because interest rates have declined. Personal saving in the USA fell continually from around 10% of income in 1980 to zero in 2005, and below zero thereafter.

This presents two headaches for the next decade:

- Dealing with the debt – through paying back or through defaults.
- Dealing with the slowing in growth as the OECD consumers slow their spending.

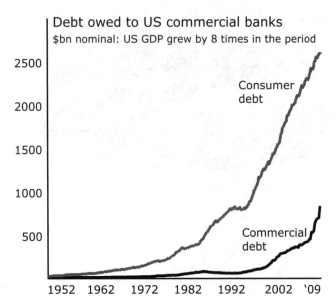

Figure 1.4 Consumer debt in the USA

Dealing with the debt

If this consumer debt generates significant default, there is absolutely nothing that any state can do to bail the situation out, because the numbers are simply too vast. The two options considered by most governments are to do nothing, which is not feasible when facing a gigantic crisis that makes 2007–9 fade into insignificance, or to print money and inflate the relevant economies out of the situation. (Inflation dilutes debt, the value of which remains constant whilst the currency in which it is denominated of course contracts in value. Ten thousand dollars would have been a large mortgage in 1970, but is less than the average outstanding credit card debt today.) Naturally, nations which did this would see their currencies collapse and their economies labour under a burden of inflationary value destruction that would last for decades.

What might precipitate a widespread default on debts? The three most immediate threats are:

• high interest rates,
• high taxes and
• high unemployment.

Unemployment is rising in all of the industrial economies, and history shows us that past recessions have a 3–4-year trough during which employment is below trend and wages are static or falling.[13] States will have to cut their expenditure to balance their books, as some are running deficits as large as 10% of GDP, unprecedented outside of wartime. This, too, will affect employment. This is a real threat, therefore. Higher taxes are also a reality, for the same reasons.

Might real interest rates rise as well? Central banks will eventually have to raise their base rates above the near-zero figures that apply today. Knowing what affect this might have, they will be extremely cautious in doing this. However, the very large sums poured into the economy in 2008, and a growth spurt – coupled with depleted supply chains – might force interest rate rises. This is probably unlikely, as assessments of pressures on both the supply and demand side of the developed economies suggest that the forces are, if anything, deflationary.

The OECD consumer
Second, the US consumer represents an enormous chunk of world economic activity. Aside from their debt position, their propensity to consume has a profound impact on the world economy. It represented 18.2% of world product in 2008, up from 14.9% in 1980. To put that in proportion, that is about three times greater than Germany's entire economy for the same year. The attitude of US

consumers, as much as their actual financial status, has a profound effect on the world economy.

Once again, debt is the key. Crudely, consumers have to cut their debt level in half to re-attain the sense of financial security that they enjoyed when house prices and equities values were high. To do this, they would have to cut their spending. That would depress economic growth. To avoid having to do this, security and house prices would have to rise. What are the prospects of this happening quickly?

House prices had risen sharply against incomes in most OECD countries. Most have now fallen to the historical average. In the USA, the numbers of new and existing family homes for sale are at a high level not seen for a generation. Consequently, a return to house price inflation will be slow.

Of course not all countries have large levels of consumer debt. Savings rates in much of Asia remain high.

The behaviour of OECD consumers during the recession shows four trends: demand for simplicity, a call for ethical business governance, a desire to economise, and a tendency to experiment with new offerings. Trends slowed by the recession are green consumption, the decline of deference, ethical consumption and extreme-experience seeking. Green consumption is expected to be a feature again beyond the immediate crisis, while attitudes to extreme experience will be altered for the long term.[14]

Equities

What about equities? Here, the issue is out of the hands of the US consumer and is heavily influenced by other factors, such as foreign interest in US securities, the value of the dollar, interest rates and so on; but most of all by prospects for corporate profitability. Companies are in much better shape than are consumers: their markets may have fallen, but the plant and people are still there and technology is racing ahead.

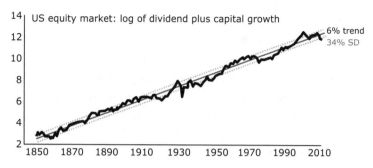

Figure 1.5 US equity market long-term trend

The chart in Figure 1.5 shows how the real-term values of investments in the US have grown since 1850.[15] It uses a logarithmic scale, and performance waivers only for the short run from the underlying trend of 6% annual growth. The dotted lines show one standard deviation from this trend, meaning that the line will walk randomly to or beyond this bound only 34% of the time. Using this pragmatic guide, we can estimate the probability that equities will revert to their former values within a given time frame. There is a 50% chance that US equities will bounce back to historical rates of return by 2020, and a 50% chance that they will still not have done so by 2030.

Assessments of this sort are no more than extrapolations, but unhappily more complex modelling activity suggests that the long-term effects of the bubble will be lasting, trimming perhaps 2% off industrial world growth until well into the 'teens of the century. US consumers are most likely to feel this cold wind, as they are far and away the most indebted group. Also, nations which have run up great debts – again, the USA but also the UK, Japan and others – will have to pay these back.

A more active government role
There is pressure from many directions for governments to take a more active role in the regulation of financial services, both

nationally and internationally. As Robert Reich said in the *Harvard Business Review*, speaking of the US economy:

> The massive failure of world economies has paved the way for government action not seen since the 1930s. New regulations will be designed to encourage desired behaviours, for instance through regulation in financial services, guaranteeing loans for small businesses and requiring employers to either insure workers or pay into a national pool.[16]

Executive Summary

- The financial crisis marked the end of a period of 'fake' economic and organisational stability, brought about by a consumer boom and a belief in the power of markets under a system of benign neglect.
- Banks took on unsustainably high levels of debt. The debt was underpinned by assets of questionable value, such as CDOs, in the belief that they had found a way to manage complexity: senior staff had very little idea what their subordinates were doing.
- There are two headaches for the next decade: dealing with the debt (through paying back or through defaults); and dealing with the slowing in growth as the OECD consumers slow their spending.
- There will be increased pressure for regulation of financial services, and the OECD debt will take some time to unwind.
- The net effect of this changing landscape is that money supply for investment in the West will be more constrained and more expensive.

Chapter 2

The New Operating Environment

Here, we introduce four of the global systemic forces which will affect the next decades and beyond. The increase in global population, centred on industrialising countries, will lead to shifts in economic power. Science and technology will have potent power. The value systems of the new economic powers are likely to be different from those of the OECD countries. And the pressure of population increases and expectations of changes in lifestyle – diet, transport, urban life – will lead to competition for resources and pressure on the environment. All of this is set against a background of military and civil insecurity, particularly in the poorer nations. These factors build on the forces described in the previous chapter to establish a map of the operating environment for the coming decades.

Demographics

The first factor that will affect the next decades is the sheer number of people on the planet: where they are, their education levels, and the ageing profile.

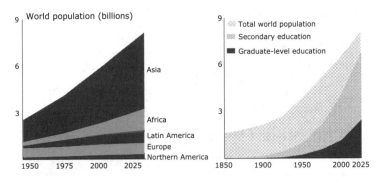

Figure 2.1 Global population growth

In Figure 2.1 the graphic on the left shows the past and projected population numbers. The world will become increasingly Asian, and the middle class from this area is expected to outnumber the entire population of the former industrial world.

In the right-hand graphic, we see the proportion of the population who have or are expected to have received various levels of education. The current Chinese and Indian 'honours student' population currently exceeds the total OECD population.

In order to assess the impact of the changing demographic profile, we use dependency ratios, which measure the proportion of economically active individuals to those who, through age or infirmity, require support from others. Industrial world dependency ratios in the 1960s were typically around 15% of the population. Most welfare systems were designed with such proportions in mind, and with life spans that ended quickly after retirement. The equivalent numbers for 2030 average 35%, with some nations such as Italy and Japan struggling with numbers 10% higher.

The OECD estimates that the typical industrial society was spending 10% of gross product on age-related support in 2000. The estimates for 2020 are double that. The old industrial world will,

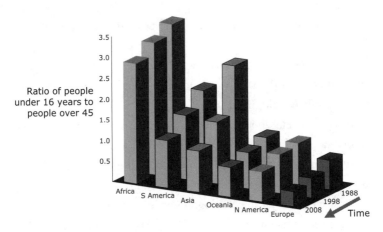

Figure 2.2 Demographic change

therefore, carry a heavy burden, as will China. However, having huge numbers of unemployed youths may make Africa's (or India's) future turbulent.

Figure 2.2 shows the number of people under 16 divided by the number who are over 45 for six regions. Europe can be seen to have a particularly small younger population, while Africa has the opposite: 40% of Africa's population is under 15 years old,[17] and the number is expected to grow.

Poverty remains a dominant issue. The World Bank believes that 80% of the world lived on less than ten dollars a day in 2005, and around a billion on about one dollar a day. Around half of all the people living in poverty are found in the growing economics of China and India.[18]

In the medium term, demographics presents a major hurdle for the rich world, as it deals with ageing and in some cases declining populations. It presents an opportunity for the poor countries with young populations if they can educate and harness their youth.

Economic development and social interactions

The demographic changes will cause deep changes in the competitive structure of the world's economies. Added to this is the effect of economic development.

It took Britain about 60 years to double its output during the industrial revolution.[19] It took China seven years to do the same during the 1990s,[20] because it could look to existing models and technologies to help it quickly move forward.

However, not all developing countries with favourable demographics have been able to do this. Africa was once far richer per capita than Asia, and in the 1950s Asia was regarded as the least developed of the major regions. African countries have since seen their income per capita decline in real terms. By contrast, Asia has grown a great deal, and in some cases – such as Singapore and Hong Kong – has surpassed incomes per capita in the old rich world.

Studies of this process by the World Bank[21] have since been confirmed by others. In essence, 80% of the observed differences are explainable as being due to three factors:

- physical location and resources (5%);
- distinctions in the quality of education (15%);
- differences in the effectiveness of government, which explains 60% of the difference between countries and is by far the largest factor.

Long-run development comes down to the effectiveness of the state in enabling economic and social life through, for example, education, health, mobility and access to information, law and property rights. The following case study illustrates the importance of horizon scanning in assessing the effectiveness of governance before undertaking major investments.

Case study – the costs of failing to gain insight: horizon scanning

A mining company invested heavily in Peru in 2007. They acquired the rights to an entire province, within which large amounts of minerals were based. The company had little experience of working outside their home region, and very little of South America. It acquired the mine from an English company that had managed to infuriate the local inhabitants to the degree that no geologist or mine worker could go out in public, at risk of being stoned. The local capital had been blockaded several times, and the country made a no-go area.

The Spanish who conquered Peru found a population of 11 million Incas, who were reduced to less than a million in a century. Imported disease, and starvation as former systems of agriculture collapsed, killed many, but so too did forced labour in the many mines. As late as the 1920s, mining companies were sending armed bands to seize peasants for forced labour.

Mining has, therefore, a heritage of bitterness, and rural communities have developed a fierce tradition of organised labour, blockades and direct action. For example, a major mining district was subject to at least a hundred dynamite attacks of facilities in a single night because it had drained a sacred lake. The 2006 elections in Peru were contested by Ollanta Humala, who lost by only a few percent. Seventy percent of the voters in the province where the investors were considering operations voted for this candidate. The principles for which he stood were a return to Andean values, a rejection of modernism and internationalism, the nationalisation of all mines and active resistance to international investment.

To this should be added that this is a frontier area, in which policing is light and drug smuggling rife. Ten police try to manage a population of 350,000. Across the frontier, central government has placed security into local hands, and into those of the army.

None of this was evident to the investors when they made their purchase. Their assessments had been made on investigations of the relevant geology, project economics, geography and fiscal issues. There had been a thorough failure of insight. A widely based horizon scan would have alerted them to the issues.

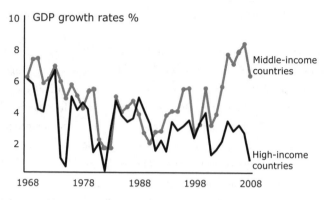

Figure 2.3 Changing balance of the world economy

A generation ago, there was no clear model of economic development. States proceeded by intuition and luck. Today, the managers and policy makers of China or India have a clear benchmark against which to set progress, and clear indications of the stages of development that each region will encounter. They can and do plan for this. Their commerce accesses the best that the world has to offer, both in terms of resource and management talent. The upshot is that there will be a veritable army of low-waged, highly skilled people based in rapidly modernising nations at the same time as the current industrial base faces demographic change.

Figure 2.3 shows GDP growth rates for the high income and newly industrialising (middle income) countries. Growth rates in the high-income countries show a decline since the 1960s. The industrialising countries showed similar trends to the end of the 1980s, then moved to high growth. Political change in the former Communist world had a major role to play in this, as it did in India and Indonesia. Growth in the poor nations (omitted for clarity) closely parallels that of the middle-income countries. Six billion people are beginning to get wealthy. The OECD countries have started to recognise this, as is suggested by the establishment of the G20 grouping.

Western societies have not grasped the implications of this. There is a tendency to see the industrialising world as essentially poor copies of themselves, or else as being worryingly efficient but ultimately helpful in the supply of cheap manufactures. Everyone in these countries is supposed to want to become just like the West. The ethical basis of Western societies is assumed to be replicated as and when these societies attain equivalent purchasing power.

But it is far from the truth that developing countries aspire to a Western ethical model. The emerging global middle classes have very different value systems to those of the old West. Values, whether in the old West or developing countries, are a vital element in any organisation, or political and economic system. We discuss this in more detail in Chapters 7 and 10.

Values of the emerging global middle class

Anthropologists like to discriminate between 'guilt' and 'shame' cultures. The former drive themselves to virtue, the latter are motivated by their public profile to acts of virtue. For the first, perhaps at its purist in Calvinist Protestantism, it is what you think and why you think it, with deeds a second and less important aspect of personal worth. For the second, what you think is irrelevant: it is what you are seen to do, or what you fail to do, which governs your worth. For example, from Latin America to India, wealthy people are supposed to display their wealth and to make charitable and communal acts, and in doing so they gain status and community approval. To fail to do this is to be seen as mean, socially inadequate and odd.

To this way of thinking, the social world is divided into 'rooms' in which often radically different behaviour is expected. The rules that govern behaviour in these rooms are set by tradition, by

Table 2.1 Five moral dimensions of society

	Traditionalist societies	Wealthy, industrial societies
Harm	Harm avoided and benefits sought but in a more atomic, less systems-related manner.	Risk/benefit and the avoidance of harm are central to policy making.
Fairness	Principal of equality is not strongly recognised. What is fair to a given individual is often predicated on their role in society. It is fair that a man has more rights than a woman, for example.	Individuals have equal rights; equality before the law. Adjudicates between collective and individual goals; central to left/right political division.
Affiliation	Unquestioning adherence to and mutual support from ethnic, caste or other group members. Regarded as immoral not to assist or promote the interests of members of the group.	Nepotism regarded as an evil and the ability of a clique to monopolise advantage or privilege is actively assailed.
Authority	Innate respect for authority, even when it is known to be mistaken. Characteristically, authorities have to establish themselves by acclaim, and must vigorously fight off challenge. Acclaim is often linked to the ability to deliver concrete benefits. Often leads to irreconcilable conflicts between rival sources of authority.	Authority is always to be questioned, mocked, eroded. Authority is granted by formal institutions or by objective knowledge or clearly displayed rational use of learning: e.g. trust in medical practitioners, respecting the office of President irrespective of the person holding that office.
Purity	Reflects a deep belief that some situations, groups of people, behaviours and foods are innately more or less pure than others. Personal levels of purity can be altered both through active measures and by association. Can lead to ghetto-isation and to complex social behaviour.	Whilst moral disapproval around concrete issues is permitted, society does not sanction public expressions of disgust about the innate characteristics of groups. Disgust focuses on hygiene, although parents keep children from 'bad influence' groups and information.

religious perceptions and by reference to the immediate social group. Added to this, there is little tradition of solidarity across social divides.

Tracking cultural differences

We can track these differences with real-world measurements. These have been conducted using the framework in Table 2.1 to compare the attitudes of traditionalist societies and wealthy, industrial societies to five basic moral dimensions.

Figure 2.4 shows outcomes from the new disciplines of experimental economics (on the right) and neural economics (on the left). Experimental economics explores people's behaviour in situations where economics makes predictions. Neural economics identifies what happens to the brains of people who are making decisions, and is able to identify specific common locations in the brain which light up when choices are being made that are heavily laden with a particular kind of issue.

The left-hand chart is based on the five dominant dimensions of choices being made about social matters,[22] found in neural economic studies. It shows that the more traditional a society is, the less that for instance 'purity' is relevant to a moral decision,

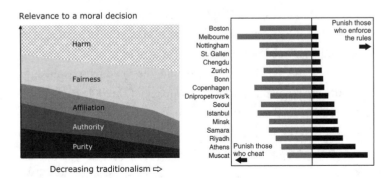

Figure 2.4 Attitudes in traditional societies

in that there is less belief that one can improve by acts or by association.[23]

The chart on the right[24] shows the outcome of one experiment consisting of a set of carefully designed 'games' that are played for money. Participants have the opportunity to cheat, to be detected cheating and to punish other players. The figure shows the relative tendency to punish those detected cheating, and those who detect the cheating (the 'police'). So policemen commit a crime against affiliation and purity, shaming the group. They remind people of how they, too, have struggled to grab what they can when it is available. Industrial societies do not much feel these emotions, and applaud policing of this sort; but other nations – traditionalist rather than monetarily poor – do not feel this way. Organisations from the developed world who do not explore and test the values of a country or region before investing may well regret their hastiness.

Implications for attitudes to governance

What are the implications of this? Two things are happening: first, a transfer of the skill base to the industrialising economies for all but the most complex and demanding of applications; second, there will be very large numbers of new middle class, who do not share the values of the developed world. They will not live and are not expected to live by the West's consensus. This erosion will be gradual, and the power shifts will greatly affect the implicit agenda of the old industrial powers.

The past 15 years has masked the degree to which power shifts have already occurred and the inadequacy of the industrial model that grew up in the 1990s. Historians will probably measure the decline of the dominance of the old powers and the old world model from the financial bubble and its breaking. What lies ahead has yet to form itself clearly.

Communications, science and technology

The third source of change over the next decades relates to science and technology. Advances in the biological sciences and technology will continue to extend life and increase agricultural yields, and may contribute to energy supply. Above all, however, organisations of all types will continue to be exposed to the direct and indirect affects of the explosion in information technology.

Nobody can easily visualise huge numbers directly, so it is helpful to use analogies. Think of a megabyte, a million bytes, as being a square metre of cloth, one thousand stitches long by one thousand stitches wide. Using this analogy, the amount of knowledge generated by the human race in 1920 was equivalent to a sheet large enough to cover the little island of Mauritius. By 1950, this had expanded to cover Madagascar, and by the mid-1980s, Africa. All of the continents were covered by cloth in 1990, and the entire planet enveloped in a duvet of annual information by the turn of the millennium. By 2020, it will cover around 1800 planets annually. IBM note that the amount of digital information currently generated doubles every 11 hours.[25] Clearly, much of this is CCTV footage; however, other estimates relating to this explosion of information are more useful.

Scientific knowledge is thought to double every two to five years in many disciplines.[26] Edwards[27] reviewed estimates of how investment into knowledge converts into economic performance. The results were discount rates that clustered around 25%. These are not just economic benefits. The US think tank Funding First[28] estimated that half of all the improvements in the standard of living enjoyed by US citizens over the previous 50 years were due to investment in the understanding of human health and investment in public health measures.

The exploitation of technology benefits from the advantages previously seen of other types of economic cluster.[29] Technology exploitation tends to occur in cities. It requires many types of infrastructure if it is to be effective: not just adjacent technologies, but law, designers, accountants, transport systems. For example, Scherngell *et al.*[30] estimate that knowledge has a predictable and extremely local effect on efficiency growth. A 1% increase in knowledge in a region would add 2% to its economy over a 10-year period. The biennial doubling of scientific knowledge has staggering implications for growth if the necessary 'social' infrastructure is in place. Nations which are able to play host to incubators of technology exploitation are likely to enjoy prosperity.

Governments have a role in creating urban, specialised societies, attractive to highly mobile talent, to commerce and to specific clusters of technologies. Naturally, there will be losers in this process: cities which fail to achieve this, people whose skills do not fit. This may be a difficult political transition to manage, particularly in the face of the many distractions of the next decades.

Resource and other systemic challenges

So far we have discussed the financial crisis, the pressure of demographics, the rising power of countries and regions with different value systems from those assumed by Western industrialised countries, and the effect of technology. One of the effects of technology plus the population pressures is that the world is going to be increasingly coupled together.

This generates systems – such as financial systems, but also crime, terror and other less welcome structures – which are pan-national if not global. At the same time, natural systems that have functioned for centuries without attention are now being impacted by human activity. These range from land clearance to pollutant emissions, depleting the sea of fish and adding tens of thousands of novel chemicals to it. (Figure 14.6 in Chapter 14 gives a view of how close we are already to – or over the edge with – eight of the most important of these.) Vast cities in the poor nations are centres for epidemics and diseases of poverty. Crime and ideologically inspired violence are fuelled by poor governance and by poverty.

These systemic issues can only be solved with international co-operation. The established rich nations will have to cede some of their power to international structures if they are to be effective. This, and the rebalancing of the world economy, will have considerable impact on both their governance and their economies. Member states of the European Union have already seen the legislative overheads of membership: a similar effect will be seen as global systems are brought into being. Security issues, for example, become crucial as biotechnology and IT-mediated mechanisms of terror and crime become widely accessible. Conventional deterrence will not work, as the protagonists are mobile and deeply embedded in civil populations. Only extensive co-operation around intelligence and policing – but also around values, goals and beliefs – will achieve security.

These are issues that have been explored in many books. For summaries spanning the issues, we recommend that readers of this book consult the Challenge Forum! website,[31] which contains a wealth of data as well as sets of scenarios with various horizons, or the World in 2025 Report from the European Commission,[32] which provides a perspective on the major trends.

All of this may sound abstract and irrelevant to senior managers in organisations. Consider, however, how they might have thought about the fall of Communism in the early 1990s. Now, such managers compete with – or collaborate with – China, and European managers depend on Russian gas, use former Warsaw pact countries for outsourcing and depend on migrant workers at all levels.

In the early 1990s, the Internet was a vague dream. Environmental issues were once the concern of a specialist minority, and terrorism was believed to be largely home-grown.

Executive Summary

- There are four major challenges over the next decade, in addition to the hangover from the financial crisis.
- The OECD estimates that the percentage of gross product spent on age-related support will double by 2020. An ageing population presents the West with a major problem, whilst the younger populations of much of the developing world have opportunity if they can be harnessed. Six billion people are beginning to get wealthy. The OECD countries have started to recognise this, as is suggested by the establishment of the G20 grouping.
- The value systems of the new middle class will be unlike those in the OECD countries.
- Science and technology will have an increasing role over the next decades.
- An increasing number of people globally will begin to expect and demand basics such as oil, and 'the good things in life', leading to systemic issues which can only be solved with international co-operation. It is not clear whether a global systems management capability will emerge to deal with these; it is currently best to take an agnostic view of this.
- The pace of change and its consequences place an enormous premium not merely upon foresight, but upon the ability to *harness* foresight.

Chapter 3

What Lies Ahead?

Let us think about what lies ahead in three time frames, and the connection between the time frames. The short run is, essentially, concerned with the way out of the financial overhang, debt and unemployment situation in the West. The medium term depends on how the wealthy world comes to terms with the new economic and political conditions, with new competitors. The longer term is constrained by the events to date and in the short and medium term, and by the capability of the world to tackle global systemic challenges. This chapter sketches three scenario frameworks for gaining clarity about potential worlds over the next decades. Scenario frameworks provide mental models of plausible, self-consistent but qualitatively different views of possible futures – and the decisions that could lead to these. They are therefore very useful in times of turbulence.

The short term

As we saw in Chapter 2, there are two financial crises that affect the environment for organisations in the short term. One revolves around bank liquidity and the overhang of the bank bail out. The second is the issue of consumer debt, the way in which it gets repaid and the potential for large-scale defaults.

Figure 3.1 How might the financial crisis be resolved?

Two dimensions of uncertainty

If we consider the effect of these two separately, a two-dimensional figure (Figure 3.1) helps us to see the future more clearly.

On the horizontal axis, we show the possibility that the banking crisis is central to the future economic situation or merely a part (if an important part) of them: consumer debt. As we have seen, is very important in some (OECD) nations, less so in others, for instance in Asia.

The vertical axis explores how quickly the banking aspect of the crisis is resolved. Once again, this is likely to be dependent on factors which are different according to country, region or type of government approach. Figure 3.2 populates the same matrix as in Figure 3.1 with representative countries based on the current position and anticipated trends.

Is there a silver bullet? Could a new technology, or a vibrant economy, act as a centre of growth? Of course, but there is no obvious replacement for the US consumer as the motor of growth in terms of sheer size of purchasing power. Economic conditions will probably be difficult, and turbulent, in the short term.

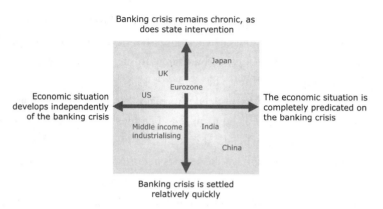

Figure 3.2 What could happen in different regions?

The medium term

Figure 3.2 suggests that not every country is likely to be affected in the same way, or for the same period. As we look further ahead, so we see that this re-division of the world's power becomes more accentuated.

Over the past two decades, the world has been undergoing accelerating, deep, socio-political and economic change. Yet these deep changes have been masked by a superficial social and economic consensus: a rational, market-oriented, democratic, secular/humanist view of the balances to be struck between the individual and the collective, of the processes of dispute settlement and of the nature of international relations. It is a view that assumes a natural order, with the older industrial powers setting the rules.

Changing balance of power

As we saw in Chapter 2, this is not the model to which the emerging billions of middle-class people necessarily subscribe, and the new stable order of the world has yet to be defined for the medium term. The succession of bursting bubbles that led up to the 2006–9 crisis has weakened the old rich world both materially and as a source of authority, and the mask has slipped. There is, therefore, every possibility of rapid changes in relative status for at least some nations and social groups, and a change in the political consensus that informs international affairs.

We have already mentioned the major global systemic challenges that will need to be managed. The means by which a consensus will emerge to handle this is far from clear. If the challenges are not addressed there will be a series of crises. If they are handled by political systems it will be costly and constraining. Either way, these factors will have major implications for nations and for commerce.

In the past, international affairs have been largely irrelevant to most organisations. This will not be the case in the medium-term future. The more joined-up the world becomes, and the more that frantic competition flattens boundaries, so we become more interdependent.

Interdependency in the 1990s and 2000s meant that low-wage workers made goods for Western – mostly US – consumers. That remains a feature of the middle-term future, but one much mitigated by other considerations, such as a relative strengthening of the bargaining position of the industrialising countries and a growing sense that power is extended far more broadly than in the past decades.

Describing a medium-term future

This brings us to two dimensions which span the medium-term future. They refer chiefly to nations, but can be applied independently to firms and other organisations. In order to describe these dimensions, we need to introduce some new terminology.

We use three narratives[33] to describe value systems, in order to discuss the dimensions of the possible medium-term future. These value systems provide the context within which societies govern themselves. So, as the world becomes more inter-connected, it is important to understand the differing value systems which will determine national and international governance.

- **Traditionalists:** retrospective in focus, taking values from the community rather than their own judgement, strongly affiliated with the 'tribe' to which they belong, deferential to authority and authoritarian towards unorthodoxy, low educational attainment, often elderly. Inclined to blame an out-group when things go wrong.

- **Consumers:** pragmatic and focused on the present, centred on themselves and their immediate family rather than 'tribe' or nation, competitive towards and judgemental of others, strongly influenced by fashions in consumption and ethical attitudes. Consumers see 'society' as a natural and given backdrop to their lives which is of concern only when it ceases to work as expected, and are inclined to blame authority when things go wrong.

- **Systems Rationalists:** future focused, their affiliations are vaguely towards those with similar views, but they do not form groups easily. They take their values from within themselves rather than from the group, and value money as a means to support a way of life determined by their interests. They are inclined to pursue power rather than status, and for the same reason. They are greatly concerned by pending or actual systems failures and many environmentalists who do not fall into the Traditionalist group are Systems Rationalists. They are less interested in allocating blame when things go wrong than in analysis of the causes of the problem.

To the Systems Rationalist, the Traditionalists seem a drain, a burden, the source of prohibitions and dissent. To the Traditionalists, the Systems Rationalists seem like the yuppies of the 1980s, the cause and vector of alarming change and of the erosion of social certainties. They are the spokespeople for frightening technologies: machines that seem to think, machines too small to see; medical technologies that reach into the nature of a person and their life trajectory; consequent regulation which seems to dictate too much of an individual life for comfort. Nations with many Traditionalists are wary of technology.

How nations might evolve

Figure 3.3 uses two axes to explore trajectories for how nations might evolve in the medium term.

The horizontal axis in Figure 3.3 defines how integrated an organisation is with the emerging world order, both organisationally and psychologically or politically. The vertical axis measures the socio-political and economic performance. At the top of the figure, the society is cohesive and cosmopolitan and the economy is able to compete on good terms. At the bottom, cohesion is lost in political dissent, and economic strategy is riddled with contradictions: the nation or organisation is playing by yesterday's rules,

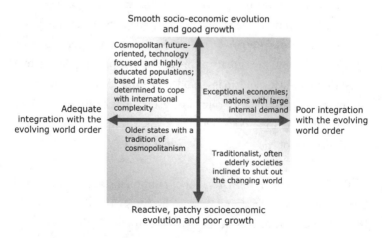

Figure 3.3 Possible responses in the medium term

is in denial about change and armoured against practical measures to renew the society.

These dimensions are not entirely independent of each other, which is why the upper right and lower left corners are shaded. It is hard to be poorly integrated with the world and still economically dynamic, for example, although a few exceptional nations may manage to position themselves 'centre upper right'. Some will be small and specialised – much as is Switzerland today – but this is a space more viable for companies than nations. Strongly national, large and established companies serving a region with a stable economy may operate in this mode, although they too will feel the cold international winds after a while. Equally, their mirror across the axis is viable for old cosmopolitan centres – one thinks of London, for example – which may embrace the new order whilst the hinterland resists change.

Two different types of nation or region

The two areas in Figure 3.3 to which nations tend to migrate are the upper left and the lower right. The caption in the upper left summarises one style. This style does not necessarily apply to all regions of a country – as London above – and the Traditionalist elements of the society, and the less capable of its population, may feel alienated by the style. These may begin to cluster around the lower right of the figure.

If we were trying to populate the lower right section of the figure today, we could use nations as the way of dividing up the world's populations. Agrarian, authoritarian and theocratic nations would dot the lower right-hand space.

In the future, however, both social and geographical parts of a nation might be scattered across the entire diagram. London or New York might be located in the upper left, whilst the respective hinterlands of the UK and USA could find themselves in the lower right. In writing this, we initially used the term 'rust belt' to describe these hinterlands: but the factors that pull regions or firms to this corner are not just obsolete heavy industry, but a lack of education or an absence of new recruits to the labour force. A source of tension in industrialised countries will be that neighbouring geographic areas with styles in different quadrants are likely to develop political friction, as London or New York above.

Tackling global systemic issues

Nations in which a successful elite has taken charge of the political narrative are carried to the upper left, as long as they can continue to carry the rest of the society with them, based on economic success. It is on this uneasy tension that success in addressing the global systemic issues has to be developed.

If these issues remain latent for a considerable period, then a gradualist set of adequate solutions will probably be stitched together across the international arena with upper-left countries in the lead. Some nations may elect not to play, and some measures may be taken against them. However, flexibility points to a viable solution. The population of the upper left will grow as more and more nations move to cluster around it. To succeed commercially, one has to comply politically.

If the global systemic issues present early and hard, then the matter is much harder to resolve. Upper-left nations – such as the USA in this time frame – will feel a 'moral equivalent of war' to be in play. They will try to force compliance on the world, for its own good. This will trigger long-term Traditionalist responses that will resist coercion on other issues, if not this. Integration will be that much more difficult to achieve, and the countries in the lower right will become more numerous, leading to an intensification of the untackled issues and a scatter shot of nationalist, authoritarian and often ineffectual actions.

To see how these tensions might play out, we need to look to the longer term.

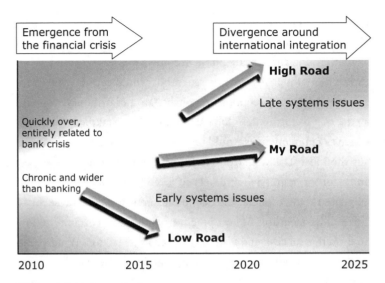

Figure 3.4 Paths to the longer term

Longer-term scenarios

In this section we sketch out three scenarios, which represent different possible futures for the world (for readers not familiar with scenario thinking, Gill Ringland's *Scenario Planning* is a good reference[34]).

The evolution of the scenarios, as the forces discussed above play out, and the potential outcomes for the world, are symbolised in Figure 3.4, which is best thought of as a map rather than a graph. That is, while time flows from left to right, the vertical axis is related to separation or partitioning. Darker areas are harder to enter, whilst lighter areas are like valleys, easy paths to follow for the journey.

The time axis is split into three zones, relating to the short and medium-term future, as discussed in the text above. Events emerge from the narrow valley of the present in directions that we described in Figures 3.1 and 3.2, relating to national positioning in respect of the banking crisis.

Low Road scenario

The lower valley is the one where the Traditionalist forces gain weight around the world. These are not necessarily caused by an early onset of global systemic issues, but would certainly be exacerbated by them. Exceptions might be: an authoritarian response by the rich countries to a global epidemic, where taking swift action which saved many lives would be seen as a positive outcome by all but the most Traditionalist. However, examples such as the 'war on terror' or aggressive attempts to force poor countries to adopt mandated styles of social and economic, environmental or 'security citizenship' measures of best practice would most certainly follow on from this success, and lead to at least some reaction. Widespread slow growth would also worsen a bad situation. Let's call this case *Low Road.*

My Road scenario

The middle valley follows on from an only moderately protracted financial crisis that is chiefly restricted to the old rich nations, and particularly to the USA. Global systemic issues are not seen as urgent. The cosmopolitan centres of the world – chiefly cities – focus on the new style and the new ethos of a billion would-be consumers. This urban and largely prosperous style is labelled *My Road.*

Ultimately, of course, global systemic forces will be impossible to ignore and *My Road* will be torn between reform and denial. As the world is wealthier, so it will have more resources to dedicate to handling these challenges, but it will also have a formidable middle class, many expert in communication skills and enabled by the extraordinary communications media of the times. They may be harder to mobilise around a common theme than were the elites of earlier in the century, and their vested interests will be stronger as they are older.

High Road scenario

The upper valley is labelled the ***High Road***. This is not traversed by all countries and regions of the world at the same pace. There are two pre-conditions for its viability. First, the major economies must emerge from the banking crisis relatively quickly and manage their debt so as to attain adequate growth and social consensus, leading to a sense amongst the communicators and power-brokers that concerted action does indeed produce sound results. Second, system rationalist values must come relatively easily to elites, and also not be too much resented by politically important populations.

When systems issues present themselves in the ***High Road***, there is therefore both the attitude of collective responsibility and the economic strength to meet these with a concerted and thoughtful response. Success in the early stages of this – and real advantages harvested around economic and quality of life issues – reinforce this style. Gradually, upper-left areas become used to this way of thinking about global systemic issues. They tend to impose the implications on their hinterlands, with some opposition and costs but also with increasing success.

High Road is to some extent a visionary scenario, in which at least some parts of the world are successful in recovering from the financial crisis and moving on to tackle the global challenges. In ***Low Road***, the world is less successful in recovering from the crisis, and is more damaged by extreme events such as terrorist attacks and earthquakes.

Global perspective

We emphasise that these scenarios are not descriptions of globally uniform conditions. Whichever may be the dominant style held by some nations, other nations will be in different conditions, much as countries were scattered across the matrix in Figures 3.1 and 3.2.

Proportion of the world's population supporting a given narrative

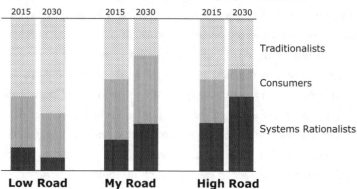

Figure 3.5 Global narratives

Figure 3.5 gives an approximation of how the three most common narratives will be partitioned across the world's populations under each of these scenarios, looking at 2015 and 2030. Plainly, these are the most gross of estimates. They are based on the Challenge Forum! 2030 scenarios which introduced these narratives,[35] but do help to underline the tensions that will exist in each of the cases and, indeed, between any conceivable case. No one of these outcomes is pre-determined, and any one of them will have to fight for its slow rise to dominance.

Path to each scenario

My Road is a projection of the past decade, admittedly with different core players; and in it, some parts of India aspire to become 'just like' the USA, with Indian differences. However, Figure 3.5 shows that even in this familiar picture, only a third of the world follows the consumer narrative, confined to urban elites and also to dynamic countries. Even by 2030, the Consumerist group has not expanded and it is instead the Systems Rationalist narrative which prospers at the expense of the Traditionalist view. *My Road* has an end game that revolves around a transition to **High Road**, a transition which cannot be infinitely delayed.

High Road starts with a high Systems Rationalist population – perhaps due to an early onset of systems-related problems – and their numbers grow, chiefly at the expense of the consumer narrative. The large Traditionalist population strongly resists many aspects of the situation.

High Road is high-minded, collectivist and somewhat authoritarian, and it is not for all nations or all groups. There will be large sections of the world's populations which cannot play and will not play. It is divisive, and despite its best efforts, divisive within nations as the best positioned take advantage of the immense technical and collective potential which is unleashed. Economic activity is tempered by a systems view, leading to what has been called the 'socio-bio-space' (SBS) in which changes in natural and human assets are tallied alongside traditional economic measures of added value, saving and consumption.

However, there will be around 9 billion people alive in 2035. The best estimates are that a 'sustainable' world can support 3–4 billion. Technology will, of course, do wonders, but the almost inevitable impact of global systemic issues is plain. The world has 20–30 years in which to have found a way to take the politically durable actions to address these.

Low Road will not achieve this. Indeed, it is hard to see how to get the world out of **Low Road**, once it is firmly and widely established. A predominantly **Low Road** world would have relatively limited 'islands' in which narratives other than Traditionalist were played. Systems Rationalists would be much hampered by international conditions, and Figure 3.5 suggests how limited their numbers would be.

High Road will exist as an island of cosmopolitanism in a sea made up of populations following the other narratives such that there is much back-sliding towards fragmentation, hostility and

jealousy. Its intense competition, immersion in technology and
fluid change are all predicated on institutional structures which *My
Road* simply lacks. It therefore permits commercial and even cultural activities which *My Road* cannot achieve. It has learned to
solve many issues of legal and political complexity which could
potentially block its progress, and can thus achieve miracles which
other styles cannot. At the same time, it is not a comfortable environment in which to live, as nothing is static and everything is open
to challenge. Remarkable new liberties opened up by new technologies are counterbalanced by many new constraints, from travel
to access to technologies deemed too dangerous for general access.
Biotechnology will have a major impact on the lives of Systems
Rationalists and Consumerists.

Table 3.1 summarises the three scenarios.

The value of scenarios

This analysis may seem rather abstract. What does it mean to the
senior manager in business, to the government policy maker, to the
activist in a non-governmental organisation, to the simple citizen?

First, the scenarios build on the analysis in Chapters 1 and 2.
They recognise that 'international' issues affect all organisations,

Table 3.1 Summary of the three scenarios

	Low Road	My Road	High Road
Early economics	Slow, divisive	New economies	Quick pick-up
Later economics	Protectionist	Urban consumer	SBS (see above)
Systems Rationalist values	Resisted	Rich cities	Aspirational
Consumerist values	Present	Strong	Tempered
Traditionalist values	Strong	Present	Segmented
Systems issue onset	Early–middle	Late	Mid–late

whether corporate bodies, nations or communities. The effect over the past decades had been – until the crisis – benign.

The scenarios deal with the world beyond crisis. By setting up mental models for how the world might evolve in the next decades, they allow us to deal with the many uncertainties ahead.

Executive Summary

- Operating in the hope that we can return to 'business as usual' is no longer realistic: there is no obvious replacement for the US consumer as the motor of growth in terms of sheer size of purchasing power.
- In the short term, the main economic concerns are likely to be the way out of the debt and unemployment situation in the West. In the medium term, the wealthy world will have to come to terms with new competitors and political and economic conditions. In the long term, the world's capability to tackle global systemic challenges is likely to be the dominant issue.
- Three scenarios describe how we might deal with the world beyond crisis. By setting up mental models for how the world might evolve in the next decades, the scenarios allow us to deal with the many uncertainties ahead.
- There is every possibility of rapid changes in relative status for at least some nations and social groups: the older industrial powers will no longer be able to set the rules in the new operating environment as the balance of power changes.
- Senior managers will need to challenge thinking in their organisation, if they are to face up to the reality of the post-crisis world.

Part II

What Organisations Can Do

Chapter 4

Organisational Design

In this chapter, we discuss the ways in which organisations have tuned themselves to past conditions, and the consequences. This tuning, we argue, has often used the same tools, methods and systems as the competition; and the nature of these has led to increased commoditisation on a reducing time scale. We start to build a picture of the additional aspects that organisations will need to have to thrive in the next decades, to adapt to the new business environment and to counter the trends towards commoditisation.

Aligned to the previous environment

A number of factors have contributed to the current way in which organisations manage themselves. Some are the result of technology, others of management theories.

Scientific management

As Peter Drucker observed in 1974:[36]

> Frederick W. Taylor was the first man in recorded history who deemed work deserving of systematic observation and study. On

Taylor's "scientific management" rests, above all, the tremendous surge of affluence in the last seventy-five years which has lifted the working masses in the developed countries well above any level recorded before, even for the well-to-do. Taylor, though the Isaac Newton (or perhaps the Archimedes) of the science of work, laid only first foundations, however. Not much has been added to them since – even though he has been dead all of sixty years.

Among the many contributions to management thought since then from business schools, analysis by Michael Porter,[37] Gary Hamel,[38] and others on the nature of competition has been seminal. It pointed to the defence of a core or set of competences as the principal priority.

These ideas converged in a new scientific management style, a rebirth of the ideas from the first stirrings of the machine age. Its tenets are:

- Change the role of people at work to meet the needs of systems, all connected and integrated by IT and logistics so as to reach around the world, through business process re-engineering.
- Take advantage of the new infrastructure: outside your organisation there is someone who can do whatever you want, so use them to handle anything which is non-core to your business, through outsourcing.
- Bind all of this with contracts that govern productive behaviour.
- Make individuals accountable for each step in the process and reward them for meeting the concrete targets associated with this.

Information technology

Information technology started to make a measurable positive contribution to productivity in the early 1990s. Business process re-engineering was introduced, indicating that if you could not match machines to people, then you should match people to machines. Processes and actions were redesigned to take advantage of what IT could offer.

The result was significant increases in productivity. The US Department of Labor estimates around 15% of total factor productivity growth – that is the growth that cannot be assigned to extra capital investment or to the use of more labour – was down to the use of IT in the decade before 1990 and 20–30% in the decade that followed it, as discussed by Corrado *et al.* in 2005.[39] These gains in productivity have been in the routine tasks in the organisation – back-end processing, enterprise-wide planning, etc.

Total Quality Management

Total Quality Management (TQM) was introduced to ensure that every act leading to a product's completion was optimised and that unusual conditions were controlled. In fact, however, its chief effect was to specify tasks so that they could be automated, opening the gate to outsourcing and remote supply chains. This interpretation of TQM allows the use of lower-skilled people who perform repetitive tasks to an absolute standard. It thus lowers wage costs and manages individual productivity. This side-effect of TQM was witnessed and regretted by Deming as it had not been his intention.[40]

TQM has many benefits, but it has two very negative features. First, it makes the individual work experience 'nothing but' a set of prescribed actions and responses, reporting mechanisms and figures. People are disconnected from the overall purpose and made to follow orders, blindly and without question. Second, TQM delays attempts at innovation.[41] True, there are styles of TQM which evolve and change to fit circumstances. However, all of these are essentially reactive, and do not think forward.

TQM is effective in dealing with the completely specified, in which what is wanted is unambiguous. It is incapable of handling ambiguous, open-ended or evolving circumstances, and it tends to fossilise organisations after a few years have passed. Worse, it lessens the habit of independent thought, innovation and flexibility, with a focus on cranking the crank of the TQM process. A cadre of senior staff emerge for whom 'doing the numbers' is all that matters and the furthest horizon is that which affects their performance bonus.

Shareholder value
The period after the 1991 recession was also marked by what was called the shareholder value movement. This proposes that a public company should focus on activities which add value for the shareholders. In theory, investment in long-term potential was equivalent to immediate cash, but this was seldom the case. Indeed, cheap funds meant that it was easier to grow by acquisition than by organic expansion, and frequently cheaper to borrow to pay dividends than to generate cash internally, as discussed in Chapter 2.

Core and 'other' activities
If your core was all that you needed to add shareholder value, then what did you do with the rest of your activity? You outsourced it. It was pointless to hire your own security guards when a contract with a specialist company would put them on site with no overheads other than cash. If a clothing manufacturer could have clothes made elsewhere by someone else, then so much the better if this generated shareholder value.

All this is to the good in one sense, that of the pin factory, made famous by Adam Smith in *The Wealth of Nations*.[42] He was able to show that 10 men working as a team, each specialised in the different stages of pin making, could easily outperform 10 nonspecialists. Outsourcing is the mechanism of specialisation and productivity displayed in a pure form. However, it has a crucial downside. The specifiers are disconnected from the details of 'doing', and the 'doers' from each other and from the habits of thinking about new things. Everyone is part of a system of targets, specifications and legal obligations. This was seen as a virtue, 'delayering' the organisation and streamlining its functions. Everything was now 'nothing but' a step in the making of metaphorical pins, and all that mattered was to count the output.

Consequences of outsourcing

In a strongly argued article in the *Harvard Business Review*,[43] Gary Pisano and Willy Shih suggest that outsourcing of manufacturing in the USA has weakened competitiveness across an array of industries such as semiconductors, electronic displays, energy storage and green energy production, computing and communications and advanced materials.

They see the need for firms to adopt six principles:

- Make capabilities the main pillar of your strategy.
- Stop blaming the stock market pressures.
- Recognise the limits of financial tools.
- Reinvigorate basic and applied research.
- Collaborate.
- Create technology-savvy Boards of Directors.

They believe that these six measures would rejuvenate innovation capabilities.

Organisations may choose to pursue economic scale or they may seek to extend their capabilities to new and complex abilities (Figure 4.1). The contour lines show the relative ease of following these two strategies. An organisation represented by the dot can increase its abilities by the amount represented by one step across

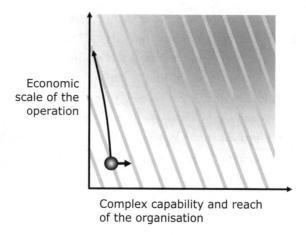

Figure 4.1 Possible trajectories for growth

these contour lines. If the organisation chooses to reduce its complexity (or 'stick to its core business'), then the strategy follows the vertical arrow to a much greater level of scale. To even retain its current level of scale, however, the best that it can do is to move horizontally, as shown by the second arrow. This is an apparently much smaller return for the same amount of effort.

But pure scale may become a less attractive option. The grey shaded area represents some of the growing constraints to pure scale. In minerals and oil, for example, there are few large deposits remaining, and each demands local tactical differences. In almost any field, complexity is increasing as more stakeholders come into play. The strategy of 'going for scale' may be less successful than a move right, along the horizontal axis. Renewal, in general, will impose an increasing horizontal movement on any organisation that wishes to adapt itself to new circumstances.

The effect of all these issues has been to drive organisations to take the vertical trajectory, and to avoid adding complexity, as illustrated in Figure 4.1.

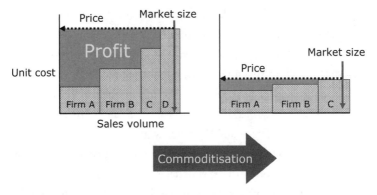

Figure 4.2 Commoditisation

Dealing with the next decades

In the next decades, the pressures in all areas of commerce which can be specified and hence commoditised will be severe. Organisations will need capabilities for adaptability that they have lost over the past decade.

Commoditisation

The next decades will see any processes that can be specified subject to commoditisation and hence extreme pricing pressures. We can see commoditisation at work in an industry in Figure 4.2, based on analysis in work by Rangan *et al.* in 'Beating the commodity magnet'.[44] It compares the division of the total market – the line at the top multiplied by the sales volume along the *x*-axis – among four companies as commoditisation takes place.

In Figure 4.2, the chart on the left shows a young industry. On the vertical axis we show the unit cost of production, and on the horizontal axis the number of units. Firms are arranged as blocks, with the size of their business represented by the block, and the firm with the lowest cost of production placed on the left. The jagged curve that rises to the right, which is the industry cost curve, shows the relative costs of each supplier. This cuts the vertical line that represents the total market size at a point where economists say that marginal revenue – the amount gained from making an additional item – just exceeds the cost of production. This sets the ceiling price, shown as a horizontal dotted line, with everything between the cost curve and the price as profit.

The figure on the right represents the same industry after several years of competition. Firm A, which was the largest and lowest-cost producer, has grown its volume and cut its costs. Firm B has benchmarked itself on A, used the same consultants, technology and business model, and addressed the same customer base. It has become very similar to A. Firm C has also improved very greatly, while Firm D has become insolvent. Market size has increased somewhat, but the price is set as before, by the point where the marginal revenue just exceeds costs, and has decreased significantly. However, these costs have been cut dramatically, and they are now roughly equal right across the industry. Profit has all but vanished.

Commoditisation is central to the competitive process.[45] It generates cheap and high-quality products. Commoditisation is therefore a Good Thing for the economy as a whole. It is less good for those who are trying to make a living from and in the industry which is becoming commoditised. Where productivity increase exceeds output growth, then by definition people, capital and other factors of production are squeezed out of the industry.

Further, the tools normally used to make a firm more productive are exactly those which hasten commoditisation. The emphasis on cost control will hasten the time when all players have the same production costs. (This is less true in industries such as mining, when geological facts have more of a bearing on costs than human endeavour.) That said, if anyone tries to delay the implementation of any of these measures they are swiftly overtaken and brought down. The effect of the large numbers of MBAs trained in 'rational management' has been to hasten the introduction of similar tools across a range of organisations.[46]

The world economy is indifferent to the fate of any one firm, for assets are redistributed and the loss of market by one is the gain for another. However, that is not how individual organisations see this, and they want to know how to avoid this process. We will come to this in the following chapter.

Successful organisations in very challenging environments

As we have seen, the next decades are expected to be turbulent, with very different operational conditions from the last decades. What type of organisation is needed in this environment?

The next decades will not usually permit the simplification of the organisation into just a clear core. There are many reasons for this, e.g.:

- The operating environment is becoming more complex, in the sense that optimisation has to occur across an increasing number of dimensions, for instance corporate and social responsibility, dealing with regulators, etc.
- The speed of change and the number of competitor or rival organisations is increasing, and there are more directions from which both positive potential and unwelcome erosion present themselves.
- Above all, the project-oriented style tends to deliver one thing – a new product, a working relationship – which the organisation continues to exploit for some time. Changes that are made are incremental. Increasingly, however, things do not last. People move on, knowledge is lost. There is no ability to adapt the product or relationship.

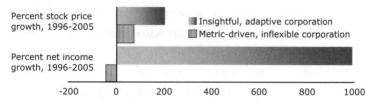

Figure 4.3 Insight and growth

So, the changes over the past decades, which have made management focused and efficient, have as a by-product made organisations less able to deal with change. The seminal work by Emery and Trist[47] suggests that adaptive capacity is what is required in times of turbulence: we observe that the changes over the past decades have made organisations less able to adapt.

The importance of insight and adaptation

Figure 4.3 contrasts the financial performance of organisations that engage in some degree of insight and adaptation with those which are assessed not to do so, based on a questionnaire responded to by 231 organisations[48] in a survey undertaken by 'Tomorrow's Company'. The organisations assessed as 'insightful, adaptive corporation' grew and generated income. Those which were not had both a smaller stock price increase and negative net income growth over the 10 years 1996–2005. These were years in which companies operated in an environment which appeared to be based on Western assumptions. We therefore need to look for evidence that these factors are important in challenging environments, including those where the value systems are changing.

Archetypes of successful organisations

What sort of organisation can be insightful and adaptive? Miller and Friesen[49] in their book *Organizations: A Quantum View* selected 81 case studies published in *Fortune*, the Harvard Case Clearing House and business policy textbooks to look for archetypes of successful organisations. As a result they hypothesised that 31 factors might describe management and organisation, and analysed the companies accordingly.

They divided cases into successful and unsuccessful firms, and separate analyses were run for each group. A successful firm was defined as 'better growth in profits and sales, stability of profits, and returns on equity relative to other forms in the same industry, over the past five years'.

They reported 10 different types or 'archetypes', four of them among the unsuccessful firms (the 'impulsive firm', the 'stagnant bureaucracy', the 'headless giant' and the 'aftermath') and six among the successful firms (the 'adaptive firm under moderate challenge', the 'adaptive firm in a very challenging environment', the 'dominant firm', the 'giant under fire', the 'entrepreneurial conglomerate' and the 'innovator').

Are any of these a model for managers in the turbulent and challenging environment that organisations face today? Yes and no. First, all organisations today need to keep their day-to-day operations competitive and focused, using all the methods and tools available to them, such as LEAN, outsourcing, enterprise systems and process management. But in addition they need to be able to adapt to the turbulent and challenging environment. So, though the 'adaptive firm under moderate challenge', the 'dominant firm', the 'giant under fire', the 'entrepreneurial conglomerate' and the 'innovator' all provide useful pointers, we suggest that the best guide to the **additional** characteristics that organisations need in the next decades is 'adaptive firm in a very challenging environment'.

We can compare the characteristics of this type of organisation with a stereotype of the organisation focused for the last decades as in Table 4.1.

The organisational characteristics that support adaptability are very different from the typical organisation of the last decades.

Table 4.1 Comparison of archetype and stereotype organisations

Characteristic	Adaptive firm in a very challenging environment	Stereotype of focused organisation from last decade
Relation to environment	Adaptive, lead competitors slightly	Tuned to last decade's benign scenario, use best practice from MBAs and gurus
Strategy	Assertive – bold innovations that are hard to imitate, new technologies	Growth by merger and acquisition
Structure	Organic/cerebral – functional, technocratic, differentiated, integrated	Strong divisional structure, weak centre
Information	Scanning environment, open internal communications, committees for collaboration	Line operations own the data
Power	Dispersed through the firm	Held by CEO and divisional directors
Decision making	Analytical, risky, bold	Strong 'me too' culture driven by shareholder pressure
Functional focus	R&D, engineering	Finance

Tensions will surely emerge as organisations try to combine these in one envelope.

We suggest that organisations think of themselves in two distinct parts, those responsible for the day-to-day operations and those responsible for adaptation. Clearly, even in very challenging environments, most people in an organisation will be working on well-specified tasks. So we looked for some role models for how organisations might do this.

Complexity and size

To define the role models we needed a taxonomy for describing organisations. Though most of our analysis in the next chapters is appropriate to organisations of all sizes and types, in some cases we found that the size and/or complexity demanded a different approach. For instance, a retailer or a mining company may be very large but have a flat structure and be less complex than a public-sector organisation which has the same size (expressed in terms of number of employees) but considerably more complexity in its operating environment.

So we used these two dimensions to describe characteristics of organisations which condition their behaviour.

- **Complexity.** One source of complexity is the co-existence of a number of cultures. The dominant culture in many retailers is purchasing; the dominant culture in many oil companies is exploration and production; in many other industries there is a tension between the engineers and the sales cultures. We believe that organisations with diverse cultures are more likely to develop the mechanisms that allow for change, as discussed in work by Ely and Thomas in 'Cultural diversity at work: the effects of diversity perspectives on work group processes'.[50]
- **Size.** Expressed by the number of employees and number of physical locations, it is well known that a 'dotted line'

relationship works if there is physical proximity, whereas a dotted line between different sites (or time zones) leads to lack of connection.[51]

This leads us to two different organisation types:

- The organisation with well-defined boundaries and with decisions taking into account and affecting several organisations with differing narratives. This is typical of divisions of large organisations or large organisations with a unified culture or relatively simple management structure. We refer to this as a '99' organisation, because the vast majority of the staff (more than 99%) are engaged on pre-specified tasks.

- The organisation connected to many other organisations, so that decisions must only be made after taking into account many defining narratives, as they will affect many stakeholders. This is typical of a large and complex organisation, and we call it a '95' organisation, because a significant number – maybe as many as 5% – of employees need to be working on less specified tasks, oriented towards adaptation.

Executive Summary

- In the past two decades, phenomena such as scientific management, TQM, outsourcing and Business Process Re-engineering have made management ever more focused and efficient.
- Products and services are now highly specified, which makes them open to commoditisation and collapse of prices.
- In the next decades, the pressures in all areas of commerce which can be specified and hence commoditised will be severe. Organisations will need the capabilities for adaptability that they have lost over the past decade. To be successful in the future, organisations will have to be insightful and adaptive.

- Organisations need to think of themselves in two distinct parts, one responsible for day-to-day operations and the other responsible for adaptation. The proportion of people in each part will depend on the type of organisation.

Chapter 5

Renewal

In this chapter, we focus on the term 'renewal'. We use this term to cover the activities which act as an antidote to commoditisation. We also talk in more detail about two types of individuals – the Fox and the Hedgehog. We then go on to discuss how organisations can separate into two parts, making renewal more effective, using a double-cone structure to represent this.

Measuring renewal

Renewal[52] is defined as 'to replace something that is worn, broken or no longer suitable for use'. Organisational renewal is the process by which an organisation achieves coherence in its responses to events. Some of these responses will consist of activities, such as product innovation, partnerships and new projects, maybe creative destruction, as an antidote to commoditisation. Other aspects will be less tangible, including the quality and nature of the many connections that any organisation has to outsiders and employees.

The purposeful coherence of renewal is deeply important. It is easy to expend resources on random activity. What is needed is directional activity. How have the goals been defined and agreed? Is it useful to have concrete goals, or rather a moving target that is never attained because it is continually extended and refined?

In thinking through how to measure renewal, we identified two factors which contribute to renewal: the change in the resources (fixed assets, capital, people, businesses, products and services) used by the organisation (the portfolio), and their ability to increase profitability, crudely expressed as the return on capital employed.

An organisation consists of a number of sectors or units, and each sector or unit has a bundle of resources. The organisation's portfolio is in general the sum of these (though sometimes the organisation has an intangible 'goodwill' associated, for instance, with a corporate brand). We can calculate the percentage of change in each sector's resources relative to the rest of the company over any time period. The aggregate is the change in the organisation's resources which are easily measured.

The second thing to assess is the desirability of any change. In a commercial organisation, it is reasonable for growth in resources to be in the profitable sectors or units, or those likely to be able to grow. Since history is not always the best guide to the future, in Chapter 12 we give some ways of using scenarios to explore future viability or profitability of sectors. The more desirable sectors should attract more investment than economically weak sectors. A crude measure of renewal could be something like the increase in return on capital employed compared with the average for the industry sector of the unit,[53] where attractive sectors have a high ratio, over the planning period.

We can now construct a figure of merit for renewal, an index which is strongly positive when the change in resource in each sector is correlated with the indications of an attractive business. Positive correlations (numbers close to unity) reflect high levels of

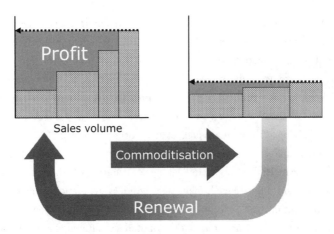

Figure 5.1 Commoditisation and renewal

renewal, because portfolio changes are tightly correlated with increases in profitability. Numbers with negative correlations (numbers close to −1) reflect perverse behaviour, where the firm is growing its least profitable activities. Numbers close to zero show investment having no correlation with profitability. The effect of a positive renewal index is shown in Figure 5.1.

The processes for renewing and managing the portfolio are less well specified than those in the line units of the organisation. They include strategy, innovation and shared vision. The case study below[54] illustrates the difficulty of renewal.

Case study – Google

In the early years, Google used an informal system for idea generation. Managers could constitute small teams to study ideas, which percolated up such hierarchy as there was. Now with 20,000 employees, this system no longer works.

In an attempt to avoid 'middle age', Eric Schmidt, Larry Page and Sergey Brin (the current CEO and original founders, respectively) hold regular meetings at which junior staff pitch their ideas directly. Projects are given more resource and independence than previously. Twelve are now running, with Google professing ambitions for a target of 50. Google Wave is an advanced discussion forum package which was developed through a typical skunk works[55] approach.

Some mainstream Google employees assert that in avoiding 'nit picking criticism' it has also missed the contribution which the organisation could offer. Indeed, many see the ideas generation process as insufficient in itself. Investment banker Piper Jaffray says, 'Google has been masterful in coming up with a lot of ideas, but none has matured to become something that moves the revenue needle'.

Google has not to date renewed itself beyond its core 'big idea'.

Firms' self-perceived weaknesses

Figure 5.2 shows the result of self-assessment by a large number of companies,[56] published by Voss in a study in 1998. They were asked to score themselves against the rest of their industry for the range of factors that are shown. The symbols show the mean for small, medium and large companies, and the line simply connects these for clarity. What is striking is that all see themselves as good at specified activities, arranged on the left. All see themselves as worse at strategy, innovation and the other less specified activities, as shown on the right. This suggests a common mindset among many managers, more comfortable with specified than less specified activities.

But at the same time, these less specified tasks are those that renew the organisation's portfolio. The cost of not getting the portfolio right is massive – in the end it is the company's survival.

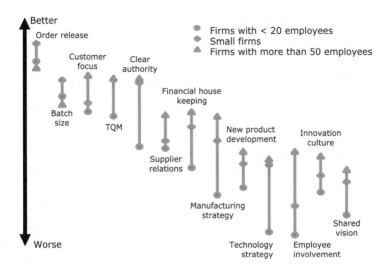

Figure 5.2 Firms recognise weakness

The cost of specification

A study by McKinsey gives a good idea of the cost of specifying a task as distinct from doing it, in the relatively well-structured environment of manufacturing. The study of the cost structure in manufacturing industry was based on firms in India, Germany and the USA.[57] The outcome is shown in Figure 5.3, in which the life-time costs are split between the actual cost of operations – at the bottom – the managerial and financial overhead – in the middle – and a third element. This last is termed the cost of gaining insight, but includes as well false starts, blind alleys and all of the unhappy events that strike poorly specified projects.

What is so striking about this figure is the absolute size of the costs that are associated with insight, here defined as developing specifications including failed pilots, cost over-runs, etc. Even in India, where the projects are likely to be less complex, these costs are nearly 40% of the total.

The processes to update the portfolio must be expected to reflect the same type of iteration since a fully specified set would

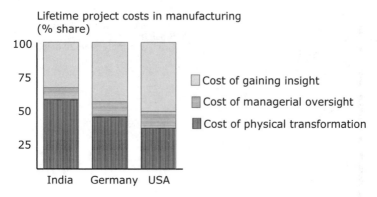

Figure 5.3 Cost of gaining insight
Source: McKinsey (1997).

be accessible to everyone and therefore instantly copied, and the resulting products and services commoditised.

Updating the portfolio
The processes involved in updating the portfolio can be divided into two categories: continuous improvement-type activities, which can have major payback for the organisation within the existing portfolio, and new departures which alter the portfolio. We focus in this book on the big, new departures which renew the portfolio, rather than the essential continuous business improvements that are part of the day-to-day operation. Innovation is the key to the leaps involved in addressing the less specified tasks in any organisation. What are the hurdles to innovation in a large organisation?

Hurdles to innovation

In large companies, normally only a few aspects of implementing a new idea require technologies or processes that are new to the organisation. Most aspects of its implementation can use proven methodologies supplied by other parts of the organisation. In a small, start-up organisation, many of the pieces may not have been put together before. This should give a higher innovation success rate in large organisations than in small organisations.

There are, however, a number of obstacles to innovation which remain in large organisations. The first of these is frictional, in which the existing organisation resists the new. In any large organisation, many senior people are in place because they have been good at 'the system', whatever that was. They are often happy to devote their time to just keeping the wheels turning, and do not want to devote energy to new things.

The second is the tension between upgrades and new things. Innovations which make it easier to sell more of the existing product are welcome, and budgets for routine upgrades are nodded through. However, the divisional line structure often hinders idea flows, either explicitly (through discouraging cross-division communication) or implicitly (through discouraging engagement in developing new ideas). This obviously hampers the ability of organisations to innovate. Third, one senior figure can, and often does, block an idea if he does not see a personal advantage in it. His motivation may be conservatism, 'if it's not broke, don't fix it'. It may even be personal concern that the new world is not one where he knows the rules. Finally, new things cost the organisation. The concerns may be about new kinds of liability, the inadequate scale of the proposed new activity, or the very real demands on management time of activities not part of day-to-day operations. And shareholders may take a view against diversification from 'core activities'.

Overcoming the hurdles: how innovation works
To look for models which may avoid these hurdles, we look at some examples. The UK Design Council's Millennium Products

initiative identified the most innovative products and services created in the UK in the last five years of the past millennium. It found that the companies able to create these products shared three capabilities: to create, to inspire and to connect with all stakeholders. They all had a strong narrative, which we will come back to later. They also, to their surprise, found that 'fun' and 'buzz' were words often applied to these organisations.[58]

Japanese electronics companies, on the other hand, often approach product innovation in a combinatorial manner, starting from available components and thinking what could be done with this or that combination of them. Then they think of a use for that, build prototypes by hand and see which ones sell. Once an idea sells, they 'squeeze' customers to see what they really like in the product and build this into more prototypes. By now, they have a good idea what they are chasing, and set up a programme to deliver a succession of models that hit the right buttons. Their car industry works in much the same way.[59]

Western food companies, perhaps inadvertently, do the same thing. Only 3% of new food products stay available for as much as six weeks after launch, and those which do survive often cross-pollinate with each other to generate new offers,[60] as described by A.L. Brody.

A semi-Darwinian procedure is at work. It is important to note that as with natural evolution, a continuity of information is required, something that fulfils the role played chiefly by genes in the natural world. The corporate equivalent is, on the one hand, collective memory and experience and on the other, the continuity of capacity and brand, customer expectation and capability that supports any initiative. Innovation has deep roots, and successful innovation needs fertile soil.

Figure 5.4 shows where new ideas come from in large organisations.[61] The key points are how much comes from outsiders, how

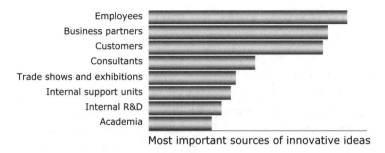

Employees
Business partners
Customers
Consultants
Trade shows and exhibitions
Internal support units
Internal R&D
Academia

Most important sources of innovative ideas

Figure 5.4 Where does innovation come from?

little from internal R&D, and what an important role is played by employees.

Some of the dynamics behind these findings may be illustrated by the case study below.

Case study – innovation from across the silos

A Korean electronics manufacturing company commissioned consultants to help with innovation. It had a strong manufacturing base in three countries and sold its products globally. It spent around 8% of turnover on R&D, but succeeded only in generating me-too products and incremental improvement in existing product lines.

On investigation, it was found that technical and marketing staff were deeply frustrated. They blamed this on the Korean temperament, which they described as unwilling to assert individual ideas or to go against what the bosses seem to want. Unhappily, nobody had any idea what the bosses wanted, least of all – save at the most general of levels – the senior management itself. Research budgets were being spent on the same issues that the business units had specified a decade previously. Marketers preferred to look to third parties for new product ideas.

The recommendation was that a set of processes was needed to get the various parties talking to each other. As a first start, interviews were conducted amongst researchers – defining technical potential and technology road maps; amongst marketers, around issues of customer preference; and amongst senior management, who were asked what the company wanted to become to its customers, and avoid becoming.

Exposure of the outcome of these interviews to mixed groups of research and marketing staff – with some production people – led to a list of ideas which were assigned priority for further development. Six of 11 products reached the market place, and two were extremely successful. Meanwhile, a more spontaneous system was put in place to ensure ongoing renewal of the portfolio.

We suggest that there is a connection between the staffing profile achieved over the past decade and the important role of outsiders. Organisations are, as a result of outsourcing and de-layering, extraordinarily more permeable to external influences than they were. The average person working for them is more educated than in the past. They will probably have worked in other organisations. They have a relatively large knowledge base, and an immeasurably wider circle of acquaintance. It was relatively rare to meet someone outside a large corporation or the civil service when you worked in either of these three decades ago; now a significant fraction of everyday work involves outside contacts with partners or suppliers.

This brings us to defining the characteristics of staff who can innovate, and who can enable and support renewal of the portfolio: what sort of staff will be open to new ideas and able to take them into the organisation?

Foxes and Hedgehogs: their roles in renewal

'The Fox knows many things, but the Hedgehog knows one big thing.'
Archilochus (7th-century BCE)

In understanding the characteristics of people and organisations that can innovate, we use a description of management styles based on Isaiah Berlin's adaptation of the quotation above. As he uses it, Hedgehogs relate everything to single concrete narrative, through which everything in life is reduced to a set of certainties. Foxes, on the other hand, distrust grand designs and absolute truths, and instead pursue many ends, often unrelated and even contradictory. They use a flexible array of insights that guide them as they experiment, play with ideas and experience, explore and, on occasion, pounce.

Recent psychological testing[62] has shown that this is a valid and powerful way of classifying people. As psychologists have defined the type, Hedgehogs are people who are happiest operating within a closed problem domain, in which standard tools and focused effort allow them to compete with their peers. They are happy with the existing system or implementing a formula to change it.

Foxes[63] are at their best exploring new terrain and re-thinking certainties. Their goals are largely self-actualisation and they are seldom concerned to rank themselves against their peers. Foxes are suspicious of commitment to any one way of seeing an issue; they prefer a loose insight that is calibrated from many perspectives. They are tolerant of dissonance within a model – for example, accepting that an enemy regime might have redeeming qualities – and are relatively ready to recalibrate their view when unexpected events cast doubt on what they had previously believed to be true.

Characteristics of Hedgehogs
Hedgehogs are exactly what organisations need to deliver against unambiguous tasks and tight deadlines. They were rightly prized in the operating environment which characterised much of the last century. Hedgehogs, however, are often stressed when asked to extend the borders of their current activities, to predict events and to mitigate new sources of risk.

Hedgehog types easily drop into over-confidence and over-focus. For example, many people who work in financial services can be seen as a Hedgehog type, with blind reliance on financial models. Almost all of those who congregate around compliance – including functions like Health and Safety and risk assessment – fit this model.

A cerebral approach is extremely seductive to Hedgehogs. The bold reduction of a problem to an over-simplified model often presents itself as a rational response to a challenge. It points to a set of practical and conceptual tools with which the typical Hedgehog feels at home. A group of Hedgehogs together may descend into 'group think' – particularly when the situation is stressful and the Hedgehog has reached his or her bounds – and a defended orthodoxy can come to reign in a company, a political movement, religion or nation.

Characteristics of Foxes

Foxes neither enjoy unambiguous tasks with tight deadlines nor perform well at them. Foxes excel at tasks which extend boundaries or are ambiguous; and consequently will frequently encounter Hedgehogs at their worst. Competent Foxes need a framework in which to operate that prevents them being undermined by, or coming into conflict with, Hedgehogs. It is Foxes, however, that are needed for renewal – the end point of the renewal processes cannot by definition be completely defined at the beginning.

The Fox-like organisation

We have seen that the Hedgehog is at his happiest when confronted with a difficult task in which everything to be done is fully specified: all that remains is the doing. This is their peak area of competence, and it has constituted much of what most organisations have had to manage over the past 20 years. It has driven the race to commoditisation. However, we are moving into a very different environment, one of swift commoditisation, ambiguity and the necessary response of renewal.

The relationship that has developed between large organisations and consultants is an interesting example of this at play. There has been an extraordinary boom in consultancy in the past 20 years. At least some of this has been a direct consequence of companies running down their capacity to think in non-Hedgehog ways. That is, if the rationale of the organisation can be reduced to a single 'thinking model' – let's say, the pursuit of shareholder value – then the organisation has its lode star, and can dispense with its Foxes. Consequently, Foxes congregate in strategic consultancies, and are brought in when Hedgehogs hit a wall.

This discussion should not be taken to establish an equation that Hedgehogs are bad, while Foxes are good. Rather, all natural Foxes need to become quite a bit more Hedgehog-like for parts of their life. The same is true of Hedgehogs. Both need to recognise their limits and natural aptitudes, and endeavour not to censor the necessary contribution of the other (Figure 5.5).

The Fox and the
Hedgehog

Figure 5.5 Foxes and Hedgehogs

We now need to set renewal, and the roles of Hedgehogs and Foxes, in an organisational context.

The double-cone: a framework for Foxes and Hedgehogs

We see many organisations which can be represented in the shape of an inverted cone, balancing unsteadily on a portfolio which specifies their activities, along with all the operational documentation, guidelines, regulatory specifications, etc. The front-end activities are at the top, as are supplier and partner relationships (which you may remember were the source of much innovation). As discussed above, most organisations have become very good at these specified activities.

But when we look at the turbulent operational environment, with the need to deal with emerging global scenarios, it is clear that organisations need to be better at activities to renew their portfolio. The insights of the people at the front end are not captured. In fact, in some organisations it is as if the cone is supported by a piece of wet string – certainly nothing to give it stability.

We suggest that there needs to be a lower cone of activities to support renewal and adaptation to the external environment, on which the portfolio and the upper inverted cone rest. These activities include those for Insight and those for developing Options for the portfolio. This is the double-cone model, as in Figure 5.6.

In Figure 5.6, the upper cone represents the specified activities that the organisation has to handle. This deals with the formalised operations of day-to-day work. It is where activity is concentrated in most organisations. It is a good environment for Hedgehogs.

Control radiates out and up from the portfolio, the ball-bearing at the base of the upper cone. This symbolises the mechanism

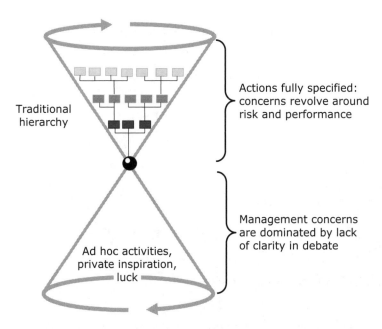

Figure 5.6 Moving from uncertainty to clarity

through which projects are selected and the portfolio of assets subject to winnowing and critique. It is the gateway between the lower cone and the upper cone.

The lower cone consists of activities that may range from the occasional away-day or routine strategic planning activity, to effective processes for portfolio renewal. It often includes vague, informal and untested insights about the operating environment. It is far removed from the customer or supplier-facing layers. This is the natural domain of the Fox. However, because of the pervasive Hedgehog culture, those who populate this domain are often unsure of their legitimacy. Some are career staff workers, somewhat alienated from the mainstream activities and not good at communicating with staff in the line organisations of the upper cone.

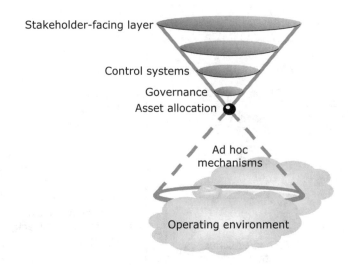

Figure 5.7 Organisational realities

This image can be redrawn to fit more closely with organisational realities, as in Figure 5.7. The upper cone now holds successive layers of activity up to the stakeholder-facing layer that deals with customers, voters, creditors, owners, regulators, suppliers, donors and others. Governance sits above the 'dot' where the two cones join, representing the mechanisms by which potential projects become part of the organisation.

The need to get the lower cone right to achieve renewal

We have seen (Figure 5.2) that substantial sums are spent on resolving issues that should have been resolved previously, in typically lower-cone activities. It follows that organisations need structures to handle these issues; that organisations need to make fewer mistakes by resolving the issues before they are part of day-to-day operations. In the software world, the relative costs to find a bug have been estimated as 1 in testing, 10 in trials and 100 in use: all being costs directly incurred by the supplier of the software and ignoring costs of lost business, customer disruption, etc.[64] Equally, if the new operating environment demands that even more ideas, insight and potential be garnered from the lower cone, then we need to find a way of making it more effective. Ad hoc mechanisms will not do, but neither will generic, rote structures: organisations are different in many ways and need to evolve their own style, processes and combinations of Foxes and Hedgehogs.

Executive Summary

- The term 'renewal' covers the activities which update a company's portfolio. It is the antidote to commoditisation.
- The cost of not getting the portfolio right is massive – in the end it is the company's survival.
- The processes for renewing and managing the portfolio are less well specified than those in the line units of the organisation. They include strategy, innovation and shared vision.
- Organisations can be represented by a double-cone structure, with day-to-day operations – specified tasks – in the top cone and the less specified processes of renewal in the bottom cone, joined in the middle by a ball-bearing which is the portfolio of assets.
- There are two distinct management types, Hedgehogs and Foxes. Hedgehogs are good at specified tasks, Foxes at dealing with ambiguity. Organisations need to evolve their own style, processes and combinations of Foxes and Hedgehogs.

Chapter 6

The Importance of Purpose

This chapter discusses the need for clarity of purpose in the process of renewal. We discuss possible sources that sense of purpose can come from, and the need for 'leadership from every chair' with 'extraordinary competence'. We introduce for the first time this book's overarching concept, a Purposeful Self-Renewing Organisation.

Clarity of purpose

Consultancy McKinsey[65] analysed over a hundred thousand questionnaires concerned with the costs and business practices of 400 business units in 230 companies around the world, in a study published in 2007. They found that three dimensions explained most of the variance in cost performance between these units. The dimensions were:

- That there were clear roles for employees, i.e. clarity of task.
- That there was a compelling insight into the direction of change, i.e. clarity of purpose.
- That the environment encouraged openness, trust and challenge.

Where clarity of purpose or task is lacking, employees often attribute its absence to poor leadership, meaning the senior management team and Board. What should senior management and directors do to set an environment of openness, trust and challenge able to bring about purposeful renewal?

Senior management and the Board

What are the roles of senior management and the Board in providing this context of openness, trust and challenge? Can senior management or the Board provide the clarity of purpose or task? We discuss below the decision-making roles of senior management.

Decision making

Senior management decision making is almost always much more informal and diffuse than the formal Board structure would suggest, and collective agreement is obtained from a consensus that is often reached by opaque means.

Quiet conversation can be more potent than formal analysis, and the pretence that project selection revolves around formal criteria and numerical assessment can be a fable. Informal and diffuse discussions are a good thing when conversations about complex matters are well informed. But when the building is on fire, command and control is the correct form of leadership to use!

Decision making in organisations cannot be democratic, but it does need to engage with the widest possible group of stakeholders to ensure robust decisions and follow-through in uncertain times. The senior management and Board can initiate such a culture.

If insight is left to the 'top', the rest of the organisation will probably perceive a strategic deficit, a sense that nothing new is happening and that all senior management are doing is squeezing the system for cash. People in the organisation may look for weak signals which could be precursors of change, and once such signs are detected, deluge senior staff with potential projects and appeals for resource. Senior management, in turn, shield their thoughts more closely.

The result is that senior managers become isolated from the body of the organisation, and matters are made worse by attempts to keep the organisation focused through a series of slogans: shareholder value, core focus, results orientation and so forth. Hedgehogs feel at home in this environment. Numerical targets – volumes, costs, prices – are unambiguous matters that can be measured, mandated and connected to equally numerical incentives.

The CEO
Meanwhile, there are many organisations in which power is tightly concentrated in the CEO. That power is sometimes seen as being synonymous with the sources of ideas and initiatives. This is not a helpful stance in a complex world, as we saw in Chapter 5.

In the USA, in particular, there is a strong myth that connects excellent results to the personal strengths of the CEO. Even in the USA, however, it is uncommon for single individuals within large public organisations to have the unilateral power to make major things happen.

It is, however, common for individuals to have the ability to block projects. Major projects therefore need the endorsement of a group of people that usually extends far into the organisation; and while a scheme may be initiated by an individual, many critical voices should be able to moderate or halt the project if it is seen to be inappropriate. Of course, this does not always happen and the root of major mistakes is often found to be the unwillingness of an individual or small group to take wider soundings before making a decision.

The role of the CEO and Board is therefore to provide a context in which dispersed power is effective in setting a direction or sense of purpose, and harnessing the activities of the organisation to that purpose.

Leadership

In Chapter 4 we introduced the characteristics of the successful, adaptive organisations in very challenging environments, which included 'Power: dispersed through the firm'. What does this imply for senior management?

The respected leadership thinker, Peter Kostenbaum[66] uses as a definition of leadership:

'The twin challenges of leadership are to develop leadership intelligence [and capability] and to universalise that intelligence throughout the organisation.'

People need to be able to 'lead from any chair'.[67]

What is added to this in very challenging times? Globalisation changes the nature of leadership and the identity of who 'we' are. Turbulence means that linear projections are unlikely to guide us sufficiently in strategic planning. The imperative for organisations to manage the lower cone effectively (and in a participative manner) is vital to developing new Values and Narratives. Turbulent environments demand changes in seemingly enduring aspects of an organisation's existence. Think, for example, of the financial services sector in which losses have been socialised while profits seem to remain privatised. Remuneration systems that were outside the purview of society at large have suddenly become the subject of social debate. Organisations need to recognise this and align themselves with society's emerging values. Emery and Trist[68] say this is a lifetime or generation-long project; there is no quick fix!

It is widely accepted that very few of the current cadre of senior managers can manage in this way.[69] The challenge is therefore immense. As Ronald Heifetz says,

'Are you waiting for things to return to normal in your organisation? Sorry. Leadership [senior management] will require new skills tailored to an environment of urgency, high stakes and uncertainty – even after the current economic crisis is over.'

He also emphasises the role of senior managers in generating leadership, giving people at all levels of the organisation the opportunity to lead experiments that will help it adapt to changing times.[70]

An example of senior management developing an environment in which people at all levels led experiments to change the organisation is given in the case study below.

Case study – leadership from every chair[71]

Julie Gilbert, senior VP at retailer Best Buy, saw a looming crisis in the company's failure to profit from the greater involvement of women in the previously male-dominated world of consumer electronics.

The company had traditionally looked to (male) senior executives for direction and innovation. But appealing to female customers meant engaging with women at all levels in the company. A successful project engaged with female staff to sell home theatre systems co-ordinated with furniture and accessories, leading to increased sales and interest from female customers. This led to the setting up of WoLF (Women Leadership Forum) packs, with two men and two women leading each group. More than 30,000 employees from store cashiers to corporate executives joined WoLF packs, which harnessed their collective experience to generate further innovative projects, using meetings, email and discussion forums.

Leadership tends to be scattered more widely within organisations than the formal hierarchies would suggest. People are acknowledged as leaders around issues and areas of insight where they are able to articulate a concrete contribution. Leadership expresses itself in specialist areas, such as technical insight; in detailed aspects of finance, of IT, of HR; as well as what are, in commerce, the product divisions. Studies based on email traffic in organisations have reinforced this view of organisational dynamics[72] – by studying the hubs of email traffic, where many connections intersect, the location of influence can be suggested. People in organisations quickly recognise and respect those who have judgement and common sense.

As we saw in Chapter 5, Insight comes from outside and inside the organisation; a role of leadership is to set the environment in which this can become information used to support decision making, and develop options for the portfolio.

Developing leaders

It is the leaders' job to develop other leaders. In particular, people will need support and feedback from many different perspectives to deal with ambiguity and develop Fox-like traits.

Managing in turbulent times requires a different type of leadership in addition to conventional senior management. Everyone, no matter what hierarchical level they inhabit, must take responsibility for leading when needed and for recognising when they should be leading. Benjamin Zander calls this 'Leading from Any Chair'.[73]

In Chapter 10 we will discuss the organisation's core values and how the desired behaviour for each value needs to be defined. In any organisation there will be conversations needed to understand and agree those behaviours because there are so many different contexts and cultures in which people work. The organisation must help people in different cultures and at different levels to live their leadership.

This can be achieved not just in formal 'learning' or development sessions, but also through example, coaching and developing others.

While leadership development in the '99' organisation is not as complex as that for the '95' organisation because there are fewer different cultures, the focus still needs to be on leaders developing other leaders.

At their best, leaders support and encourage creativity and innovation, which brings about renewal. They use any method to hand for this – encouraging contributions from across and outside the organisation to bring additional diversity into the organisation. This could be making use of drama, art or storytelling, innovative presentation methods and ideas for research. Their role is not only to develop the leadership tools in their team, but to create an environment in which innovation can come from any role in the organisation.

Competence

Employees can be competent if they have clarity of role as we saw earlier. The CIPD (Chartered Institute of Personnel and Development) defines competence as:

'the behaviours that employees must have, or must acquire, to input into a situation in order to achieve high levels of performance'.[74]

Competent individuals understand their working environments, what is wanted of them and the limits to the response that they can make to these. They have the tools and 'permissions' – legitimacy, rights – to do what is required of them.

Furthermore, a group can be much more capable than a cluster of competent individuals.[75] In R. Meredith Belbin's work with teams in the 1970s he was able to show that teams can perform better than individuals do separately;[76] the essential factor was that a team was in balance and contained all the team roles he had identified. A person could play more than one team role or they could play to their secondary rather than primary team role if there was another person better suited for their primary team role. For a team to be extraordinarily productive and capable, all team roles need to be present.

Extraordinary competence

Positive-sum games are defined as those where a win is for everybody, all players benefit, and the chances of a win are greater than the possibilities of a loss, as distinct from a zero-sum game where one person's win is somebody else's loss. An example of a positive-sum game environment is that of everybody fulfilling their role to the best of their abilities in a high-potential project. The leader is pleased with everyone, nobody loses out (for instance any redundant staff are redeployed), and the organisation is in better shape after the work is done than it was before.

This is a step that goes beyond collective competence. It is readily recognisable, and we call it 'extraordinary competence'.

Extraordinary competence allows dispersed leadership to contribute to the direction – the purpose – of the organisation. Extraordinary competence is enabled by a clear set of Values of the organisation, as discussed further in Chapter 10, and by a strong Narrative to harness innovation, as discussed in Chapter 12; and it requires a positive-sum game culture. It was described in Rosabeth Moss Kanter's early work *Maintenance and parallel organisations*,[77] which observes that this parallel activity (lower cone) releases potential which generates a positive set of feedback loops for the individual:

- Breaks from routine, revitalising individuals.
- Interactions with others beyond the normal horizons, leading to reciprocal learning.
- High opportunity around valued contribution, leading to high self-esteem.

The extraordinary competence of the organisation is reached by

'self-esteem and freedom of expression linked to social interaction through cooperation with others and the achievement of identifiable results'.

Setting a purpose

The answer to the question 'who do we want to be?' involves a complex series of concerns and is best answered through a broad, continual process; a journey. It is a journey of many small steps, with the destination gradually growing clearer just as new – perhaps alternative – destinations appear faintly further off, requiring course corrections. This is very different from the strategy-setting processes of the past decades, but is essential in turbulent times.

Figure 6.1 gives us some idea of what is happening on this journey. Figures of this sort must be drawn in order to reflect the most important issues as they affect the organisation. We will use competition as an example, though of course for public-sector organisations the issue could be service levels or disruptive technology.

The left-hand side of the figure represents the present. The two axes are the factors which matter the most to the organisation. In a marketing company, for example, one of these might show how strongly the organisation links its brand to 'green' issues, as

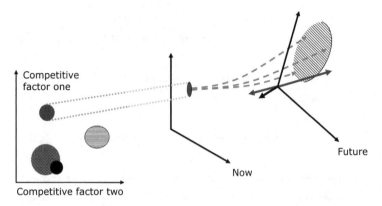

Figure 6.1 Plotting a course

compared to its rivals. The other might represent the balance which it strikes between cost and quality in its retail offer.

Each competing organisation sits at a defined position on this plane. The size of the spots which represent each of them is proportional to its absolute scale, measured by sales, capital employed or employee numbers. It is then easy to see who dominates which aspects of what are defined as being the most important factors which affect the organisation.

The right-hand side of the figure represents the future. We have omitted the competitors for clarity but each of them will, of course, be making similar assessments and choices. The original dimensions are now skewed, because what is now meant by the original form of words – for example, 'Green positioning' – has changed. Equally, there could be more axes shown because the world has changed. The new axes might, for example, represent segmentation of the market by consumer age cadre, or perhaps a new issue facing this industry.

The blob that represents the organisation is much larger than before, representing not growth but rather the range of potential destinations that are open to it. The nature of this potential is set by competitive considerations, but also by all sorts of other issues, such as the Values to which the organisation adheres, its asset base, the quality and nature of its people and its geographical range.

All of this, taken together, suggests a 'fuzzy destination' towards which the organisation might want to travel. This is not a discrete target, but a directed journey. This *purposefulness* is what has to be captured in the Narrative of the organisation. It is also what the Options process has to embody and advance when it selects new projects, and when it closes down existing activities. It is the root from which renewal will grow.

How to describe the destination
It is worth asking what constitutes a 'destination'. There are two factors that describe the destination. The first is that it is what the organisation *does* in the future, what units or sectors it has, targeting which customers or fulfilling which services. The other is that it is the *bundle of assets and capabilities* that allow it to do these things, its portfolio as already described.

The many small steps of the journey are each concrete changes in the assets and capabilities of the organisation. This collection of physical assets and cash streams, intellectual property, licences and rights, tools, permissions, contracts and contacts is part of the portfolio.

Destinations, expressed through the portfolio, are useful ways of representing positions on the overall organisational journey. Leadership's role is in providing an environment in which the journeys can be successfully travelled to a well-chosen, though fuzzy, destination.

A Purposeful Self-Renewing Organisation
An organisation which can adapt to turbulent times needs to have good Insight. It needs to be able to develop Options for renewal. It

will have strong Values and Narrative to provide purpose and set the context for extraordinary competence, as discussed above.

The organisation which combines these is one which we call a Purposeful Self-Renewing Organisation, or PS-RO.

A PS-RO can be any size of organisation and PS-ROs can exist within organisations as well. If the organisation as a whole is not (yet) a PS-RO, a group can still be one within it. They can act like a skunk works. It is highly likely that they will then experience the 'When Harry Met Sally' effect: people will notice how well the group is working and want to have some of what *they* have.

Executive Summary

- The role of senior management is to set an organisational purpose, guide the organisation towards that, and ensure that the operating environment supports extraordinary competence.
- High performance standards often emerge best in 'positive-sum game' cultures.
- The key role of leaders is to develop other leaders such that leadership becomes dispersed throughout the organisation.

Chapter 7

Five Qualities for Renewal

In this chapter we bring together leadership, competence and adaptability to describe the five essential qualities necessary to drive the kind of purposeful self-renewal needed in the new operating environment.

The journey and destination

We have highlighted the important role of clarity of purpose in achieving extraordinary competence. The first two qualities that must be in place are a wide understanding across the organisation of the core **Values** against which the organisation calibrates itself and a wide understanding of the true proprietary capabilities and important gaps in these, the **Narrative** of the organisation.

This is because in a time of changes in the external environment, the Values and Narrative of the organisation provide stability, a sense of purpose. The expression of Values may of course change – albeit slowly – over time, as society changes. Narrative is likely to evolve, but slowly as well – maybe over a 10-year time frame – as new activities enter the organisation's portfolio. A coherent Narrative facilitates innovation in pursuit of renewal.

Clearly, in volatile times, there needs to be the capability to understand the operating environment, current capabilities and gaps that exist within that understanding, i.e. **Insight**. Given Insight, what **Options** does the organisation have to respond to these insights in line with its core Values and Narrative? This is perhaps the issue most complex to deliver in an organic, informed manner.

The **Machinery** to support these includes processes, communications and people. In the absence of this machinery – or infrastructure – success will be achieved only by accident.

The flow of the Insight and Options generation activities is continual and parallel. In a PS-RO, it harnesses the experience and knowledge from across the organisation rather than being limited to a separate or elite group. How can people in different parts of the organisation become involved, informed and enabled to achieve extraordinary competence? The five qualities of a PS-RO model which contribute to this are connected as shown in Figure 7.1 and discussed separately below.

Values

Values are the beliefs of a person or social group in which they have an emotional investment (either for or against something). They provide stability in uncertain times because core Values do not easily change.

Values set the terms on which an organisation makes choices. As an example of this, it is a value judgement as to what level of quality an organisation is to pursue: the legal minimum, the level that only one customer in a thousand will find defective? One in a hundred thousand? The answer depends on a host of other judgements and there is no unequivocally correct answer.

There are, usually, a number of such dimensions on which the company has to place itself as 'not more than this, not less than

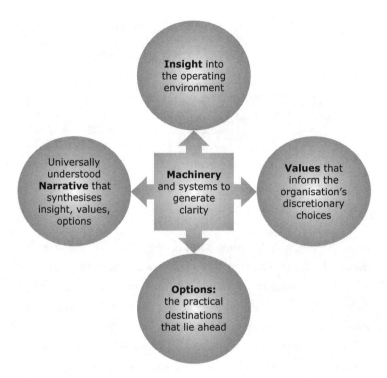

Figure 7.1 Five qualities of a PS-RO

that'. We call these limits 'book ends' in Figure 7.2. Positioning an organisation in this 'value space' defines its identity with respect to its competitors, since the organisation and its competitors are all governed by similar rational calculations, technologies and outsourcing. Typically, such choices are not independent of each other if the positioning is to be coherent. Consequently, differentiation, brand and general positioning depend sharply on coherent value-related choices. The figure shows the intersection of an organisation's desired position on the spectrum of attitudes to employees and that on the spectrum of approach to customers. Both would be the subject of audits as discussed in Chapter 11.

Organisations have a specific position in this value space, and individual units will always have a clear position. It may be a poor

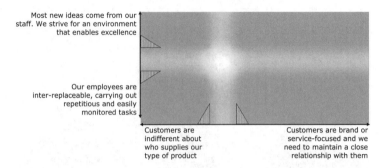

Figure 7.2 Finding a position in value space

position, they may be ashamed of it or hypocritical about it, but they will have it. There may be clashes with other units, with the overall organisational position or with external stakeholders. Nevertheless, there are always values present and restricted to a more or less clearly articulated locus in value space.

The organisation needs coherence: 'We are like this; this is how we behave', in order to behave predictably towards its customers, suppliers and staff. It needs cohesion such that all of the component parts of the organisation must be aware of and subscribe to this. And finally, it needs utility; it must have a realistic connection to reality.

An agreed set of Values steers the organisation through minor and major decisions, pronouncements to the public, ways of working and attitudes displayed. Whether renewal is able to take place or not will depend on the cohesion, coherence and utility of the Values-related choices that are being employed.

Fitness of Values for purpose
The analysis of Values raises some important points: their coherence, as already discussed; their uniformity across the culture and, above all, their fitness for the current and longer-term operating environment.

To this end we suggest that among the values held by PS-ROs are three from among the 12 defined by the Brahma Kumaris[78] which they believe to be common across all cultures: Peace, Respect, Co-operation, Happiness, Honesty, Humility, Love, Responsibility, Simplicity, Tolerance, Freedom and Unity. Of these, those most central to a PS-RO are:

Respect – enabling staff with different working styles to work together and strive for the best they can be in a supportive environment; a necessary adjunct to the recognition of Hedgehog-like and Fox-like styles.

Co-operation – creating a positive-sum game environment, as discussed under Competence in Chapter 6.

Responsibility – in which individuals are pro-active in putting forward ideas and implementing change, also discussed under Leadership in Chapter 6.

The last value, responsibility, has heightened effectiveness at harnessing the energies of staff in the context of a strong Narrative.

Narrative

Sociologists use the term 'Narrative' to mean the encapsulated insight that a person or group has about its experience in specific situations.[79] It tells a person what is expected of them.

A shared and articulated Narrative in organisations makes it much easier to communicate and take group decisions, because most of the underlying issues are summed up in the Narrative as a given. When challenges present themselves, the rules of the game – and the 'assets' that can be deployed – are clear.

As an example, it is hard to recall that the idea of gross national product was only enunciated a hundred years ago and only addressed formally in the 1920s. Today, we use this intangible as a common benchmark by which to estimate all manner of future performance, from energy demand to unemployment. The idea of the organisational Narrative is similar to this. Once it is clear what it is, you can see it. You need only think about an organisation's brand and some of its Narrative should be clear. It is that sinewy combination of mechanisms and morality, options and operations that is as indefinable as a scent, but as unmistakable.

Organisations which lack a single over-arching Narrative may exist as a legal or pragmatic entity, but they will lack cohesion. While conglomerates do not have a single 'corporate' Narrative, they often delegate financial and most other aspects of control to the units, each with their own Narrative. Organisations that do not have a single over-arching Narrative and do not delegate financial control are likely to be indecisive, internally conflicted, and find that plans need to have every detail spelled out, with response from staff grudging and slow. This is the exact opposite of a PS-RO.

How Narratives work

There are a number of things which it is important to understand about Narratives. Narratives are powerful structures that have quality parameters. Narrative at the organisational level will be augmented by Narrative at the group level. The organisational Narrative may not be made explicit because it consists of shared assumptions. People value their Narratives and they do not like having them challenged or changed. Hedgehogs are particularly fond of surrounding their Narrative with spines: 'there is but one way to see the world and we know what it is'.

A bad Narrative can be very strong. Totalitarian societies have been exceptionally powerful in instilling suitable Narratives in everyone, from school children to soldiers.

In order to be engaged with the over-arching organisational Narrative, people need to hear it expressed in terms relevant to them. It will need to be expressed differently for different audiences. A Narrative told from a shareholder relations expert's perspective will not necessarily go down well with a bench research scientist or a salesman.

An organisation which has no integrating Narrative cannot be exceptionally or even ordinarily competent, because its working assumptions and goals are fragmented. A clear example is when an option or idea is put up for discussion. It can be discussed constructively only when all involved share a common Narrative.

Narratives can be brought into being, but they cannot be assembled like an engineering project by an off-site team, and delivered to the door. This is why former styles of strategic planning went so frequently wrong; wrong not usually in the sense of being incorrect about the situation, but wrongly attuned to what the organisation was prepared to hear and act upon, and ineffectively communicated.

A Narrative, as we've said, can be both strong and wrong. When an incorrect Narrative has taken root, it creates what a psychiatrist might call a neurosis, a set of deep conflicts whereby what seems to be the right action for a given circumstance always has to be tempered, blunted, held back. The organisation has perpetually to explain to itself why it should not do what its instincts tell it to be right. In a PS-RO we choose 'the right' Narrative as that which assists renewal, that which is in tune with the realities of the operating environment and the particular capabilities of the organisation, that which the organisation is prepared to hear and act upon.

Case study – failure of Narrative

The leader of an Asian country had been impressed by the outstanding performance of the Tiger economies. His country needed to make the transition from a primary production-based economy to growth based on services. The productivity of agriculture would have to be increased and workers taken off the land and put to work in factories and offices.

In addition, however, the country had profound ethnic divisions. Such service industry as existed was in the hands of one such group. Agricultural workers, by contrast, belonged predominantly to another.

The way forward was, therefore, seen in terms of pouring concrete. That would make work for the former agricultural workers, and would also 'build Singapore'. A state-funded property boom began which radically changed the main cities and which influenced behaviour in neighbouring countries. The crash in 1998 brought all of that to an end, when it was found that occupancy rates in many of the new buildings were under a fifth, and that new freeways ended abruptly in rubber plantations.

As a result of this, policy makers began to examine their assumptions. Did the state need to continue to borrow huge sums internationally in order to support the profits of construction companies? Was the lobbying and cronyism of the previous long-lasting regime helpful to balanced development? Above all, was the country telling itself the right story about who it was and what it wanted to be? This last issue became crucial as Islamic influences came to bear on politics.

No simple answer emerged, but a debate had begun that had been suppressed by over a generation of populist nationalism, central planning and fake modernity. A more plural society was to be encouraged. The state was to generate knowledge and insight. Markets were to operate under greater transparency and to fund themselves by conventional means. The national Narrative evolved through being tested.

Finally, Narrative helps to prepare the brain to see patterns, which enhances the effect of the innate innovative capability by aligning it to the Narrative. Since Narrative is so powerful, this emphasises that an out-of-date Narrative can act as a set of blinkers, and an inconsistent set of Narratives causes confusion. The role of Narrative and innovation will be picked up again under Options.

Insight

Insight is the ability to make sense of the external world and its future, and harness that understanding to assess the organisation's strengths. This provides a basis for generating Options for taking the organisation forward. As such, it provides the context for Board discussions, taking them above the level of shareholder management and turf wars. Insight can also give senior management shared mental models of the current and future world, using imagery or scenarios (see Chapter 11). These facilitate discussion and sharing of assumptions by setting out rational views of the external world and possible futures.

Case study – getting senior staff to use Insight

D2D was a manufacturing business which among other things made the terminals for the UK's lottery company, Camelot, and for a number of PC, telecoms and computer suppliers. D2D's management team wrote a business plan, as part of assessment for a trade sale.

When the HQ planners discussed the business plan with the management team, they realised that the plans were based on a set of assumptions very like a scenario that we had seen before; *Coral Reef* (Figure 7.3), in which the ICT industry was driven by innovation. This reflected the attitude of the team, who had joined the computer business because they enjoyed innovation and a rapid pace of change.

So then the planners asked the question – what happens if the world is more like the *Deep Sea* scenario (in which the industry is driven by 'the blame game' and suppliers expect to be sued)? Are the customers of subcontract electronic manufacturing mostly in markets which are very innovative or are most of the markets characterised by risk avoidance, outsourcing of manufacturing to minimise risk in existing business?

> The team realised that the overall shape of the subcontract electronic manufacturing business was dominated by risk minimisation. So a number of the characteristics that D2D had taken for granted, such as European Quality Awards, were of more interest to the customers than the team had assumed. The business was well positioned for low-risk manufacturing.
>
> Using insight gained from this exercise, the business plan was rewritten and the business sold to a multinational contract manufacturer.

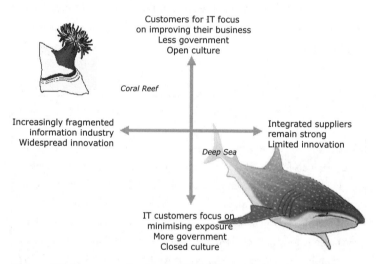

Figure 7.3 Two scenarios for the ICT industry

Insight is a way to harness the intelligence of people focused on specified tasks in the upper cone – people who will be chosen for their capabilities in those tasks and tend to be Hedgehogs – to the purpose of the organisation through giving them opportunity to develop Fox-like approaches.

The process of renewal is iterative; Insight describes the bundle of tools and methods which allow for course correction, when used with the other tools and methods of a PS-RO.

Internal and external insight

Much of the focus in any discussion is on external insight – anticipating trends and new competitors, exploring the impact of global systemic challenges on the organisation, its suppliers and customers: the activities traditionally called Foresight.

However, a PS-RO will put similar focus on the less glamorous activities associated with understanding internal capability – auditing the organisation for its skills, knowledge, reputation and relationships. An audit of the organisation's current capabilities is a baseline for current gaps and gaps against future needs. This should result in an understanding of the areas of distinctive competence that may have been dormant and can now be revitalised. An audit of potential fulcra and break points, through technology or other sources of change, will help anticipate disruptive technology.

Generating Options

The process of making an unspecified idea into a workable Option involves a great deal of formal work to explore the implications of the idea and turn it into a formal, costed plan. It also involves dialogue around the Narrative. The two stages of the process can be thought of as the innovation stage and the stage of incorporation into the organisation's portfolio. Both of these are discussed further in Chapter 12.

Below we sketch out how these processes are shaped and relate to the upper and lower-cone parts of the organisation.

How decisions are made

The Options process should ask a number of questions, such as:

- Can this be done?
- Should this be done?

- Should we be the ones to do it?
- Should we do it now or later?

Given all of these things, how does it stack up to all the other things that we could do but cannot, through limited resources?

Plainly, each of these questions is repeated over and over, and many of the answers to them are provisional.

Grand plans seldom succeed; but seedbeds, suitably prepared, tended and harvested will yield surprising and spontaneous results. The prime preparation for this seedbed is a 'good' Narrative. The nurturing consists of processes that include the right people at the right time, motivated by targets and reward structures, tasked appropriately and delivering what they have done to a further step in the process. That is, making use of the Machinery that fits into the upper reaches or specified part of the double-cone structure.

This is symbolised in Figure 7.4. The cones remain the same as those introduced in Chapter 6. The lower cone is now populated with a set of processes which review the operating environment as free-standing activities, which are brought to bear on real-world issues that affect the upper cone – that is, the fully specified, day-to-day business (the left-hand arrow).

A typical interaction in an energy equipment manufacturer might be a workshop to develop a product offer that is targeted specifically at the infrastructure of a particular country. The outcome might be such a product, but there would also be considerable learning on all sides about – let us say – the economic development process, regulation, attitudes to bribery and corruption and their mitigation plus, of course, the core engineering issues as seen in a completely new light. Further, the insight gained from the workshop exercise re-enforces the Narrative.

There is a similar loop that is shown on the right of Figure 7.4. This refers to the issues of new project evaluation that we have

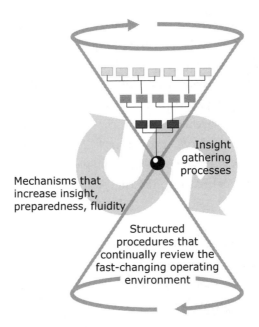

Figure 7.4 Linking the cones

already discussed. In much the same way, knowledge is pooled, tested and integrated in ways which isolated project development cannot touch. Plainly, most of the work in the project remains entirely conventional, but now informed by thoughts that avoid the false starts that we noted in Chapter 5, where the cost of not using Insight proved so high.

Machinery

Last, but certainly not least, we encounter the necessary Machinery. The term 'Machinery' here is used in the same sense as in the phrase 'machinery of government'.

The Machinery that is needed, over and above that needed in all organisations, is the processes, people and tools that facilitate the conversation across and between the cones. We consider these under the headings of processes, ICT, communication, knowledge management and people.

Some of the machinery is specific to the '95' or '99' type of organisation introduced in Chapter 4. There are also processes specific to smaller groups which can themselves be a PS-RO; they are also important to the conversations and are covered in Chapter 14.

PS-RO processes

In the specified, upper part of the cone, defined processes like 'sales' engage with sales targets. PS-RO processes, however, engage with intangible factors, such as:

- A desire for new things, renewal.
- Openness to possibility, curiosity.
- Creativity, a sense of open horizons, linked to a sense of purpose.
- The desire to understand, to learn.
- The wish to tame an uncertain terrain, while accepting ambiguity and the fuzziness of the future.

While these intangibles are essential to a PS-RO, they can lead to effort which seems to have no useful output. PS-RO processes therefore need clear targets, which:

- engage with the organisation's needs;
- are tasked from identifiable authority, which preferably sets a budget, success criteria and time scale for the activity and defines the 'playing field';
- are connected to existing activities, so that some aspects have in-house 'experts' who can advise;
- are in line with the organisation's core Values and purpose.

Renewal – how and when to change processes

Most of the processes in an organisation will be in the specified, or upper, cone. The processes here need to be reviewed less frequently than those in the lower cone, but they certainly shouldn't be forgotten. The processes for establishing Values and Narrative are also likely to be relatively stable, while the Machinery will evolve more quickly.

The lower-cone processes that need to be reviewed frequently are those for Insight and Options. These are the processes that directly drive renewal, and need to be absolutely relevant – and aligned – to the needs of the organisation. Here the focus in terms of products, markets and customers, and the time scale of interest, can change very rapidly and needs to be reviewed every few months.

Executive Summary

- A PS-RO depends on five organisational qualities: Values, Narrative, Options, Insight and Machinery.
- Insight gathered from the external environment and about internal capability is used to generate Options, the choice of which Options to follow and implement is made through the lens of Narrative.
- Insight is a way to harness the intelligence of people focused on specified tasks in the upper cone to the purpose of the organisation through giving them opportunity to develop Fox-like approaches.
- Machinery provides the underpinning infrastructure for making it all happen.
- Whether renewal is able to take place or not will depend on the cohesion, coherence and utility of the Values-related choices that are being employed.

- Among the core Values held by PS-ROs are Respect, Co-operation and Responsibility.
- A shared and articulated Narrative in organisations makes it much easier to communicate and take group decisions.
- A PS-RO harnesses the experience and knowledge from across the organisation rather than being limited to a separate or elite group.
- The process of renewal is iterative, with ongoing course correction in the turbulent operating environment.

Chapter 8

The Structure of Renewal

So far we have identified the need for adaptability in challenging times, and the five qualities needed for renewal. Now we need to see how the elements of a PS-RO link into the overall organisation and its planning system to provide purposeful self-renewal.

Organisational change

A PS-RO knows that it has to change to survive and prosper, while the core Values and purpose of the organisation remain unchanged, providing a rock-solid foundation to help give direction and define the right Options to choose and implement.[80] Change can be incremental and/or transformational depending on what is needed. For any change to be successful, however, it needs to engage the whole organisation and harness the energy of the people within it towards its implementation; towards making it happen.

Changes may be primarily geographical or product-led; they may relate to *how* things are done (processes, technologies, plant and partnerships) or to *what* is done (products, markets, brands). In short, anything can be considered for change bar the organisation's core Values and purpose.

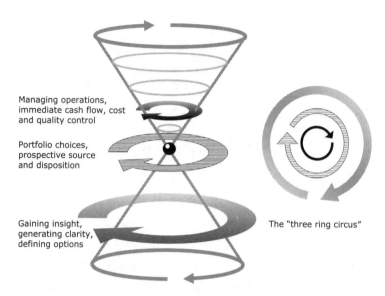

Managing operations, immediate cash flow, cost and quality control

Portfolio choices, prospective source and disposition

Gaining insight, generating clarity, defining options

The "three ring circus"

Figure 8.1 The Three Ring Circus

An essential issue for a PS-RO is linking portfolio management together with innovation. In order to see how these two levers can be connected, we need to add to the double cone that we introduced in Chapter 6. Figure 8.1 shows the double cone with the addition of three sets of processes.

The Three Ring Circus

The processes added to the double cone are drawn as loops because they are iterative. As the organisation repeatedly addresses broad cloudy issues, so the learning increases. Additionally, as the issues become less cloudy and the learning increases, the organisation is often more predisposed to listen to the outcome. For industries with a short product life cycle, iteration of issues means keeping up-to-date.

In the discussion that follows, the time periods are benchmarked to an industry with a product life cycle measured in 3–5 years: car manufacture, for example. Very long-lived activities – such as water or drainage provision – will need to think longer-term thoughts. Fast-moving industries can think in the shorter term, though these are often underpinned by industries changing more slowly: for example, fashions may change but textiles change far more slowly; and while the sewing machines have moved from Middle America to Mexico to China to Vietnam, they still sew standard stitches with familiar thread.

In Figure 8.1, the outer loop/bottom cone concerns itself with how the operating environment 'works' and how this may change. Scenario planning, competitive and stakeholder positioning, corporate and social responsibility and communications, human resource development, succession planning and talent management, long-range Option generation and innovation are connected into and from this loop. Cycles are of different duration in different industries, and may be related to the planning cycle – for instance, only every second planning cycle, although parts related to a specific issue in a business unit could be much shorter with a faster reporting time scale.

The financial cost of carrying them out is extremely small, both in absolute terms relative to corporate turnover and in terms of the scale of the errors they avoid and the renewal that they enable.

The middle loop is focused on the portfolio in the medium term, and on concrete plans, rival projects and competition for scarce resources. It assesses the source and disposition of assets and flows over the annual to 5-year period. It has a strong operational characteristic, employs many of the tools of finance and is home to resource flow planning, road mapping and the assessment of volatility, discount rates, risk mitigation and related activities. This is typically an annual cycle, although it also includes many ad hoc events, such as project proposals, acquisitions and the like.

The inner cycle/top cone consists of established operations and their financial and other reporting. This will have a cycle time that is typically monthly or quarterly, with an annual contribution to the middle loop.

The revolutionary effect of linking the outer loop/bottom cone

On the right of Figure 8.1, we look down from above the cones, and see the three cycles as concentric rings. We have called this the 'Three Ring Circus', and the processes in each ring need to synchronise and communicate with those in the other rings.

None of the mechanisms in the outer loop are revolutionary. Some companies have carried out at least parts of them for decades.

What makes a revolutionary difference, however, is the integration of the processes and their engagement with sources of knowledge from across the organisation. In our experience, this is exceptionally rare. Indeed, the streamlining of organisations during the 1990s and 2000s stripped out much of the capacity that had once existed to do this. This means that the ability to sense what is happening outside the organisation and generate a timely response has all but been eliminated. This Fox-like trait is essential for organisations wishing to thrive and succeed.

Information flows

Each organisation will have its particular structure and methods for planning and renewing the portfolio. Figure 8.2 gives a sketch of some of the flows that are needed. The arrows symbolise the flow of time, with the cycle beginning at the left of the figure. The organisation consolidates what it has learned in the last cycle, capturing the knowledge by interviewing and surveying people, by

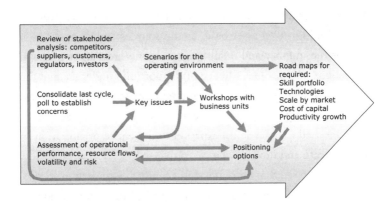

Figure 8.2 Renewing the portfolio

taking a hard look at unit and sector performance, and by thinking what external stakeholders may want from the organisation.

This generates a list of key issues. Of course, one has to ask: key for whom? How are they established? Though the Board and senior management have a formal role in closing the debate and making the final decision, the issues should be widely debated by the dispersed leadership, keeping the organisational Narrative in mind.

These key issues feed into a mechanism for taking a structured look at the prospective operating environment. Scenario planning, for example, could be one such mechanism. This may question the default assumptions, add to them or may change their very nature. Iteration is needed, both around the emerging ideas and their relevance and validity; but also politically. The outcome is tested on the operating units. Once again, one has to ask tested how, by whom, with what remit and permissions? The answers depend on local circumstances, strengths, weaknesses and priorities.

The outcome of this procedure will be a set of scenarios or other models such as those of the competitive space (see Chapter 11). It can be the starting place for an assessment of Options for investment or divestment. It could be used to analyse the strength of the medium-term asset base, or the sources and disposition of cash, or the number and quality of the human resources that will be needed, and/or the resilience of the portfolio under each of the scenarios. It can be used by operational units to test their business plans for assumptions, and for decision points between scenarios. It can be used to cascade information to the entire organisation so as to educate and develop the Narrative.

It is easy to see that there is a significant value to such processes. They provide a framework for harvesting ideas, for critiquing latent connections to external bodies and for discovering potential show-stoppers, such as other people's intellectual property or regulatory changes.

What has emerged is the potential for generating generic Options. These sit within a flexible context, within the Narrative. When projects come forward, therefore, they are assessed against questions such as: 'That's a good idea, but does it go where we want to go?' The Narrative, capturing much of this, means that potential will be recognised and opportunities grasped only when they satisfy the overall purpose and direction.

Linking the Three Ring Circus

Figure 8.3 looks at the same items, now arranged around a sketch of the Three Ring Circus, as in Figure 8.1. Each of these rings is revolving at a different rate, as symbolised by the 'ticks' running off to the right. The inner operational loop ticks at a quarterly/annual rate, with every fourth tick being followed by the annual results and operating units' plans and bids for resource. This is often consolidated into a 3–5-year budgetary forward plan.

The loop that assesses the portfolio and generic Options usually ticks annually. However, many projects cannot wait a year, and so

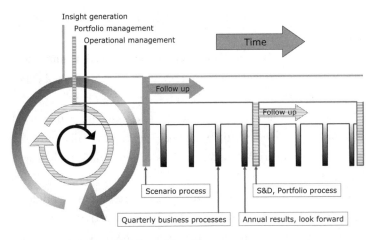

Insight generation
Portfolio management
Operational management
Time

Follow up

Follow up

Scenario process

S&D, Portfolio process

Quarterly business processes

Annual results, look forward

Figure 8.3 Linking the Three Ring Circus

the development of Options and their presentation as candidates for the portfolio is almost continuous.

The Insight generating or outer loop revolves biennially, as symbolised by its single tick in the period shown. What it has to say about key issues and long-term trends is taken formally into account within the annual plans that emerge from the operating units and inform the portfolio/Options procedures.

Figure 8.2 showed a small number of the many key issues which these various processes require and deliver. To put these in their correct places, and to trace all of the connections, would require a vast version of Figure 8.3 which would be different for each PS-RO.

Processes in a PS-RO

Any organised process needs the equivalent of a project plan, with defined inputs, time scales and outputs; and a project manager. Similarly, each of the modules of work needs to be staffed. We have stressed the importance of business unit participation in these activities. It is crucial, however, that the project manager ensures the engagement of the right mixture of Hedgehogs and Foxes.

Experience of Insight, both internal and external, is important; that is to say, experience in the organisation or industry, and experience as measured by aptitude and track record of handling issues of this nature. A team might include people who have experienced this sort of process many times before, people who really know the issues and a collection of others such as young high flyers in learning mode.

Projects need more than purely human resources in order to generate new knowledge. An early stage in any activity is to identify the important factors about which the group is ignorant. To replace that ignorance with knowledge costs money – seldom large amounts, but sums which are rarely in an initial budget. The project manager acts as budget controller and impresario: this is an important role, and needs have social skills in abundance.

Specific attributes of a PS-RO are:

- Strong future-orientation. This shows up in its cognitive focus – the best is still ahead! – and in its concentration on renewal.
- A coherent Narrative and set of Values that provide a stable context for innovation and renewal, and HR criteria aligned to the Values and Narrative.
- Information as a shared tool, not something with restricted access.
- The leadership to become extraordinarily competent; senior staff who own and legitimate the renewal process.
- Schedules and linkages of lower cone processes to other processes: awareness of the stages in a process, and the different needs of each stage.
- Projects spanning divisional structures, ability to manage network-type structures.

Case study – renewal[81]

Cisco, a telecoms company which was successful in the 1990s, realised that its core market was mature. They decided to tackle 30 non-traditional areas, of which half were expected to be successful and generate 25% revenues within 5–10 years. They have achieved this, with products new in 2000 such as optical networks, space-based communications, Internet telephony, now bringing in 25% of earnings.

They set as their destination 'We want to be the Microsoft of the physical internet', and 'supplying the connected economy'.

Cisco has a portfolio of technologically coherent products, a family of inter-locked software and hardware that drives demand for extensions of this. They include industry-specific offers: e.g. software plus hardware for electricity utilities and general business applications like absolute fidelity video-conferencing. They use their own tools in-house – wikis, tele-conferencing and automated collaboration processes, with about 5500 tele-presence meetings a week. This has halved the travel budget. They are pushing tele-presence into the home, spending $7bn on a set-top box distribution company to provide match-day experience in the living room, and mobile video streamed to a home console.

They have maintained their market-oriented structure, with inter-locking managerial groups, based on projects, where the managers retain line responsibility. Councils are in charge of markets greater than $10bn; Boards $1bn. Today, Cisco has 50 Councils and Boards with about 750 members. Working groups are created as needed: they span the whole company and are ephemeral.

Cisco has evolved a culture of collaboration. The CEO of 14 years has a collegiate style, and most managers have a role on both a function – e.g. manufacturing – and a Board or Council. Senior staff are part of a minimum of five and often many more such groups. 30% of bonus pay is determined by team work score. Major work is in progress on how to effortlessly assemble and disperse teams, even though the system has been under development for 9 years. They have a blueprint for how to set up and manage these structures, called 'replicable processes'. There is a formal common language in which activities are described: a group must have a 5-year vision, 2-year strategy and 10-point execution plan, which makes decisions transparent. New projects go through successive screens: does the customer want this and do they want it from Cisco? Is it big enough for Cisco? Does it create demand for other Cisco products? Can Cisco be leader in this market?

The cost of this has been a reduction in its staffing requirement by 20%. The downside is endless meetings, persuasion, listening. But it has allowed for agile response to new ideas, market changes; allows scale with agility; allows true global integration.

Cisco has moved from command and control to cultivate and co-ordinate.

Executive Summary

- A PS-RO's five qualities are linked together in a 'Three Ring Circus'.
- The Three Rings are the renewal processes, the portfolio processes and the operational processes.
- The Three Ring Circus enables changes of the portfolio of assets, both physical and intangible.
- Attributes of a PS-RO are a strong future-orientation, a coherent Narrative, a set of Values that provide a stable context for innovation and renewal, information as a shared asset, leadership determined to support extraordinary competence, senior staff who own and drive the renewal process, and the ability to manage across silos.

Chapter 9

Managing Renewal

To complete this part of the book, this chapter provides some guidance on practical aspects of creating and managing a PS-RO. It tackles the thorny issue of how to motivate people to make time for renewal activities. At the end of this chapter we direct you to a web-based tool which can diagnose aspects of an organisation that could benefit from first intervention.

Getting going

It is in many ways much harder to get such a system going, even in embryo, than it is to run it at maturity. Here are some pointers from our experience:

- There is no 'correct' design for any one of the rings discussed in the previous chapter, except that which matches the needs of the organisation.
- That said, the design needs to be formal, documented and it needs stability.
- The structure needs to be clear, agreed and seen to be useful.
- It needs an overall owner who has a budget and the skills to use it.

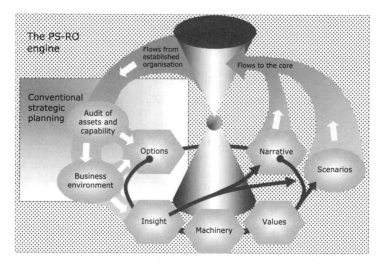

Figure 9.1 A typical planning cycle

Figure 9.1 shows the now-familiar double cone. Ringed around its base are the five qualities which we have shown to be essential to renewal. (Of course, these really apply everywhere in the system, but they are placed at the base for clarity.)

Two structures lie on either side of the double cone. One represents a flow out from the established business, located in the upper cone, and acting chiefly where the two cones meet, and where decisions about targets are taken and assets allocated. Almost all organisations employ these flows, which generate assessments of present and future assets. On occasions they may also involve surveys of the competitive arena. This area is boxed, in order to show the typical bounds of conventional strategic planning. The full image, shaded grey, comprises the much wider domain of the PS-RO approach.

The second structure is unique to the PS-RO. It takes what has been learned through the workings of the PS-RO machinery and feeds this back to the upper cone, informing and extending the horizons of the established activities. It does this principally through the Narrative, and also through tools specifically designed to embrace complexity, such as scenarios.

The descending processes – on the left of the cone – are, of course, much enriched within a PS-RO. Prepared minds are busy spotting new things. Rich conversations are in play about 'what might be'. New investment ideas are assessed against the complexity of the operating environment, and solutions are recognised for their full potential.

Staffing

Renewal project modules should be staffed to have diffuse envelopes, with a manager, who has resource, knows what is wanted, when and why. He has access to a cadre of people who can help. In some cases, these people may be more or less full time, and in others, the majority will be on call, to contribute directly or to offer critique. Usually these will be internal staff, though outsiders have an important role in scenario generation, to raise the unasked questions and challenge the default assumptions.

The case study below illustrates the first stages of one organisation, Christian Aid, towards developing insight in their senior management group.

Case study – getting started

International development agency Christian Aid works with over 600 NGOs in 48 developing countries, to 'expose and root out poverty and change the systems which favour rich over poor'. Its success in pursuing its goals depends increasingly on continual anticipation of, and adjustment to, changing operating environments.

For many years Christian Aid had followed a traditional 5-year strategic planning horizon, but in 2007 it began to feel that its senior management group (SMG) was not collectively surfacing its thoughts about what the future might hold for Christian Aid, yet was working to these individual views in its respective functions.

The process chosen involved Christian Aid's SMG meeting quarterly, facilitated by external consultants The Futures Company. As a first step, members of the SMG identified critical drivers they felt would impact Christian Aid's work. Drivers were defined as external influences outside the organisation's control that would impact either positively or negatively on its ability to achieve its goals.

From the drivers, two 'axes of uncertainty' facing the sector were eventually arrived at, one consisting of political and economic power (leading to more or less equality within and between societies), the other expressing different directions for social and cultural meanings (more or less fragmentation within and between societies). 'Scenario Narratives' were then developed for each of the four quadrants in the model.

These four 'Scenario Narratives' now underpin Christian Aid's strategic planning approach, describing the different worlds they may find themselves operating in, and so need to respond to. Common issues across all four scenarios will be addressed in renewing Christian Aid's strategic framework beyond 2010. The narratives also identify scenario-specific issues – or 'early indicators' – that Christian Aid will need to respond to if it felt the world today was exhibiting signs that it was moving towards one scenario over the others. By tracking these early indicators of where the world might be heading, the scenarios can be kept alive amidst the distractions of day-to-day operations.

Those involved generally fell into two camps: people who loved it – who enjoyed being imaginative and welcomed the chance to think more widely and deeply; and people who struggled a bit to have confidence in the drivers or who found the process unduly time-consuming and drawn out.

Overall, the insight process has helped unlock managers from thinking in terms of *one* 5-year strategy based on *one* world view and helped SMG examine its assumptions about what needs to happen to bring about change.

Source: Contributed by Aidan Timlin, Corporate Performance & Accountability Manager at Christian Aid.

The role of Narrative and Values

Many people find change stressful, as discussed earlier. Organisational Narrative and core Values, once articulated, provide a stable reference system which reduces the level of fear, uncertainty and doubt about the future among the workforce.

Gain legitimacy

The absolute key to success in becoming a PS-RO is to start small, and to start with legitimacy granted from the highest source of power available. If the president, CEO, Board, owner, Secretary of State says that 'Something Needs to be Done', and points in your direction, then there is a good chance of getting something to happen. Under these circumstances, it is essential to know how this enabler thinks: what matters to them, how they express this, what their underlying mental models are – their personal narrative – in order to align your efforts.

Evolution of a PS-RO

One of the more convincing criticisms of evolution is the unlikely nature of the mature organ. So many things have to come together to make a functioning eye! How could that happen all at once? The answer to that argument is that it does not have to happen all at once. Light-sensitive patches become directional pits, pits cluster and retreat to become proto-retinas, protective membranes take on optical properties and, as a result, four or five distinct eye designs have come about.

Much the same is true of the systems of a PS-RO: the parts are useful in isolation, but a lot more useful when all are joined up. Evolution consists of both creating the 'islands' of capability, and also joining them up into a coherent whole.

Overcoming objections

One hurdle to change is near-universal. It is embodied in catch phrases such as *'if it ain't broke, don't fix it'*, or the more common *'I know exactly what I am doing but I don't have the time (resource, support) to do it properly. Please don't distract me with this stuff that doesn't help me at all'*. Thinking about alternative and fast-changing futures, or assessments of the organisation in which at least some units must appear less than optimal, can be seen as an unjustified criticism. It can also be seen as a further burden on already overburdened staff.

This explains why change has been discontinuous in many organisations. Things have to go badly wrong before fixed positions are abandoned and people are prepared to discuss new options. Organisations in which there is no over-arching Narrative – or a Narrative that is no longer connected to reality – are aggressive when challenged, seeking people to blame as being insufficiently enthusiastic or actively subversive.

In such a situation, it is truly hard to get traction and achieve anything significant. The art is to find a still, quiet corner of the organisation and be helpful within it, so starting small, challenging nobody, demonstrating practical outcomes and building momentum: for instance, to set up dialogue between the research function and senior management about 'what might be'. (One note of caution – hypothetical discussions are only of interest to senior managers with some Fox-like traits.) Other approaches in the starting small and non-threatening mode could be to build maps of the competitive environment, or interpret legal or regulatory issues into language that brings out the implications for the organisation.

The workshop as a mechanism

An unthreatening procedure is the workshop. This can be preceded by interviews, from which the findings about agreement and disagreement, areas of focus and gaps can be captured. The participants engage in structured debate and set priorities on what they have found. This is guaranteed to be 'relevant', understood and, if the results are challenging, legitimised by the group.

We cite the psychologist who is changing the light bulb, as long as the light bulb really wants to change. If the organisation does not want to change, it will not. If it does want to change, it is up to the senior managers to advance by steps towards a full integration of PS-RO processes, with articulation of the cost/benefit of this.

Managing a PS-RO system

It is not possible to generalise the Three Ring Circus, as the entire point is for the organisation to become unique, ideally fitted to purpose for future challenges. But one key plank is the unexceptional but rarely exploited statement that the level of unarticulated or tacit knowledge is high in most organisations. This knowledge is readily accessible if tackled through PS-RO machinery. The second key element is that it takes effort to express a new thought; further, it takes still longer to set the context. Once formed, the thought needs a home.

The role of conversations and processes in harnessing the talents and articulating the insights in a PS-RO is discussed below. Here are some pointers from our experience.

Anticipate change

Just as the world does not stay still, so the Machinery and techniques of a PS-RO also need to keep up-to-date, become familiar to those parts of the organisation that are most in need of help. Many challenges will not wait for a 2-year cycle to complete itself. However, one of the advantages of thinking about the future systematically is that the big structural issues change slowly, and seldom surprise the organisation once they have been explored. It is the surface manifestations which alter quickly and – if the organisation has not thought about them – unexpectedly.

There is a good explanation for how advance exploration reduces surprises, based on physiological studies. Ingvar, a Swedish neuro-biologist,[82] found that the human brain is constantly attempting to explore options for the future even while we are asleep, and called these options 'memories of the future'. These 'memories of the future' act as a filter to external signals, helping the brain to discard irrelevant factors. So, if the only model of the world that is the basis of these explorations is a forecast, many signals are rejected. This explains the physiological basis behind the observation that a pre-pared mind picks up early-warning signs and weak signals which others just do not notice.

Establish networks with wide competence

The overall PS-RO structure should be able to process the wide range of issues articulated during an innovation project. Each issue needs to be challenged several times during its development, and pass quality tests before delivering its product. What is a quality test for an intangible set of thoughts? Essentially, the good opinion of outsiders to the project who find it illuminating, unexpected and resonant with what they already know. Scrutiny panels are to be defined at the same time as the issue itself is listed for analysis, using the capability of the networks.

Identify emerging issues

Issues are intended to analyse specific targets, often as steps in a process. For instance, if the organisation wishes to generate renew-able electricity in China (setting up a project internally known as the Green China project), one issue is the regulatory regime that will permit this. Thus, the issue manager has a clear issue to develop, and a 'place' to put his or her findings, defined within the overall project plan by which the Green China project is managed. An early stage of that project is one in which all of the modules to tackle specific issues are defined, mapped, prioritised and resourced. It is important that each module, when reporting, reports on all of the relevant corporate dimensions. That is, not merely on the bare facts, but the implications of working under – using the above example – Chinese regulatory systems for human resources, commitments to 'clean' business practices, information technology requirements, etc. In other words, each module needs to draw on and report to a multifaceted group of potential stakeholders, who (as with the contributors) may be in either the lower or upper cone.

What about the workers?

There will be a core cadre of individuals dedicated for most or all of their time to managing a PS-RO structure and processes. There is often a temptation by the Board or senior management to outsource this work. This is a mistake. Knowledge that is generated is endlessly recycled and it is not good practice to lose this, or pay to regain it repeatedly. However, joint teams of in-house staff and experienced consultants can be an effective form of knowledge transfer and increasing insight.

Participation and motivation

A PS-RO tends less to task people with minutiae than to give them a set of general remits – to expand sales in Asia by 20%, to ensure that the following IT upgrade is in place – and reward them for the excellence with which they do this. This compares with a set of detailed targets by quarter by product, or the number of people trained in the upgraded IT system by quarter by department. It is not possible to operate in the detailed targets style and simultaneously force people to give time to what they may see as diversions. People need to know that they are trusted to act responsibly in setting their own targets and doing a good job.

There are some ways which we have found effective in engaging an organisation of any kind. One is to set aside a portion of employees' time in the line units to be engaged in renewal: they are then judged and rewarded for their contributions. This may generate grudging acquiescence, a minimal engagement if it is seen as a diversion from their chief tasks. The second way, complementary to this, is to make the renewal tasks relevant to their day-to-day work. That is, if they are charged with market extension, then thinking about markets and competition in a structured way must be helpful to their 'day job'.

Finally, some people need to be tasked with PS-RO activities as their core work load. They are needed to tackle issues for which the organisation has no operational response: for example, think who might usefully have got themselves involved in a debate about renewable energy in an oil company during the 1980s. These people come in two kinds: younger people who are in need of broadening and individuals who have proven themselves in areas such as external relations, technology and research, finance, aspects of HR and systems design. It is important not to let them get stale. They should be cycled through such posts, much as the military send promising officers to work with the civil service on, for example, research management, procurement or intelligence; both the individual and the organisation will benefit.

Useful ideas from knowledge management

Knowledge management is defined as the way a company stores, organises and accesses internal and external information: narrower terms are 'Organisational Memory' and 'Knowledge Transfer'. Sharing of information – co-operation – is a key value of a PS-RO. Here, two ideas from the knowledge management movement are useful. One of these is communities of practice, networks of people who operate in specialist fields, who know one another and are encouraged to interact around current issues. Each is aware of the others' specific skills, often as described on a page on the intranet. The other role is that of the 'domain spanner', people who are good at bridging between communities of practice, or perhaps going a level higher and enabling IT experts, for example, to talk to risk assessment engineers.

A more general approach to the important task of setting the culture to encourage participation and motivation can be found in Chapter 14.

People who are good Insight generators tend to have had a long and plural career. They have an overview which has been developed across organisations, functions and time, and can get to the heart of an issue quickly because in one guise or another they have been there before. But many organisations have lost these people over the past decade, as discussed in Chapter 5.

However, Insight generators can become as crusty and resistant to change as any other society or organisation. They can become *prima donnas*, expecting people to dwell upon their words. They can become Hedgehogs, wrapped up in an all-encompassing interpretation of the world that is often of their own making. In order to exploit their excellence and avoid the down-sides, professionals need new challenges. These may include periods of line management, to prove to them that they can still be surprised and make mistakes, or through assignments to areas where they need to gain new knowledge or skills.

Knowledge transfer from external sources

We have discussed the role of outsiders to the organisation in several places in this book. We have emphasised that most of the renewal we talk about builds on the strengths of people in the organisation. However, outsiders can have three catalytic roles.

First, people who have had a lot of experience of working with organisations on aspects of renewal – Value, Narrative, Insights, Options or Machinery – will be able to see patterns and bring out the talents and experience of people in the organisation: they know where to look and what questions to ask.

Second, they bring fresh eyes to a situation, unclouded by familiarity and history (baggage). As such, they can provide a valuable independent forum where old sticking points can be aired, analysed coolly and discussed neutrally. This lowers tensions and allows for movement within previously strongly defended positions; the resulting dialogue can be seen as the first steps towards renewal in its simplest form.

Third, they can ask the naïve questions which it would be difficult for a member of staff, especially a senior member of staff, to ask. These 'stupid' or basic questions can help reveal gaps or misunderstandings or misalignments in any aspect of the organisation's operation. Voicing them is often a cathartic experience for staff members, allowing them to discuss issues in a non-judgemental environment. Almost always, this results in further questions, leading to increased dialogue as staff members seek to solve issues through co-operation.

The diagnostic tool

Renewal should make an organisation tuned to its specific operating environment and ambitious in its innovation. A PS-RO is the embodiment of these ambitions.

Not everyone works in anything like such an organisation. The first step to renewal is the objective identification of weaknesses. That is what the diagnostic tool is intended to help achieve.

We invite you to go onto the Internet and visit the following URL:

http://www.chforum.org/book/index.html/

This offers you a way of mapping the issues which you face. When you have completed the exercise, you are taken to a web page that gives you a number of items of information. It describes how your organisation is assessed in terms of the five qualities of a PS-RO:

- Values: what the organisation wants to be and does not want to be.
- Insight: how things work – external assessment and internal capabilities.
- Options: generic areas of potential – innovation and bridging the gap from innovation into the portfolio.
- Narrative: the stories that the organisation has, for alignment and engagement.
- Machinery: how to harness the potential of the organisation.

Executive Summary

- Narrative, Values and knowledge management motivate people and generate the energy necessary for a PS-RO.
- Getting going will involve gaining legitimacy through small steps.
- Managing a PS-RO once established requires continuous course correction.
- Engaging with talents working in the upper cone is key, though there will be at any time a small set of individuals dedicated for most or all of their time to renewal activities.
- The Diagnostic Tool can be used to provide help and guidance on how to do this in your organisation.

Part III

A Toolkit for Purposeful Renewal

Chapter 10

Values

This chapter is concerned with Values, both personal and organisational, and their alignment in a PS-RO. It will help you to see how you can implement agreed, aligned Values in your organisation. A successful, sustainable organisation needs employees who are aligned with its core Values. Core Values give people a sense of stability when the organisation is undergoing course correction and operating in uncertainty.

Values provide a framework for senior managers to have rational discussions which rise above day-to-day agendas, particularly in allocation of resources. They set the organisational agenda on a range of matters from competitors and product quality to handling staff. They provide a sense of purpose for the organisation.

In this chapter we introduce a number of tools, in the form of simple exercises, to help you identify which Values exist in your organisation:

- A day in the life
- What has motivated me?
- Aligning personal values with the organisation
- Energy matrix
- Why is that important?
- 'Random Corporate Serial Killer'

Core Values

Core Values underlie our behaviours. People may not be aware of what they are, but when they behave against them, they will feel uncomfortable. An organisation's core Values also underpin its behaviours, hence the importance of understanding your own core Values and how they link into (or don't link into) the core Values of your organisation.

Core Values and principles

We use the term 'Values' despite our belief that the term has had its meaning debased over time. Many people speak of 'Values' but there is rarely a consistent understanding of what is meant.

For our purposes we shall use the following definition:

> In general, important and enduring beliefs or ideals shared by the members of a culture about what is good or desirable and what is not. Values exert major influence on the behaviour of an individual and serve as broad guidelines in all situations.[83]

Therefore, we will talk about core Values as the basis for people's – and the organisation's – actions and behaviours.

In Chapter 7 we suggested that, although organisations may well have differing core Values, among the core Values of a PS-RO there will be three that are always present:

- Co-operation
- Respect
- Responsibility.

These are core Values which will not be compromised either in the short or long term. They provide the justification for people in the organisation to start work each day, eager to do their work in service of the organisation, its core Values and purpose. They help people to see what can and should change and what cannot. Core Values almost never change, while operating practices will change all the time.

Research indicates that organisations which have core Values that they live through their day-to-day operations enjoy greater success than those that don't. This is measured by long-term performance, including financial returns as well as contributions to the society around them, as described by James Porras and Jerry Collins in *Built to Last.*[84] Companies bounce back from adversity and develop things that become ubiquitous to our society, such as Post-It Notes by 3M or Band-Aids from Johnson & Johnson.

Applying core Values

The importance of relationships
Whatever we do in organisations is based on relationships. Constructive, long-term relationships require trust and respect, based on both parties living up to each other's expectations over the long term. These expectations in turn are based on core Values that will not change or be violated. Shared core Values help leaders to build their teams; organisations to build their culture and to create alignment throughout the organisation. Values set the tone of the conversation with all the stakeholders. They define the way we behave towards each other.

Agility and adaptiveness: Responsibility
PS-ROs nurture the ability to respond quickly and pro-actively to whatever is happening around them. This means that their leaders have developed some Fox-like characteristics. Values are a filter to

help make confident choices and robust decisions. You apply the organisation's core Values, to help you see where the boundaries are.

In all aspects of life you can be pro-active, making things happen – a Master of Circumstance – deciding how to react to external events and taking responsibility for the consequences. Or you can decide NOT to act – a Victim of Circumstance – instead, letting things happen to you, giving you an excuse for not being responsible. People who live by their Values have confidence, commitment and take responsibility for their decisions. They know they have done their best. They take a lead themselves and provide a good example to others. Organisations that live by their Values share these attributes.

Organisations that are aware of their core Values attract the right people – it is easy for people to tell that 'this is the right organisation for me!' Because they know what the Values are and like them (else they wouldn't be there), they can act in line with those Values. An aligned organisation is an effective organisation which operates within the framework of 'Commander's Intent',[85] which can be defined as:

> ... a concise expression of the purpose of the operation [which] must be understood two echelons below the issuing commander ... It is the single unifying focus for all subordinate elements. It is not a summary of the concept of the operation. Its purpose is to focus subordinates on the desired end state. Its utility is to focus subordinates on what has to be accomplished in order to achieve success, even when the plan and concept of operations no longer apply and to discipline their efforts toward that end.

Recruitment: Respect

An organisation's core Values should be evident from the hiring practices of the organisation.[86] What does your organisation do to ensure 'fit'? To make certain that there is a match between the individual's Values and those of the organisation?

This can save money in the long run as the new hire will be happy in the organisation and behave as the organisation desires, in line with its core Values.

Case study – the cost of hiring someone who didn't fit

An SME grew steadily until they were of a size that they needed to add a layer of management. They had a distinctive culture with a strong USP, a great family feel and they looked after their staff well. People worked hard, but they were respected and rewarded for their work.

Growth meant either hiring new people at the level below the Directors (who all had a day-to-day role in the organisation as well) or developing them from within the organisation. However, while there were a few internal people who could take over the new roles, their growth was such that they needed to hire from the outside as well, and they needed to do so quickly.

The management did not take the time to explore core Values with these new hires and as a result the new hires did not act in line with the implicit assumptions and Values of the organisation. The organisation tried development, they tried coaching, and they tried performance management – all to no avail. In the end, they had to fire several of the new hires. There wasn't a good fit.

The cost to the organisation was not just the wasted recruitment costs, but also motivation in the organisation – especially in the teams these people had led, lost clients, the costs of training and coaching and the final separation costs.

Employees who do not share the organisation's core Values will cause problems and costs. When an employee leaves due to lack of fit, they may have cost the organisation business, they may have cost severance pay and they will certainly have caused problems within the organisation, not to mention the cost of recruiting a replacement.

Values and strategy

Core Values have a strong relationship with an organisation's strategy. It is not just the 'what' of the strategy, but most importantly the 'how it will be achieved' that is guided by core Values. A question that should be asked when reviewing strategy progress is, 'Were we consistent with our core Values in what we have accomplished and how we accomplished it?'

Values will be reflected in the set of behaviours of employees, how business is conducted, what kind of business is acceptable, and how people both inside and outside the organisation are treated.

Clearly defined core Values are especially helpful for those who aren't quite at the top of the organisation, by giving them confidence in making decisions. Having made a decision in alignment with the organisation's core Values, a leader can explain it to any stakeholder in the organisation, making it easier to stand behind any decision they have made.

In the 'Three Ring Circus', the Board-level debate about what the core Values are – what is unchanging and cannot be violated – mapped onto the purpose of the organisation helps people to decide and be clear on the direction that the organisation needs to go in. It also helps identify the goals it needs to achieve while de-personalising the discussion and thus avoiding turf wars. But just *how* the organisation chooses to get there – what the different parts of it need to do – will be aligned so long as people are clear what their boundaries are (what they can and cannot do); the core Values that are inviolable, and also what the shared Narrative is – discussed in Chapter 13.

The origins of Values

How can you start the conversation to articulate the organisation's core Values?

Comparison with competition

One route is as part of the Insight activities, where comparison of the organisation against the competition will bring out differences, not only in the product lines, but also in the approaches to customers and other stakeholders. This should be treated as an objective enquiry and entered into with as open a mind as possible – what might bring these differences about? As with all Insight activities, you start thinking widely before narrowing your thinking down. What assumptions might you be making? What assumptions might the competition be making?

The choice of a brand name and images will bring with them certain 'brand values' as in the cigarette or snack foods industries, where they are disjoint from the actual product (so you don't connect them with the fact that using the product might be bad for you), or in the computer or communications industries which may have descriptive brand names, such as International Business Machines, Microsoft, Twitter. Values need to be aligned to the organisation's purpose, whether expressed through the brand or through other media. What Values do you see expressed? What ideas does it give you for expressing your own Values? What are their approaches to Co-operation, Respect and Responsibility?

Regulatory, stakeholder demands

Some Values are laid down by the regulator, as in the financial services sector. In Chapter 2 we discussed some of the likely regulatory changes over the next decade. In addition, stakeholders have displayed resolve over the past decades, pushing companies to adopt Values such as 'our products are not tested on animals'. These pressures are felt less outside North America and Western Europe, and may reduce further as the global economic tectonic plates shift.

Reward and recognition

People like to be recognised for their efforts – a Values system lets them know what the organisation regards highly and in a PS-RO the rewards are aligned to this. Everyone – even those at the very top – needs to be recognised and praised for their contribution to the organisation. Values help people to see what is praiseworthy and can and should be recognised.

Articulating organisational Values

If the core Values of the organisation are not sufficiently articulated, by working with your team/organisation (or perhaps some of your peers) you can uncover what the organisation's purpose and Values are.

• What do the guiding Values need to be in order to achieve that purpose?
• Do you see the organisation living those Values? What stories or Narratives do you see?
• Do your Values (and your team's Values) align with what the organisation's Values are?
• Are the organisation's Values what they need to be?
• In one hundred years will these core Values still be the same, regardless of the external environment? Even if the organisation is no longer rewarded for them? Or perhaps even penalised?

During the exercise, capture what is truly and clearly believed and lived. Remember, this is for internal use and guidance only.

These core Values need to be the same across the organisation although the way the business runs (the *how*) can be different in different places *as long as it adheres to those Values*. After all, different cultures live the same Values with different behaviours. To test if the Values are true core Values, think about whether or not the organisation would be willing to give up business that would force it to go against the Values.

For instance, Motorola would turn down business if bribery were required. It was against their core Values and no one would have even thought to suggest it. That is indicative of a core Value: it is a gut feeling, recognised as true throughout the organisation.

Aligning your Values with a PS-RO

The core Values that all PS-ROs share are Co-operation, Respect and Responsibility. How do these and other Values of the organisation match up to your own Values? How can you discover your Values from your behaviour? How do the organisation's Values contribute to achieving the right balance and harnessing people's – and especially your own – energies?

Discovering your own core Values

Below are some exercises to help you discover your own – and your organisation's – core Values. While they may seem simple, if you really work with them, you will find them powerful. They are, however, only a snapshot in time. To be consistently useful to you, you need to revisit them and repeat them as time goes on. Not because they will change – core Values should not – but to see if you are living them and to correct your course if you need to, so that you can get back on track.

Tool: A day in the life

Here is a simple exercise that you can do to lead yourself through 'discovering', articulating and confirming what your personal fundamental Values are.

Start by examining how you spend your time. We call this exercise 'A day in the life'. In it you start by mapping your activities over a typical working day. How much time do you spend doing which things?

Think about what spending your time like this means to you.

- Is the majority of the time spent on things that are important to you?
- What is missing from your day?
- What are you communicating (with your actions) about yourself as a leader and about what is important to you?
- Does this match up with your Values?

Mapping organisational Values

We discussed above the processes to articulate a set of Values which support the desired long-term position of your organisation. Chapter 11 discusses an audit of the organisation's current reputation and hence the extent to which the Values are implemented. This can usefully be represented on a spider diagram, see Figure 10.1, using the 12 core Values that research has indicated all cultures share,[87] as discussed in Chapter 8. Clearly, for a PS-RO the Values of Co-operation, Respect and Responsibility are a focus.

From the entries on your spider diagram, you will be able to see where there are gaps, where some work and development on core Values is needed. On an organisational level we find that the steps needed to bring the workforce to engage with and implement the core Values typically consist of:

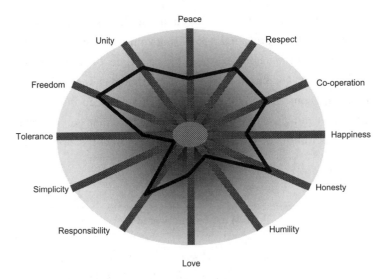

Figure 10.1 Mapping organisational Values

- Widespread awareness-raising of the reputation, Values; what is its desired position, and why. Identifying the gaps and how to remedy them. This is an iterative process, using different methods, not a one-off workshop. We explore methods in greater detail, especially for large groups, in Chapter 14.
- Training of leaders in desired behaviours.
- Developing activity levels, sharing learning and implementing required changes, for example supported by Action Learning Sets.[88]
- Monitoring of progress, followed by course correction. This can be achieved through 360° feedback, appraisals, and online sampling of staff and customers. This will take years and is ongoing and iterative.
- Reward for the desired behaviours through bonuses, remuneration, etc.
- Games and awards, competitions, etc.

From this you can start to think about the Values that drive your leadership. Discovering and recognising your true Values is a powerful and often revealing exercise. This is a time for reflection and perhaps even keeping a journal of your thoughts and Values. In thinking about which Values are your drivers, keep questioning what lies behind each Value and what lies behind that, going deeper and deeper until you reach the fundamental Values that are dearest to you.

Tool: What has motivated me?

You could also think about a time when you felt most satisfied, motivated and valued at work. Reflect upon the Values that were being expressed and satisfied, when you lived your Values and get feedback from others to check your view of reality. Often there is a gap between our true Values and those we exhibit to others through our behaviour. It is revealing to find out if this is so, and where the gap lies; once you are aware, you can choose to do something about it.

The importance here is for you to be clear about your reasoning, what your Values are and therefore where your boundaries are. Think, too, about what you will do if you are required to cross or defend them.

Tool: Aligning personal Values with the organisation

Do the Values discovered in the exercise above suggest that those which matter to you as a person differ from those you have as a leader in your organisation?

- If they are different – why? Does this lead to stress, inconsistency?
- If so, why can't you take your Values to the office?
- What would be the benefit to the organisation if you did take your Values to the office?

• How could you and your organisation benefit from having a common set of shared Values?

Aligning your Values with your organisation's Values takes deep thought. Firstly to have an understanding of how you would have to act in order to honour and be aligned to the organisation's Values and, secondly, whether or not you are willing to do that.

As a leader it is also wise to regularly consider the organisation's Values explicitly. Have your behaviours (AND your team's behaviours) been consistent with the Values? If not, are they the right Values? Or do you need to change and if so, how? It is your job as a senior leader to remain focused on the organisation's core Values and make sure that whatever you and your team do is in line with them.

Tool: Energy matrix

Understanding your own Values and connecting them to the organisation's Values and your behaviours – how you live your Values – gives meaning and energy to your life. There is a spark of enthusiasm when you are living 'on purpose'.

Taking the activities from 'A day in the life', plot them onto the Energy matrix (Figure 10.2) and add the personal activities as in the example.

How can you navigate yourself to where you want to be? Once you know where you ARE, you can consider how you got there and what you might learn from that. Then decide what you need to do to close the gap between where you are now and where you want to be. As in navigating a ship, you need to check your course and correct it on a regular basis or you may find that in your journey from London to Stockholm you end up in Gibraltar.

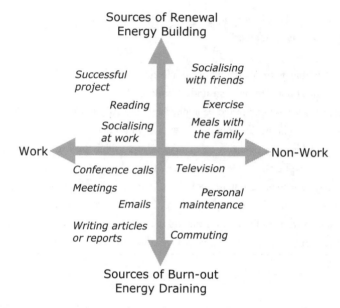

Figure 10.2 Energy matrix

Unlocking extraordinary competence

An enduring purpose,[89] combined with core Values which do not change, provides the framework for developing strategies, operating practices, policy and day-to-day running of the organisation. Values provide a framework for developing policy based on evidence, ensuring a consistency of approach in the face of current pressures. They enable rational conversation with stakeholders.

Any idea or product can become obsolete; however, guided by core Values, the organisation can **evolve** beyond what exists today and ensure that it continues to exist in the future, even if the products are different. The organisation will continue to do something of Value – and therefore continue to be effective, profitable and successful – because it has guidelines to follow in making decisions on the direction to follow. Its cultural norms may change, products, goals, competencies, policies, organisation structures and design, reward systems – all may change, but the central, enduring core Values and purpose do not. This ability to evolve is an extraordinary organisational competence which is part of any PS-RO.

Alignment and cohesion

Organisations that wish to make the most of understanding their Values need to work together in groups to articulate shared Values through the entire organisation. The way to live the Values needs discussion, development and interpretation for each team and each individual. Just as we each embody leadership in our own unique way, the way that each person lives their Values – and the organisational Values – is unique to them and their own Value set, even while they are aligned.

An organisation's Values are the most important drivers for its success, as they transcend individual aims and ambitions and provide a cohesive, shared view. Ultimately core Values, together with organisational Narrative, are the compass that guides the organisation to achieve its purpose: facilitating conversations between parts of the organisation that have very different roles and outlook.

Tool: Why is that important?

An exercise you might try for uncovering the organisation's purpose is the 'Why' exercise. Begin by starting with a descriptive statement about what your organisation does or produces. Then ask 'Why is that important?' Repeat the process with the answer several times until you can't go further. That is likely to be the fundamental, underlying purpose of the organisation. It should be inspiring and motivational; together with the core Values, helping to guide the organisation forwards to success.

There is an apocryphal story about a janitor at NASA in Houston who, when asked what she was doing, proudly stated, 'I am helping to put a man on the moon'. What you want to achieve is that every person in your organisation understands and appreciates how what they do works towards achieving the organisation's core purpose.

Tool: 'Random Corporate Serial Killer'

Another way to uncover core purpose is to play this game as introduced in *Built to Last*. Suppose that a person was willing to buy your company and pay a fair price, taking all aspects into consideration. Employment would be guaranteed at the same level of pay, but there wouldn't be any guarantee that jobs would be in the same industry. The new buyer would 'kill' the organisation – it would cease to exist, along with all of its products and outputs.

- Would you sell?
- Why (or why not)?
- What would be lost if you did?
- Why, therefore, is it important that the organisation continues to exist?
- What does the organisation contribute and to whom?

The discussion will surface shared and divergent assumptions, and will give insight into the core Values and purpose.

Handling ambiguity and paradox

Today's world is increasingly uncertain and ambiguous. Leaders have to handle ambiguity – to hold two conflicting ideas and respond to them at the same time. For instance, how do you balance short-term needs (e.g. shareholders) vs. long-term needs (e.g. people in the organisation and the organisation itself)? Where does the balance need to be? Does it change with the situation?

Often leaders will choose one side over another because of their own preference, skill set or comfort zone. It isn't always right to choose to stay in the middle; leaders need to be able to judge what is correct, effective, useful and profitable in each particular situation even if it is outside their comfort zone. And each situation will be different. Moving quickly to choose the right point on the continuum from which to work gets the best out of the paradox and minimises the downsides. You need to learn to be versatile, flexible and agile in changing your approach to deal with different situations; add more Fox-like behaviours to your skill set. Clarity on what you will and won't do (guided by your Values and what is right/wrong), and what the organisation will and won't do, will help you to narrow the available Options down so that you can more easily make a robust decision.

Managing clashes of Values

Paradox also exists between different parts of an organisation. For instance, a classic Values clash is between the Functions (Finance, HR, IT and Facilities, etc.) or between central parts of the organisation and the line units or between parts of a merged organisation after a merger.

Case study – managing clashes of Values

An Indian company had grown from local origins to be the owner of many national brands. It entered into a joint venture with an international soft drink manufacturer to make and distribute their equally venerable product. Both companies had deep Values, but Values that were completely distinct from each other.

The local company had begun trading as the provider of food of guaranteed religious purity to people of the Brahmin caste. No non-Brahmin workers were allowed. Later, in separate facilities, it provided halal food to Indian Muslims. Later expansion completely transcended these product lines, but the work force was still selected on ethnic and religious lines, and all manner of segregation was applied to facilities, purchasing and retailing.

The international partner had long adopted a multi-cultural, inclusive approach to its branding, employment policies and general ethos. It had projected itself in bright primary colours as the space where children dance together in harmony. It was strongly committed to high business ethics, excellent environmental performance and community relations. Precisely what it meant by those terms was set in Value judgements formed by its US headquarters.

Neither partner could see why the relationship was not working. The Indians saw one thing, the multinational another when looking at the same issue. For example, the Indians gave priority to family relations of workers when hiring new staff. The internationals saw this as nepotism. The Indians saw brand continuity over generations as a stamp of authority on their products; the internationals saw it as fusty and vaguely repulsive. Then, when it came to ethnic segregation and the refusal to buy from open markets, the relationship collapsed.

What was to be done? In effect, one or the other would have to cease to be the organisation that it had been throughout its long life. On recognising the nature of the problem, they also recognised an incompatibility that made the joint venture impossible to support. The partnership was dissolved amicably.

In the case study above, respect for the different cultures underpinned the decision and allowed each firm to stay true to its core Values.

Measuring behaviours

Behaviours flow out of core Values, both for the individual and the organisation. In order to ensure that everyone understands the behaviours that are required, in a PS-RO these behaviours are explicitly defined, agreed, measured and are part of the reward system.

Values and behaviours

To act in line with the organisational Values, organisations need to have identified the behaviours that exhibit their chosen core Values. Then the task is to communicate, communicate, communicate – not just about the desirable behaviours, but also examples of how people live those Values by their behaviours. These examples can be incorporated into the induction process and performance management system as well as the organisational Narrative. The organisation's systems and processes need to support these behaviours; so if one of your Values is Co-operation, then people should be rewarded on the basis of Co-operation. Recognise and celebrate the people who do it well. Build it into discussions between senior management. Ensure that support activities like procurement are aligned with your Values. Celebrate success. Celebrate your core Values. Make them part of everything you do.

Competences – required behaviours

As the discussion above suggests, Values themselves are hard to measure. The behaviours and processes carrying out the Values, however, can be observed and measured. The behaviours you monitor need to be aligned to your core Values so that you measure (and reward) what you wish to see. Just because you do not see a behaviour exhibited, however, does not mean that the person you are measuring is not able to behave in that way, only that they have not yet done so. With a good, agreed description of what the desired behaviour looks like, productive and helpful feedback can be given to enable the person to improve and/or change their behaviour.

Conflicting Values and behaviours

Organisations sometimes have Values which are contradictory in the behaviours they imply, as our case study below illustrates.

Case study – conflicting Values and behaviours

A computer company had tight management control of finance as one of their Values. Another Value was to empower individuals dealing with customers to resolve problems 'on the spot'. If the problems could be resolved with software changes, or with items held in the individual's spares collection, the two Values were compatible. But the finance Value meant that drawing items from the spares store needed next-level management approval through a written signature on a standard form. This could easily take several hours or days to organise, depending on the availability of the manager and the location of the stores.

The processes were changed to give customer services personnel a level of budgetary discretion. This modified the Values governing the company, giving the Value of empowerment, and of customer satisfaction, primacy.

Assessing competence

Competences are observable behaviours and these come from a person's core Values, so organisations need to use formal assessment of behaviours in order to improve alignment to its own core Values. For instance, a company that had a core Value of 'Constant Respect for People and Uncompromising Integrity' might have assessments for three different levels of customer-facing staff as in Tables 10.1 to 10.3.

The staff got feedback on their conformance to these behaviours. There were development Options if there was a gap between what was expected and what was observed, and it was unlikely that a person would move to the next level before the competences were observed under even stressful conditions.

Table 10.1 Level 1

Competence	What it looks like	What it doesn't look like
Commitment and integrity	Has the confidence and trust of others	Lets dates slip
	Shows consistency between words and actions	Blames others for own lateness
	Lives up to commitments	Inconsistent
	Keeps word – if a promise is made and cannot be kept it is renegotiated	Doesn't take ownership for issues
	No surprises for stakeholders – keeps clients and suppliers up-to-date	Doesn't keep word
	Shows constant respect for people, e.g. listening to them, respecting their time and treating them respectfully	Manipulates others
		Says things behind others' backs but not to their face
		Has a hidden agenda

People at the next level of staff were required to exhibit the behaviours in Table 10.2 in addition. And the most senior staff were expected to exhibit the additional behaviours in Table 10.3.

From the example, you can see how the important behaviours to monitor will change depending on a person's level of seniority in an organisation.

Implementing the alignment processes

The behaviours that align people in various parts of the organisation with the organisation's purpose and core Values need to be discovered through discussion and dialogue. Often it is easier to uncover undesirable behaviour; however, this will carry the seeds

Table 10.2 Level 2

Competence	What it looks like	What it doesn't look like
Own development	Accepts responsibility for own mistakes Actively seeks feedback to enhance own performance Adapts behaviour in response to feedback and experience Demonstrates awareness of own strengths and weaknesses Takes the initiative in learning new skills in order to be more effective	Doesn't accept criticism Refuses to change Own training plans not met
Developing others	Accurately identifies strengths and development needs in others Lets people know promptly when they are performing well and also when they are NOT performing well Mobilises people to take action, inspires them to excel Rewards people for good performance Gets agreement and understanding for the need to change	Fails to gain agreement to or understanding of the need to change Does not give feedback Tells not sells Follows 'Do as I say, not as I do' De-motivates people

Table 10.3 Level 3

Competence	What it looks like	What it doesn't look like
Interpersonal sensitivity	Promotes team objectives and fosters team and organisation spirit	Works to meet own agenda
	Engenders an environment of co-operation both inside and outside area of responsibility	Does not consider own impact on others in the unit
	Tempers activities of self and team in line with the organisation's goals	Being dismissive of others
	Able to manage group dynamics in a 'heavyweight' environment	Trying to manipulate and use your own position to influence outcomes
		Disrespectful body language

of what is desired – as you can see in the example above – 'what it doesn't look like' has a flip side.

Crucially, it is not worth having a system like this unless it is *used*. That means measuring how people are doing, using the system to give feedback, actively developing people in alignment with the system; encouraging and enabling the desirable behaviours.

Case study – respect for people

A firm wanted to develop a core Value of 'respect for people'. An organisational audit identified that one of the Executive VPs shouted at his people and shamed them in public. He was proud of the fact that he was a 'tough guy' and the stories that were told in that part of the business were all around how terrible he had been to people. Even in Europe, with well-developed processes for handling disputes, he would attempt to fire people on the spot if they displeased him. Before a presentation was made to him, the numbers would be adjusted so that he wouldn't hear bad news.

For an organisation that professed to a Value of respect for people, this behaviour was not acceptable. The CEO coached him on the expected behaviours, but he was not able to change, so eventually he was asked to leave. The organisation was very serious about its Values and acted on them.

Behaviours supporting a PS-RO

While the exact behaviours exhibited by people in a particular organisation will differ – depending on their particular core purpose and Values – there are some that are key for the success of a PS-RO. How each person behaves contributes to the extraordinary competence of the organisation and the following three aspects are particularly important. Each is underpinned by the core Values all PS-ROs share, of Co-operation, Respect and Responsibility:

- Ability to listen to the outside world and see what is happening on the horizon – what global trends are out there and how they might affect each person, what is coming their way (Insight, see Chapter 11).
- Agility – seeing the need for course change and implementing it as quickly as possible, bearing in mind that an organisation is like a ship: course corrections need to be delicate and take time to come into effect.
- Reflection – each group or team needs to take time out on a regular basis to examine what is happening and see if their part of the organisation is on course. Equally important is for each person to reflect on whether they need to change course or not,

based on the core Values and organisational Narrative. Tools for this include Narrative, see Chapter 13.

Legacy

Finally, a PS-RO is concerned with its legacy, in what the organisation as a whole stands for and what it can create – and, perhaps more importantly, keep creating – for its employees. It is about contributing not just to its own life and success but also to the community in which it lives. This comes out of the core Values of Respect and Responsibility that PS-ROs depend on.

To do this, each person in the organisation needs to be a champion, living the Values and 'being the change' that is needed. It means that the organisation has dispersed leadership and people lead whenever it is necessary, enlarging their sphere of influence, being clear about where they have control and where they only have influence.

Part of your legacy and contribution as a senior leader and manager will be developing new leaders from those who work with you. Enabling people to lead and supporting them in their leadership journey is a profoundly rewarding element of living your Values, making a difference and finding meaning in your life, both on a professional and personal level.

Executive Summary

- Core Values give people a sense of stability when the organisation is undergoing course correction.
- An organisation's core Values should be evident from the hiring practices of an organisation. Employees who do not share the organisation's core Values cause problems and costs.

- Discovering your own core Values and aligning them with the organisation's Values is a powerful and often revealing exercise.
- A PS-RO contributes not just to its own life and success, but also to the community in which it lives. It is concerned with its legacy as well as the here and now.

Chapter 11

Insight

In the last chapter we discussed the role of Values in an organisation, and the fact that they were deep and slowly changing. In addition to Values, organisations need Insight, defined as the ability to make sense of the external world and its future, integrate it with internal capabilities and harness that understanding to assess the organisation's strengths, and so provide a basis for generating Options for taking the organisation forward. Insight fits with the other four qualities to help the organisation move from ambiguity and uncertainty at the bottom end of the lower cone to a place where it can use Insight for its survival, success and advantage.

Insight provides the context for Board discussions, reaching above the level of shareholder management and turf wars. It also gives senior management shared mental models of the current and future world to facilitate discussion and sharing of assumptions and information.

Insight is a way to harness the intelligence of the people focused on specified tasks in the upper cone – who will be chosen for their capabilities in those tasks and tend to be Hedgehogs – to the purpose of the organisation. This allows them an opportunity to develop Fox-like approaches and to handle ambiguity.

Achieving Purposeful Self-Renewal is bound to be an ongoing journey – this chapter describes the bundle of tools and methods which allow for course correction, when used with the others of a PS-RO. Specific tools are:

- SWOT and SOAR
- Boston box
- Horizon scanning
- Scenario creation
- Skills audit
- Relationships audit
- Reputation audit
- Knowledge audit

Scenarios as a source of Insight

The directions in which an organisation looks for Insight are conditioned by its view of the world. Many organisations have a limited view of their potential directions, based on their default assumptions. Scenarios provide a framework for exploring and challenging assumptions (as the case study on 'Getting senior staff to use insight' in Chapter 7 illustrated). For this reason, considering more than one potential scenario will facilitate the organisation looking in directions that might not have been included under the default assumptions of the organisation, which tends to be *one* preferred future.

It is useful to look for signs of change which would be relevant to each of the scenarios; these may inform the organisation's mental model by helping it to find evidence of scenarios previously dismissed as 'impossible'.

The scenarios described in Chapter 3 (*Low Road, My Road, High Road*) provide a possible set of framing scenarios: others are to be found on a number of websites, as discussed below. The use of framing scenarios provides a low-threat way of introducing scenario thinking: 'these are in the public domain, what are the implications for our organisation?'

Relationship of Insight to the other PS-RO qualities

Insight is provided focus – and has boundaries set – by the core Values and Narrative of the organisation. The Insight processes link into methods for generating Options and analysing the overall organisational position.

Tools: SWOT and SOAR

These are two of the many tools for analysing the overall organisation.

SWOT stands for Strengths (i.e. internal capabilities), Weaknesses (again, internal capabilities), Opportunities (the external possibilities) and Threats (from the external world, such as the competition, from technological change or demographics).

SOAR stands for Strengths, Opportunities, Aspirations and Results,[90] and is a process designed to take organisations in a group environment through the Insight processes and to use a whole systems approach to strategic and tactical planning.

Tools which additionally suggest diagnostics include the Boston box or Market Attractiveness/Capability (MA/C) matrix. (The MA/C matrix is used with scenarios in Chapter 12 and discussed there.)

Diagnostic tool: Boston box[91]

The growth/share matrix – commonly known as the Boston box – was developed by the Boston Consulting Group (BCG) in the 1970s. It is a tool of portfolio management. The Boston box evaluates the products of an organisation according to their market share and growth prospects. On that basis it can reveal insights about their financial needs or their ability to generate cash.

Products are described as Stars (high growth and high market share), Cash Cows (high market share and low growth), Dogs (low market share and growth) and Problem Children/Question Marks (for products entering a market, with low market share but potentially high growth).

Chapter 14 on Machinery describes a number of the underpinning methods and processes, particularly those which link the upper cone – where people are assigned specified tasks and the lower cone – in which people are tasked with less specified assignments with the inner ring, the management of the portfolio.

Methods for developing Insight

The constituents of the Insight processes can be divided into two groups.

First, methods for exploring the external and future worlds, including horizon scanning/understanding the environment, forecasting (e.g. Delphi) and creating possible futures (scenarios). These are collectively often referred to as Foresight. Good examples of Foresight can be found on a number of websites, e.g. the World Economic Forum,[92] UK Government Foresight website,[93]

Challenge Network[94] and the US National Intelligence Council website.[95]

Second, an audit of the organisation's current capabilities is discussed as a baseline for current gaps and gaps against future needs, in terms of skills, reputation and alignment to Values, relationships and information. This should result in an understanding of the areas of distinctive competence that may have been dormant and can be revitalised. An audit of potential fulcra and break points, whether through technology or other sources of change, will help anticipate disruption.

How Insight is gathered

We discuss in Chapter 14 the factors that will motivate people in the operational, specified parts of the organisation to contribute to renewal: the need was established in Chapter 5.

Though we have been writing as though participation in Insight processes came solely from individuals, it need not: teams can interface with the processes. And the domain spanners (called 'Connecters' by Gladwell in *The Tipping Point*[96]) are important to Insight – they are human telephone books – if they do not know the person who can contribute, they are usually only a hop or two away from them. You need to be aware of people's strengths for Insight generation and use these strengths and people to best advantage.

This chapter describes how, and most importantly when, to use the Insight processes; we provide references for designers and implementers of the processes.

Horizon scanning

Horizon scanning is designed to help identify the external and long-term issues and trends facing the organisation. Ideally, horizon scanning is based on knowledge of futures, of a range of information sources and expertise in information science, to reduce the risk and cost in identifying and tracking long-term issues and in scanning a wide range of potential factors. A good description can be found in Wendy Schultz's article, which also includes a thoughtful analysis of the difficulties of getting horizon scanning results accepted in large organisations.[97]

Tool: Horizon scanning

When to use it?
As well expressed by consultancy McKinsey,

> 'Almost all large companies undertake a time-consuming strategic-planning process that leaves many executives frustrated with the results. One approach is to start the exercise not by examining the numbers but by identifying the long-term issues facing the company.'[98]

Who can benefit?
- Organisations concerned that their annual strategy cycle or new business development activities may be missing major opportunities or challenges.
- Organisations in government which are concerned at the ability of pressure groups to over-influence policy and strategy – and need evidence about the happenings outside their walls.

Outcomes
Horizon scanning has a number of clear benefits, including:

- A framework for harnessing the capabilities of people from the upper cone as well as the lower cone, to pool expertise.

- The ability to explore a wider set of influences than in day-to-day competitor or customer analysis, going for instance outside the normal geographic or industry domain. This exercise frequently proves to be a source of illumination, a major source of 'aha's'.
- Thinking out of the box increases the ability to see new opportunities. People exercise the 'thinking muscle', developing creativity and increasing their awareness of what might happen, and therefore carrying that thinking through to contingency plans.
- Requiring dialogue at senior level about strategy and the assumptions behind strategy, it creates a shared vocabulary and understanding of the issues.
- Setting a framework for strategy.
- Identifying early indicators of trends or drivers, for instance newspaper headlines. These increase the ability of the organisation to recognise when change is happening and then respond appropriately to that change.

Case study – sharing Insight: getting it wrong

One government department spent a year on a major horizon scanning process, finding over 800 different factors affecting the department's future. They wanted to discuss these with senior management, so wrote over 800 Post-Its and put them all round a conference room, arranged a day in the diary of the senior team and invited senior managers to walk around and comment. The senior managers did not know where or how to start, and had no structure or process to help them think through the future issues. They quickly left the room and did not come back, or accept any further invitations to explore the important future issues facing the department.

> ### Case study – sharing Insight: getting it right
>
> Arup, the consulting engineers, have developed a deck of cards, each describing a factor affecting the built environment – widely interpreted. The card packs are available on request and used extensively in government and universities, where a selection is provided to kickstart a discussion on a specific topic. The cards can be quickly read and also give good backup data and sources. When used as part of a facilitated process they allow a group to quickly focus on the key issues.

Forecasting as part of Insight

Forecasting is the process of estimation in unknown situations, commonly referred to as estimation of changes in values over time. Risk and uncertainty are central to forecasting. They form an important part of Insight for those variables that can be forecast, particularly in the short term. Forecasting is used for all *short-term* planning, for instance in everyday customer demand forecasting for manufacturing companies. The discipline of demand planning, also sometimes referred to as supply chain forecasting, embraces both statistical forecasting and a consensus process.

Technology and demographics are two areas where forecasting is important: technology availability in the market place is forecast from knowledge of developments in the laboratories; while demographics are derived from knowledge of medical advances and birth rates.

How does it work?

Delphi forecasting methodology
Delphi is named after the famous Delphic Oracle who was consulted about the future by supplicants in Ancient Greece. It is the

most widely used forecasting technique for technology availability. The methodology involves iteration among experts until they agree on a forecast. This can be done electronically, though it was also extensively used by the Japanese during their Foresight exercises, where they used a mixture of meetings and correspondence through a facilitator. The role of the facilitator is to set the time scale for responses, to précis the consensus and highlight outliers and reasons.

A review of accuracy of outcomes was undertaken after 25 years of Japanese Foresight projects using Delphi processes. What they found was that accuracy was better when a wider range of subject experts were included in the process. So, for instance, if the subject was the future of surface chemistry, the best result came from consulting surface chemists, together with chemists from other branches, **plus** chemical engineers, physicists, biologists, economists and mathematicians, as discussed in *Research Foresight: Priority Setting in Science.*[99] The reason for this is that changes in a domain come from breakthroughs or discoveries in neighbouring domains and these are often not visible to people in the core domain.

It is also worth remembering that adoption of technology often takes paths surprising to the technologist – as in the take-up of text messaging. And now that people are so mobile, demographic forecasts are much more uncertain in any specific geography.

Forecasting in other domains

Do the same guidelines apply to forecasting in other domains? While Delphi is mostly used for scientific forecasting, could it give good results in the social sciences? Would consulting a wide range of experts provide good forecasts?

The best evidence on this is from a study covering regional forecasting exercises from hundreds of experts in dozens of countries, covering topics as wide-ranging as transition to democracy,

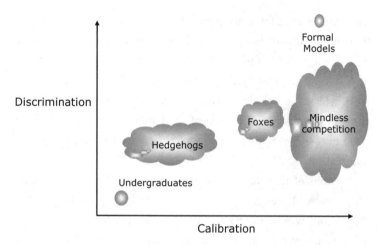

Figure 11.1 Modelling does best

economic growth, interstate violence and nuclear proliferation. In Figure 11.1, the axes are discrimination and calibration.

Discrimination is the ability to get better than a simple 'predict the base rate' strategy, and so a discrimination score for a person is 1 if he always predicts events that do happen and always gives zero probabilities to events that do not happen.

Calibration is the correspondence between objective probabilities and subjective probabilities, so to maximise calibration it pays to be cautious and assign probabilities close to base (or historic) rates. High calibration is 'good' and at the right-hand end of the scale.

Formal economic models did best of all in forecasting across this range of social, economic and political data (top right-hand corner). Mindless competition (including chimpanzees selecting balls from a bag) did quite well. From this study we can also compare the performance of our two archetypes, Foxes and Hedgehogs, in prediction. What it found was that Foxes are considerably better at forecasting than Hedgehogs in this type of domain, crucial to gathering Insight for the organisation. Hedgehogs tend to have a fixed view of the world and are unable to pick up signals of change.

The ability to anticipate high-impact, hard-to-predict and rare events beyond the realm of normal expectations (Black Swans)[100] is infrequent, and is often found in science fiction. The ability to anticipate these extreme outliers is more frequent than the ability of organisations to prioritise their planning: for instance – how much planning should an organisation do for the possibility (foreseen in a movie) of a plane crashing into the World Trade Center in New York?

Forecasting is important because forecasting is the basis of much of modern society. Experience is, after all, our guide. The trick is in knowing when it is right to forecast – and expect the results to be accurate – and when forecasts cannot be relied on. And, even when forecasts need to be made – because budgets must be set, plant built and people recruited – it is worth remembering that a forecast is a point in a sea of possibility – see Figure 11.2.

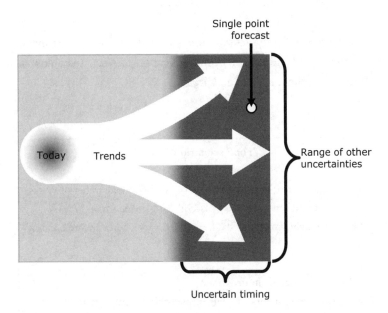

Figure 11.2 Forecasting the future

The scenario process

Scenarios, unlike forecasts, provide alternative mental models of possible futures. Thus, they can play a far more open-ended role than forecasts.

Scenarios as context setters

Scenarios provide an integrative mechanism for the external world, futures and the competitive environment. In addition, they provide a process for handling possible futures and so can create models of the world based on a range of answers to questions such as:

- Will there be extremely fast change, or blocked social change?
- Will the current crisis be a chronic drain?
- Does the will exist to find painful solutions?
- Can we organise transnational complexity?
- Can we cope with obstructive politics?

Scenarios not only act as a tool for analysis, but have a major role in internal and external communication, as discussed below in 'Insight and the Three Ring Circus'.

Tool: scenario creation

The scenario creation process is well described in a number of works, of which the most widely used is Gill Ringland's *Scenario Planning*.[101] Below we identify some of the factors to be considered before creating scenarios.

When to use scenario creation?

Scenarios, being mental models of plausible futures, are useful when the external world seems confusing or turbulent. They are not useful when there is a single major discontinuity hitting an industry. One example would be the abrupt change in the computer industry as it went from proprietary design and components to one based on semi-conductors, with a reduction of the margin from 40% to 5%.

Who can benefit?

The scenario creation process itself is a very rich learning and team-building experience. Using pre-built scenarios, exploring the implications for a business, organisation or industry, is a more analytic exercise, though often one rich in new understanding.

How long does it take?

Scenarios can be created in a day workshop, and if this involves a team with a shared database of information and a clear focus, it can produce useful results. An example is described in *Scenarios in Marketing*,[102] with a group developing new men's grooming brands. Often, scenarios are created during a project which has the aim of setting the context for detailed research into options for investment, or for testing project proposals. For these purposes, it is important to ensure that the input to the process includes interviews inside and outside the organisation, that the data is well researched and calibrated by experts, and that the scenarios are described appropriately to the audience (see Chapter 13).

The core scenario creation process is shown in Figure 11.3.

Next we touch on some of the ways in which scenarios are used in organisations.

Synthesis of the external environment and internal capability

Astounding yourself

The generation of Insight – in the form of scenarios or other forms of foresight – will often lead to unexpected perceptions,

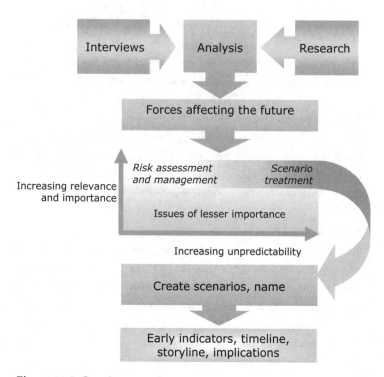

Figure 11.3 Creating scenarios

called the 'aha!'s'. One example is that of the D2D management team discussed in Chapter 7, who realised that they shared a view of the world (default assumptions) which was not aligned to their business's capabilities.

Being useful to others

The prime purpose of Insight is to be of use to the organisation. The various methods that can be used to communicate Insight are discussed in Chapter 13, but without coherent and plausible insight, communication effort will be wasted.

The basis of being useful to others is:

- A time scale which people can relate to.
- A scope that is relevant to the organisation or the issue being studied.
- A set of relatively short-term potential impacts.
- A well-expressed set of early indicators (see below).

Early indicators

Early indicators are possible events which would happen under a given scenario, in the relatively short term. They are often expressed as newspaper headlines, and provide a focus for the team to discuss the evolution path of a scenario – often as important as the scenario itself.

They are one of the most important tools for connecting the upper and lower cones of the business process. They should be visible through the normal processes of the organisation, and understood to be significant. In this role they are effective at engaging harassed and busy line managers in watching for their appearance and hence contributing to the strategic conversation.[103]

Case study – early indicators

A university had developed four scenarios for the future of higher education, in order to provide a context for planning their future. They wanted to engage academic and support staff from across the University in order to facilitate debate. They chose to do this via one-day workshops, with 50 to 100 participants at each.

The format chosen meant that each scenario was introduced by a different person, using the words 'It is obvious that my scenario is going to happen', showing a slide of a recent newspaper headline or photograph which was consistent with their scenario. This made the point that the world is complex and all four scenarios might develop, as well as relating scenarios to the current world and current decisions.

Practical deliverables

Legitimisation and framing
A well-structured Insight process gives transparency to the perceptions delivered – they have an evolution and audit trail. This becomes important as the focus turns to evaluating Options and a Narrative.

Style and accessibility
The output from an Insight process will normally include:

- A report, outlining the methodology, citing sources for key data and describing the storylines and possibly also an analytic form of description. A good example can be found on the Health and Safety Executive website.[104]
- A set of communication tools as discussed in Chapter 14.

Presentation and workshop combination
Most people find it difficult to engage with futures thinking, Insight or scenarios, through a presentation. It is more effective to have a short presentation followed by a workshop in which participants explore the implications of each future for their organisation. This allows them to 'get inside' and imagine possible different futures from their own point of view.

The essentials of successful workshops are described below, under 'Practical aspects of gathering insight', and detailed agendas for 'implications' workshops are discussed in Gill Ringland's *Scenario Planning.*[105]

Describing the organisation

A sense of direction
Achieving a sense of 'where we are going' is a process which balances views of the future – from foresight – with examination of

current reality and strengths. We now build on our previous discussion of the elements of foresight – horizon scanning, forecasts and scenarios – with a discussion of the methods for understanding the organisation's competitive position.

We will also discuss the iterative nature of the process, and the ways of harnessing ideas to generate innovation more in Chapter 12.

Analysing the current position

The discussion below is based on the analysis used in Michael Porter's *On Competition*[106], in which he identifies that in addition to established rivals, four additional competitive forces can hurt prospective profits: his thoughts were based on the decades before the crisis, and our comments on the new world order are in *bold italics*.

- Savvy customers can force down prices by playing you and your rivals against one another; for instance, using the power of comparison websites. *This is of increased importance beyond the crisis.*
- Powerful suppliers may constrain your profits if they charge higher prices. *This threat is increased beyond the crisis as suppliers go out of business, leaving others dominant. For instance, one of the two factories supplying batteries for a laptop range suffered a fire, and the price of replacement batteries subsequently increased by a factor of two.*
- Aspiring entrants, armed with new capacity and hungry for market share, can ratchet up the investment required for you to stay in the game. *The effect of this is lessened beyond the crisis, as investment is in shorter supply.*
- Substitute offerings can lure customers away. *Beyond the crisis, there will be substitute offerings which redefine price brackets, as the Tata Nano will do in the auto industry.*[107]

These headings are also useful in the public sector, e.g. for a National Parks sector:

- What competes with this sector now?
- Who are the customers (who may not be end-users) and how can they change pricing structures?
- What are the dynamics of the supply industries, e.g. infrastructure providers?
- What new entrants might offer services, e.g. international vacations?
- Will there be specific challenges, e.g. from virtual reality?

Insight: in which areas do we have activity/exposure?

For the private sector, industry or market analysis needs to be at a sub-segment level in order to realistically assess competitors – as discussed in *Marketing Management*.[108] For the public sector, agencies often have a defined focus akin to that of a private sector organisation, whereas central and state/local governments have a much wider remit and are more exposed to pressures from political masters. Figure 11.4 illustrates the 'Five Forces'.

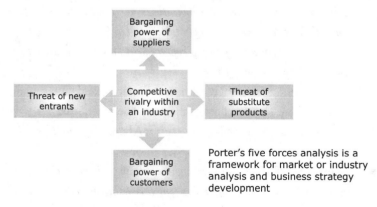

Porter's five forces analysis is a framework for market or industry analysis and business strategy development

Figure 11.4 Based on Porter's Five Forces

What are the key variables for these areas?

In addition to considering the competitive position through the supply chain, competing organisations and the power of customers, underlying factors include:

- total market size, and geography in relation to the organisation's footprint;
- relative market share, where relative ranking in the market is correlated with profitability;[109]
- rate of change of market, which is an advantage to a small player and a threat to incumbents.

In the public sector, where organisations are state-owned but operating in a market, such as national flag carrier airlines, the above are also relevant. For other public sector organisations the equivalent could be:

- total value of services delivered, or budget if not citizen-facing;
- relative value of services delivered to other, e.g. private, providers;
- rate of change of citizens' attitudes and social changes.

Evidence-based policy

In the public sector, this type of analysis can be alarming, as it leaves no place to hide. As public sector budgets come under increasing attack, such gathering of evidence will become more and more important, leading not just to evidence-based policy but to evidence-based budgets.

Audit of exposure to risks

Approach to risk

Many organisations have processes to assess risk. These often sit at the operational level and relate to financial risk or operational risk from staff, customer and partner delinquency or fraud. Very few address the systemic risk to the business from either the internal capabilities or their impact on the organisation's ability to be adaptable, to purposefully self-renew, or to the effect of failure of other actors needed for the organisation's operations.

While adaptation – encompassing new business areas or new customers – always carries some risk, a careful audit providing insight into the skills, information, reputation and relationships of the organisation will limit the areas of exposure.

Risks to how each area works and may come to work
Each aspect of the organisation may be subject to change. For example:

- Business-to-business or business-to-consumer – this may change due to changes in the market, for instance the growth of DIY has meant a new marketing style to target individuals rather than building firms.
- National or local markets vs. international or global (whether due to regulation or other factors) – this may change due to changes in regulation, as in financial services in the 1990s.
- Changes in the supply chain, with 'Just in Time' supply reducing the stock held in retailers and warehouses; and a potential effect of pressures to reduce air cargo being a return to sea transport for many goods.
- Changes in the funding of public services, for instance the introduction of scaled fees for public services.
- Changes in the regulatory regime, as in telecommunications in the 1990s and financial services over the next decade.
- Changes in government's role and approach, as in Eastern Europe and India.

- The role of ICT in disruptive change, as in the telecoms and media industries.
- The role of biotechnology in disruptive change, as in the health care and potentially the insurance industries.
- Global systemic risks such as climate change, environmental pollution, security.

All organisations will need to form their own list of the areas of potential future risk to their organisation, through horizon scanning and other Insight activities.

The audits sketched below focus on capturing the current basis in order to be able to ask the questions: how might these change? Some potential types of change are discussed under the paragraphs on fulcra and breakpoints, and the effect of technology.

Organisational audit

An organisational audit looks at the organisation as a whole system. It looks for evidence of core Values to identify where there may be dissonance between these Values and the Values which are lived and evident in the organisation. It explores the different Narratives in the organisation and assesses whether these fit with the core Values and are fit for the organisation's purpose. The main tools used for organisational audit are interviews and workshops with groups of varying sizes. It is useful to map how the organisation actually works – depending on the area you are enquiring into, you might wish to add a focus on skills, knowledge and/or relationships (see below).

Tool: Skills audit

A skills audit is typically based around existing data in the organisation. It should particularly look for skills created through job moves and combinations of skills from previous roles. This follows the thinking in Denmark, where the retraining of the unemployed is actively undertaken to build a workforce of multi-skilled people, through the social security system.[110]

The data could be HR information, development information, assessment centres or information from appraisals. It can be augmented by interviews and/or questionnaires if the information is not available otherwise. The audit should look to ascertain a description of the skills, competences and behaviours that exist in the organisation as well as the number of people in the organisation who have each skill, competence or behaviour.

If possible, the data should also include both the age of the person and their time in the company. This is because, while young high-flyers are an important part of the organisation's human capital, it is important to tap into the experience built up by staff who have seen the organisation through previous changes. These staff are important for their corporate memory as well as for their actual previous positions.

Case study – multi-skills

The increasing importance of people with multiple skills acquired through a range of assignments and the difficulty of capturing all relevant skills in a database are illustrated by a call to a strategy company: can you help with strategy for the dairy industry? Have you experience in country X? Can you talk to farmers? By using the company network, it located staff members who had all of those, including direct experience as dairy farmers – which did not appear on their CVs – and experience of the country – which was buried in the CV under 'various roles at consultancy Z'.

Tool: Relationships (primarily business-to-business) audit

The starting point of a relationship audit is the mapping of the relationships of the organisation, focusing on business-to-business relationships, both current and required for potential new activities. The audit is therefore essential as part of the Options processes (see Chapter 12). The WonderWeb tool to map relationships is described in Chapter 14.

Once the organisation has captured its relationships via a WonderWeb or similar tool, the strength of each relationship can be assessed. This can be done via online surveys, workshops, phone calls or personal visits. The essential tasks are to ask the other party to the relationship:

- What do we do for you?
- What do we do well?
- What do we do badly?
- What else should we offer to do for you?

It is important after an audit that feedback is given to the other parties on the overall results and what in particular the organisation plans to change as a result – and how they will monitor and feed this back.

Tool: The reputation audit

An audit of the organisation's reputation needs to involve at least five key groups of stakeholders:

- customers
- current and past employees
- competitors
- suppliers
- regulators and/or auditors.

The aim is to find gaps where management attention can improve the reputation, in areas important to the organisation.

Alignment of Values to behaviour

In Chapter 7 we discussed the role of core Values in supplying stability in a changing world. It is important to audit both the knowledge of the organisation's core Values with stakeholders (as for reputation) and with staff, and to audit the alignment of behaviour with these values, see Chapter 10, in the section 'Measuring behaviours'.

Case study – tacit knowledge

An outsourcer was asked to capture user requirements for a new system. The methodology was well designed, but the final product did not meet the expectations of any of the users – much of the tacit knowledge had been cultural and not picked up by the outsourcer.

When the same outsourcer was asked to create an exact copy of a legacy system – handling all input and output the same as with the old system – the project delivered a system which was well documented, ran on new equipment and had a payback time of less than three months. No tacit knowledge was needed.

Knowledge management is defined as 'systems to support the creation, transfer and application of knowledge in organisations'.[111] Effective knowledge management will be based on a good understanding of the knowledge in the organisation.

Tool: Knowledge audit

A knowledge audit consists of four steps:

- To analyse what knowledge assets are used by the current organisation and its businesses, to support their core Values and Narrative, to harness Insight and create a set of innovative Options that can be used to purposefully renew the organisation. A knowledge map is a useful output of this stage.

• To identify which practices work well at present, and whether or not there are any associated issues or gaps in information or knowledge in moving forward to a PS-RO.

• To establish what improvements could be made to the sharing, the security and protection of knowledge, whether sharing between silos or different divisions.

• To identify additional knowledge needed for new challenges: this will be an iterative process, as the knowledge map gets extended over time.

Detailed processes for each of these steps, starting with creating a knowledge map of the organisation, have been developed by the Henley Knowledge Management Forum.[112] The essential points are:

• Be clear about the purpose of the knowledge audit.
• Use the effort needed to capture information on knowledge maps and flows as an indicator of the knowledge health of the organisation.
• Integrate the knowledge map with representation of knowledge flows – actual and needed – in a form which senior managers can visualise.

Identification of changed fulcra and break points

How can external changes that will alter the course of an organisation be anticipated? How can the timing be anticipated?

Clayton M. Christensen, in *Seeing What's Next*,[113] has suggested useful approaches to this. He starts with his disruptive innovation theory, which holds that existing companies have a high probability of beating entrant attackers when the contest is about innovations which bring better products into established markets. The theory also states that established companies almost always lose to

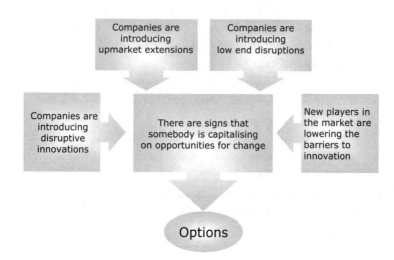

Figure 11.5 Signals of change

attackers who provide disruptive innovation, which is an innovation either bringing in lower-cost business models or targeting new customers. He applies this to the telecoms industry as a role model, spanning as it does high-tech supply, business and individual users. He suggests a framework for looking for signals of change, as in Figure 11.5.

The signals of change above relate to changes in market behaviour. It can also be appropriate to consider disruptive change specifically from technology too. An example is in health care, where within the space of a few years, new drugs and technology for insertion of stents – plastic tubes – have revolutionised heart surgery, with the almost complete demise of open heart surgery, and major cultural and practical impact on hospitals and their staff as well as on patients.

Early anticipation of the effects of disruptive technology is difficult to get right, but it is worth setting up and monitoring early indicators for potential developments.

Distinctive competence and vulnerability

The Insight processes above will have identified some areas of the organisation which are either strengths or weaknesses. Gaps will generally be under five main headings.

- Reputation gaps: our stakeholders' perception.
- Market gaps: where we can invest to improve market position.
- Information gaps: what we need to invest to learn.
- Skill gaps: people and capabilities that we need.
- Relationship gaps: blocked potential, hidden foes.

These can then frame a number of discussions, e.g. on

- The balance between social responsibility and other values. Consider, for instance:
  - Are people assets for development, or cost centres which would be best outsourced?
  - What is the centre of gravity of the organisation,[114] the unique element that enables them to accomplish their objectives? This determines which skills absolutely need to be near to home, and which parts of the organisation can be specified and outsourced.
- Where stakeholder perspectives surprise senior managers or the Board, why is this? Which are crucial to a PS-RO and which can be held at arm's length?
- What sort of workforce does the organisation need in the future and what sort of working environment and reward system will they react well to? (See also the discussion in Chapter 10, 'Applying core Values'.)
- How can the organisation work better with suppliers to learn from the intelligence they have from their perspective? At what

level should interchanges of information take place, and what processes should underpin these?

A programme of feeding back the Insight from the audits to shareholders and the Board to frame discussion will allow them to feel in touch with the organisation, without pre-announcing strategy.

Practical aspects of gathering Insight

Creating Insight is an ongoing process, which encompasses course correction. One organisation which started to explore the possibility that competitors could introduce products providing low-end disruption actually found that one competitor was about to make a move to do just that.

Insight gathers traction as more parts of the organisation are involved.

Workshops and interviews

Workshops and interviews have a key role in helping to identify forces, and prioritise analysis. They need to be backed up by high-quality desk research if the resulting scenarios are to be widely used to develop options for action.

Workshops also have a role in embedding analysis and scenarios in the organisation. A format which combines briefing on the scenarios with workshop activity to explore the implications for the organisation or unit allows for internalisation and adoption of scenarios and their use in discussion.

This format also engages with participants: it is much easier to accommodate new ideas if they are being used in discussion – as studies on learning styles suggest, the best way of learning something is to teach it to another person.[115] It provides for harvesting feedback and facilitating participants' use in their working roles later. It also increases group energy and is fun, while integrating the Insight with the organisational Narrative.

Using workshop output
Workshop output may have several different forms depending on the purpose of the workshop. If the purpose of the workshop is to engage a wide range of participants – as for instance with an OpenSpace[116] event in which participants define the agenda and self-organise into groups to discuss the topics, or an Appreciative Inquiry event,[117] which tends to be used to increase community engagement – it may be that capturing the discussion materials with a camera and posting on a website is part of an ongoing process. Or it may be that participants in these events take away specific learning or action points. Such workshops must not be seen as a one-off; they need to be part of an ongoing process. And in all cases it must be extremely clear who is going to do what as a result of the workshop and what follow-up will occur, as a review of the Scotland Future project showed.[118] The project had organised a series of very well-received workshops in communities around Scotland, to discuss Scotland's future. However, after the workshops no actions were followed up. It turned out that both the communities and the Scotland Future organisers expected the other party to follow up and were disappointed when they did not.

Normally, the results of a workshop provide most value when set in context before being widely used. While the output can collate the views of participants and may bring out important new points, it needs to be calibrated within the overall process, including desk research in – for instance – developing the cost/benefit analysis for options.

There is a particular danger in workshops with people who do not control or influence strategy. They may become de-motivated if they contribute to a workshop expecting the outcome to be an immediate change in their environment, and this does not happen.

Case study – realistic expectations

An example was a central government department, who at the beginning of the workshop thought they could influence the direction of their department. They realised through discussion that their department's purpose was set by politicians and that the best use of the workshop was to explore possible ways of implementing potential policy directions.[119] Therefore, it is very important to set clear expectations around outcomes before the workshop is run.

Mental models
A powerful set of mental models will allow for fruitful dialogue across the organisation, leading to organisational change and renewal.

Case study – mental models

Man Group is a world-leading alternative investment management business. It manages over $70 billion and employs 1800 people in 13 countries worldwide. The ED&F Man Group's origins go back to the 1700s, when it traded sugar from the Caribbean. The business extended over the years into other products, from trading to refining and sourcing, and into stock broking, investment management and insurance.

The Group wanted to anticipate changes in markets through scenario planning – for instance, to reduce losses on trading in sugar derivatives. After discussions on the underlying causes, it was decided to engage the management team to think about the future and uncertainties, using scenarios.

The scenarios chosen were 'London in 2020' (see Figure 11.6), on the future of financial services in the City of London. These four scenarios looked at how the City, as a leading home of financial services companies, might respond:

- If the world is 'global' and Information Technology (IT) becomes pervasive (*Globetech*).
- If Europe, Asia and North America divide into competing trade blocs, all using IT successfully (*Fragtech*).
- If the world is global but there is very little use of IT (*Slowglobe*).
- If the world is broken down, with fragmentation of trade and little use of IT (*Fourth World*).

A workshop for four divisional directors and their immediate teams asked each divisional team 'What are our strengths in each of the four scenarios'. The answers were very different for each business. The division trading sugar products felt comfortable with Slowglobe. Other businesses had built their business plan on assumptions corresponding to Globetech, Fragtech and Fourth World.

The discussion after each divisional team reported back was very revealing to the teams. They had not realised the differences across the Group, perhaps due to the underlying dynamics of the businesses, their history and tacit assumptions. In particular, the division concerned with ownership of land, refineries and the logistics needs of handling the sugar products had a very different dynamic from the other businesses, which relied on trading using IT. In 2000, the Group divested the sugar products division, followed later by aligning the insurance and stock-broking arms to the derivatives business, along the lines seen in the discussion of the scenarios.

This shows the value of scenarios in bringing out implicit assumptions through explicitly considering possible mental models.

Mix to match the problem being solved

In organisations which have not developed the processes necessary for Insight – or have forgotten them over the last decade – it is useful to engage with a Board sponsor, perhaps the member with

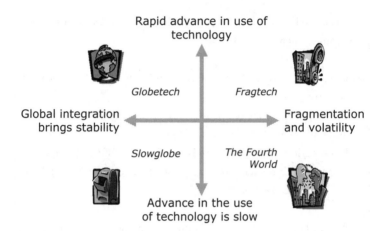

Figure 11.6 Scenarios for the City of London 2020

responsibility for new business development, or with a specific strategic challenge. This will provide a focus for an initial iteration.

In organisations which have attempted to develop Insight but in which this process was not altogether successful, it is important to understand the reasons – whether because of lack of Board support, because the Insight itself was not felt to add value, because not enough people were engaged in the process or because of lack of preparation at the start-up step. This will provide you with a 'to do' list for renewing the processes and making them succeed.

Getting senior staff to communicate

The Insight process can be effective in getting senior staff to communicate, in that many senior-level discussions are by their nature about territory – budget, people, priorities – where it can be difficult to get win/win decisions. By sharing mental models of the external world and possible future challenges, implicit assumptions are surfaced and queried and defensive behaviour is reduced. After all, who would expect to be in the same job in five or ten years' time? This can provide a way forward that is not personally threatening.

The role of a set of shared Values is clearly central. The Narrative will be built through sharing mental models, to create a coherent and shared set of assumptions and meanings (see Chapter 13).

Debate within the full organisation

People in senior roles in organisations often feel very isolated. Informal meetings are rare, even one-on-one to clear a specific issue, so it is difficult to 'try out' ideas on colleagues. Many managers have been running line units before being promoted to the Board – or may combine the two roles, and have never explicitly been asked to redefine their approach and behaviours for the new role. And finally, management and Board meetings have fixed agendas and time slots. This means that it is difficult to find a context for discussion of the important issues for the longer term of the organisation. One study for the magazine *Fortune* found that:

- 40% of time is spent thinking about issues outside the company
- 30% of this is spent thinking about future challenges and strategic issues
- 20% of this is spent in dialogue with other senior managers
- Therefore only 2.4% of senior managers' time is spent collectively discussing strategic issues for the future of the business

Insight is a powerful basis for the narrative that links organisations together and allows exploration of structural issues. Using Insight – articulated through scenarios – provides a context for senior managers and politicians to discuss structural issues. One good example was the Wanless Report,[120] which used scenarios to highlight to politicians and practitioners that the UK National Health Service would not be able to meet demand through increased internal productivity: that change in the demand pattern from citizens and residents would be needed to keep costs within control.

The full organisation also includes young recruits and those new to the organisation. Insight processes are good at harnessing their energies, whether formally (though inclusion in a scenario team earlier) or less formally through capturing their Insights, as discussed in Chapter 14 in 'Five interlocking parts of the PS-RO machinery'.

Insight is a powerful basis for the Narrative that links organisations together. This is discussed more in Chapter 13.

The deliverables from the Insight process

One output of the Insight process can be mental models of the possible future competitive environment, or scenarios, as discussed above. The Insight process also delivers a number of tangible and less tangible benefits to the organisation.

These shared mental models provide a framework for the various analyses that go on in organisations, allowing them to be integrated into views of the future rather than floating independently, and for people from across the organisation – wherever in the cones their jobs are – to show initiative. It is obvious that staff at the front end will be the best source of information about customers and competitors, few organisations have the Machinery to harness their Insight.

Other specific deliverables are:

- Competitor analysis (including anticipating potential new sources of competition).
- Wild cards, or low-probability, high-impact events that could disrupt the organisation.
- A better understanding of the gaps between the existing reputation, market position, skills, information and relationships and those needed in future.

Quantifying scenarios

Scenarios are often described through storylines, perhaps backed by a table of political, economic, social, technological and environmental data. A good example is regional strategic scenarios, which need to map through to the economic implications and hence to planning. They are a good way to present models in a manner that is easy to recall and work with.

There is a wide literature on the use of Monte Carlo techniques to quantify scenarios,[121] on the number of scenarios to choose,[122] and on positive and negative feedback systems.[123] These are more technical subjects than we wish to cover in this book, but there are papers surveying these on the Challenge Network website.[124]

Insight and the Three Ring Circus

The Three Ring Circus was introduced in Chapter 8, where the inner two rings represent respectively operations and the existing portfolio. The outer ring includes the set of processes for talking about the issues, for gathering Insight.

Insight has six important characteristics, discussed below, which connect it into other parts of the Three Ring Circus.

Informing but not prescribing the internal discussions

The Insight processes should provide a sorting mechanism through peer assessment so that special interests and trivial projects are discarded without taking senior management time (see Chapter 14). They set ranges to variables, such as 'this Business Unit will be subject to new competition from about 20xx' or 'demographics will swamp us by about 20xx'. They should show dependencies between influences, such as 'the increasing price of raw materials will increase our costs and also drive inflation'. They should allow for debate right up to (but not beyond) the point of a decision, without fear of the 'finger of God' from the Board or elsewhere.

Influencing, hearing and tapping into outsiders

Insight creates images of the world external to the organisation, its relationship to the world and possible futures. With these articulated, it is possible to bring these to bear in many ways.

Insight allows an organisation to influence its external environment through sharing images and models of the future, providing a context for a dialogue about desirable futures and for expanding its circle of influence.

Case study – influencing, hearing, tapping into outsiders

To help think about the future of energy, Shell has developed two scenarios that describe alternative ways it may develop. In the first scenario – called Scramble – policy makers pay little attention to more efficient energy use until supplies are tight. Likewise, greenhouse gas emissions are not seriously addressed until there are major climate shocks. In the second scenario – Blueprints – growing local actions begin to address the challenges of economic development, energy security and environmental pollution. A price is applied to a critical mass of emissions giving a huge stimulus to the development of clean energy technologies, such as carbon dioxide capture and storage, and energy efficiency measures. The result is far lower carbon dioxide emissions.

These scenarios were explicitly developed to set up a wider stakeholder dialogue around energy futures, engaging e.g. the public, governments and industry. The value of this process has been information gained from the debate of 'hot topics' which can be used by Shell in decision making and planning.

The benefit of using scenarios to engage multiple stakeholders is that it allows for people with diverse views to start discussions and reach a consensus.

Stakeholder relations, CSR, regulatory relations

Insight can provide a context for a more informed and fruitful dialogue with stakeholders. When a pharmaceutical company wanted to think how to develop its Corporate Social Responsibility (CSR) policies, it used Insight from a UN project UNAids.[125]

Case study – CSR

A pharmaceutical company which has a reputation for social awareness and with a number of CSR projects in Africa wanted to develop its CSR policies for Africa to anticipate future demands.

They used the UNAids scenarios for Africa. These scenarios were developed over two years and involved workshops and interviews in many African countries. Once the scenarios were developed, it became clear that different countries followed different scenarios. This made the scenarios extremely suitable for the pharmaceutical company, who realised that 'one size fits all' would not be appropriate for their African CSR policies.

The scenarios and possible CSR responses were briefed to the company's CSR team during a two-day workshop, and they reached agreement on CSR priorities for each of their target countries in Africa. The scenarios allowed them to have an informed discussion about the differing characteristics of the target countries and appropriate policies.

Means of surfacing senior staff preoccupations

It is observed that senior managers spend much of their time on current, internal issues. A study of the Fortune 500 companies in the USA found that senior managers only spend on average 2–3% of their time collectively discussing strategic issues, derived as follows:

- 40% of their time spent thinking about issues outside the company;
- 30% of this about strategic and future challenges;
- 20% of this talking to colleagues about these.

Individual and group reflection

In Chapter 6 we introduced the concept of extraordinary competence, arising from not just individuals but groups working effectively together. Insight provides a framework for this conversation in several ways:

- By focusing on looking to the future, defensiveness in the management team is reduced (moving away from 'my patch' into a shared future); it is too far away to be personal.
- By exposing group assumptions so that they can be questioned, as in the D2D case study in Chapter 7, in which the team realised that their common set of assumptions did not match their business environment.
- By providing a bridge between cultures – we identified in Chapter 5 that a major source of complexity in organisations was the number of different cultures – both functional and national – that were needed to create their product or service.

Understanding complex systems

Insight processes provide a structure for tying together topical intelligence – at the front end/top cone of the organisation – with structural work – often done in the bottom cone. By sharing information from horizon scanning, forecasting and scenario exercises with the eyes and ears of the organisation, true insight is gained and made accessible to the organisation.

Chapter 14 discusses the underlying processes to achieve this.

Executive Summary

- Insight needs to be linked to the core Values and Narrative of the organisation, into a process for exploring and agreeing Options.
- Insight can be provided through tools such as forecasting, horizon scanning and scenario planning.
- It is also important to gain insight into the organisation's capabilities through audits.
- Insight is the basis for deriving choices or options.

Chapter 12

Generating Options

Options are derived from the information generated by Insight together with innovation, in the framework of core Values and organisational Narrative. The purpose of the process is to identify clear choices.

A transparent process for harnessing innovation to generate Options and make decisions is important for a PS-RO. There are four over-arching reasons for this. First, transparency encourages *all* staff to volunteer their time and energy to contribute ideas and innovation to the overall purpose. In this way, staff achieve self-development and job enhancement as well as contributing to a more purposeful organisation. The transparency also allows senior management to assess the overall strengths and weaknesses of their staff (see also the 'Skills audit' in Chapter 11) and encourages the Fox-like behaviour essential to a PS-RO.

Second, a process for changing the portfolio of the organisation is essential to prevent drift and decay[126] and the feeling that the organisation is 'out of control'. It provides information that enables senior managers to discuss the impact of changes.

Third, only by being able to discuss concrete Options and trade-offs in a context which considers the future of the organisation, can the Board make a proper contribution (see Chapter 6). These

Options encompass those of the many ideas generated which have survived the process of first and second screening that will be discussed in Chapter 14.

Finally, and perhaps most important of all, it reduces the likelihood that the organisation will blunder into costly ventures which take money and management time to unpick.

The Options processes fit within the overall PS-RO structures as described in Chapters 7 and 8. They are concerned with generating and choosing what goes into the corporate plan and business portfolio. The Options process therefore connects Insight with the standard strategic planning process or the two outer rings of the Three Ring Circus.

The Options journey has two key aspects:

- Processes around innovation, and the links throughout the organisation to harness new ideas and turn them into part of the organisation.
- The analysis and management of the portfolio, including the role of scenarios in improving decision making and making it more robust, see below.

It can be seen that these processes are cyclical and iterative, so that analysis of the portfolio may lead to requests for innovation in specific areas. They are an essential mechanism for course correction. We show you six tools that can help with this journey:

- Questions to drive the generation of Options
- Idea champion
- Research management toolkit
- Backcasting
- Viewing the initiatives
- Assessing the portfolio.

The Options journey

The Options journey is a journey with ongoing course corrections, by which the organisation identifies the Options that are viable, that fit with its Values and Narrative, and moves these into implementation.

General ideas, sparks of potential

The culture that looks for and rewards ideas is a key part of a PS-RO. How can this culture be engendered? There is a vast literature on this; we particularly like some of the ideas in Johansson's book *The Medici Effect*.[127] The key aspects highlighted in many studies are:

- The need to inspire people and have fun – linked into reward systems: monetary, developmental and recognition.
- Having a formal system for capturing ideas and managing and sharing know-how, as discussed in Chapter 14.
- Having a well-managed process for staying close to customers and markets.

Options need to develop through exploration and discussion, identifying a range of people across and outside the organisation who have contributions to make and ensuring they are involved. We saw in Chapter 5 the evidence from a study by IBM that innovation comes from both inside and outside the organisation. The culture of the organisation needs to be that of co-operation, as discussed under core Values, before groups can develop new ideas.

Getting into a new line of business is disruptive for both those involved and those in the 'old' businesses. A widespread understanding of the core Values, Narrative and Insights behind the new directions helps to achieve understanding and co-operation.

If a small, dedicated group is formed to move ideas forward, they are more likely to be successful if they have tested these ideas against the widest set of stakeholders. They can also be the first port of call for suggestions from the Board, to calibrate the effect on the organisation.

Case study – exploring Options

An Australian mining company considered its route into China: joint venture? Purchase? Direct start-up? It was cash-rich and staff-light, so it favoured a trial joint venture with a Chinese company in which it held a majority of the shares.

The result was not happy: local standards meant that injury statistics mounted, environmental standards were breached, ethical considerations ignored. Unquantifiable risks appeared on every side. On top of this, the rush into China meant that the company paid a very high valuation.

The company sat back and asked itself what it mean by 'getting into' China, and indeed why this was such a priority. China is an enormous market for minerals, but it pays the world price. The company had no downstream manufacturing interests for which cheap labour or access to markets would be attractive. Plainly, the right thing to do about China was to do nothing, and instead invest in worldwide mining from which it could sell to China without complications.

The chief lesson that was taken from this was the need to avoid fashionable topics until there had been long, deep conversations about them and all the options had been fully explored, taking on board expert opinion as needed.

Learning your way forward

Iteration will lead to gradual clarification of the original ideas and maybe spin-offs. It will clearly be a journey which is going to a fuzzy destination but has features that can be described, derived from the work on Insight. The fact that the journey takes place over more than one planning cycle, in the context of an articulated and desired future, acts as a counter-weight to the pressures of today's business.

The processes can use formal networks – such as functional groups – or may use high-potential new joiners or leadership development programmes as sounding boards – again, the wider the qualified exposure, the better. It is important that mechanisms are found for combining the insights and capabilities of those working in the specified, upper cone with those working in the unspecified, lower cone.

The benefits of this are fourfold:

- The proponents of the idea learn from the iteration. Visualising the future state of the organisation helps to innovate and to discard parts no longer needed. This harnesses people from across the organisation and connects them to create an engine for change.
- Other people in the organisation learn from what is being proposed and there is a story to engage senior management and the Board.
- While the direction may be general, the impact on specific parts of the organisation will be very practical and may well lead to ideas for enhancing the business offer or reducing the effort spent on unnecessary activities.
- Many senior managers have reached the Board or senior roles through being good line managers – Hedgehogs par excellence (Chapter 5). As part of their training for senior roles, working with the processes for weighing Options at an organisational level is an excellent introduction.

The characteristic sector time scale
Clearly, sectors work on different time scales for planning and investment. Capital-intensive industries may plan payback over

many years, and have a limited time window when new projects can be accepted. In some sectors such as education, policy initiatives take a long time to mature, so that consistency over a long time frame is important, with Narrative playing an important role (Chapter 13). Other sectors may be able to take a 'try it on the consumer and see' approach, as in the Japanese approach to new consumer goods discussed in Chapter 5.

Innovation

Innovation is not one thing, but many

Much of the innovation in the organisation is necessary to keep the products, services and processes in the specified, upper cone, competitive. Upgrades to products and services are needed to keep pace with the competition. The innovation in this cone is very different from that in the unspecified cone.

George Day's work on 'Big I and small i' is relevant here: he makes the case that a balanced approach between big and small initiatives is the way to go for most companies trying to close the growth gap (big and small are based on size, but also on how far the initiatives are from the core regarding their target market and technology). He reached this conclusion by studying the innovation portfolios of many companies and estimating the success rates and incremental revenues/profits for the different types of initiatives.[128]

Big innovations include those which create new markets and/or destroy others, or change lifestyles.

Innovation to achieve more with less, an issue facing the public sector, is often thought of as in the upper cone, but can to great effect be driven using lower-cone thinking.

Case study – innovation to cut costs

A public sector organisation was asked to reduce its budget by 40% over a year, while maintaining services. By asking basic questions about the standard of service and how to achieve it, the organisation was able to reduce one of its units – responsible for issuing licences – from 100 people to six, while decreasing the turnaround time for applications from six months to two weeks.

Context for non-routine innovation

One of the defining characteristics of a PS-RO is that it acknowledges the need and space for non-routine innovation, ideas and activities in the lower cone.

In a PS-RO:

- Idea generation is not seen as taking the eyes off the ball, but as an important part of people's work.
- Idea generation and propagation is part of staff KPIs.
- Idea generation is not 'controlled' by the line manager but encouraged by him.
- The resource costs are seen as meeting an urgent and important need for the organisation.

The role of scenarios in generating Options[129]

At the stage of generating Options, the first step is to think expansively, to generate as many potential initiatives as possible. The important thing is not to be bound by the current condition of the organisation or 'frames' around the industry: scenarios provide different potential views of the future.

Organisations generating strategic Options for purposeful self-renewal in turbulent times will face problems in estimating profit and revenue volatility. There will be large downside and upside risks depending on the scenario anticipated for the future. So, some of the guiding principles for generating, assessing, selecting and executing Options under uncertainty are:

- Add flexibility during the generation of Options.
- Take a portfolio view during the assessment and selection of Options.
- Implement the Options with continuous course correction.

There are several 'templates' which guide managers through the initiative generation process. These templates serve the purpose of reminding managers of the different strategic levers and potential moves at their disposal. They are often linked to the frameworks used during the external analysis phase of the strategic process, e.g.

- Porter's Five Forces, see Chapter 11.
- Value innovation, a strategic approach to business growth, involving a shift away from a focus on the existing competition to one of trying to create entirely new markets. Value innovation can be achieved by implementing a focus on innovation and creation of new market space. The term was coined by W. Chan Kim and Rene Mauborgne in 1997.[130]
- Disruptive innovation, see below.
- Knowledge maps, see Chapter 11.
- Hub and spoke,[131] based on a 10-year study of 2000 companies conducted by Bain & Company. This suggests that three factors differentiate growth strategies that succeed from those that fail: (1) reaching full potential in the core business (the hub); (2) expanding into businesses adjacent to that core (the spoke); and (3) pre-emptively redefining the core business in times of market turbulence.

> **Tool: Questions to drive the generation of Options**
>
> - What initiatives are clear winners in each of the scenarios? (In other words, if one scenario were certain to occur, what would the winning strategic moves be?)
> - What initiatives could win in more than one scenario (called robust initiatives)?
> - What initiatives would resolve current competitive issues of the business?
> - What initiatives would allow building the required capabilities identified in the strategic vision?
> - What initiatives would allow testing new lines of business?

Throughout the generation process, it is important to distinguish between a number of conflicting aspects, e.g.

- Short-term vs. long-term actions.
- Incremental and bold moves (scenario-dependent) vs. robust moves (applicable in all scenarios).
- Bet-type initiatives (large investments in time and money, applicable in only one or two scenarios) vs. flexible options (scenario-dependent but able to be implemented flexibly).

It is also important to make sure that enough information on the initiatives is captured in the process, for example when considering alternatives for execution – build, buy or partner, payback periods, relevant scenarios – and type of uncertainty: internal or market-based.

Mechanisms to accelerate non-routine innovation

Innovation is often defined as taking useful ideas and implementing them. One mechanism we have found to accelerate non-routine innovation is having idea champions.

Tool: Idea champion

An idea champion is identified with a particular idea and takes respon-sibility for marshalling it through the organisation. This can be very effective in a PS-RO, when the 'licence' granted by the organisation gives:

- The right to access and convince a panel of peers – who will prob-ably cross functional and divisional lines.
- The right to go 'off line' to develop the idea, usually with minimal budget: for example, many technology companies allow Distin-guished Engineers one day a week to maintain their specialist exper-tise – the panel of peers can award this status for a period of time.

At the end of this period (or when the idea champion is ready), he has the right to access a senior panel that can move the idea into whatever next stage of exploration is required. Probably, by this stage, budget is required. The idea description and its progress should be visible on the organisation's intranet, to encourage the formation of informal networks for its development.

Why would people become idea champions? Clearly it is a very visible role, whether the idea succeeds or is rejected. The reward system must be aligned to recognise the value of the idea cham-pion, even if a particular idea was not, in the end, taken into production.

Extraordinary competence

The best idea champions are those who can inspire a group of people to become disciples, helping to sell the idea across the organisation. See the discussion under 'People' in Chapter 14. The ability to identify and engage these individuals is a necessary capability of a PS-RO.

Mechanisms for picking up gap-filling ideas

A widely dispersed knowledge of the core Values and purpose of the organisation, of its Narrative and of the Options generation process will mean that more people are able to see the gaps needing to be filled.

Social networking systems provide organisational 'space' for debate, pre-idea generation or during its process. A mechanism to discuss ideas, and assess them, at an early stage – even before they appear before the jury of peers – is very helpful. Software tools can automate the process for gathering comments and canvassing for views.

It is people, however, who are the driving force of innovation, who are at its heart; culture and processes provide valuable support.

Tools: Research management toolkit

A research management toolkit can be divided into four parts, of which the first gets most attention in terms of existing supportive tools and the others are comparatively neglected. We believe they need to be considered here.

1. Management of research material

Tools designed to aid in gathering, managing, storing and publishing information. Newer tools combine 'traditional' reference management systems with the open knowledge communities increasingly characteristic of Web 2.0. Specialist tools manage citations and references. A guide to some of these can be found on the web tool[132] supported by George Washington University.

2. Management of the research process

The research process has traditionally been in one place – the laboratory. In a PS-RO, research activity around a specific idea will often span divisional boundaries. To manage this needs the full facilities of an intranet with areas for communities to interact, plus ideally a system to progress research projects across and outside the organisation. There are a number of software tools that provide this progress monitoring and tracking, for instance the FutureMapping system.[133]

3. Management and development of people

To many senior managers, research is 'foreign territory' and the people who are good at generating and following through potentially disruptive ideas are treated with suspicion.

In a PS-RO, people who generate ideas are key; senior managers need to understand how to best harness their energies in service of the organisation. What is needed to enable such ideas generators to contribute to the full? What practices will develop and leverage their knowledge and ability to create value? While the specific practices need to be tailored to fit different industries and occupations, they generally include:

- Selection, with an understanding of Foxes and Hedgehogs.
- Training and development programmes, with self-selection by participants. Online training has an increasing role here.
- Mentoring, often used as a way of creating cross-organisational links.
- Incentives, which for most scientists and engineers include money (e.g. a bonus or raise) but more importantly time to follow specialist interests as for Distinguished Engineers above.
- Knowledge-sharing and shared decision-making mechanisms.

These practices are most effective when they are implemented together and in concert with new capital or technological investments,[134] and aligned to organisational strategy.[135]

4. Roadmaps for exploitation of innovation

Organisational change is less disruptive when there is clarity of the direction, as discussed in Chapter 6. The distant elements will be the least understood and the closest perceived in detail. How is a balanced perception of the way ahead to be achieved?

Tools for this include the road map. This comes in a number of types. One common form, invented by BHP Billiton Plc (see Figure 12.1), lists the projects that an organisation may have queued up over the next 5 to 10 years – new mines to be developed, or car models to launch, or a new government initiative to be implemented – with those furthest in the future usually being the least defined.[136] This gives an 'at a glance' 5- to 7-year calendar and allows others to start their sub-plans, for people, cash and so on.

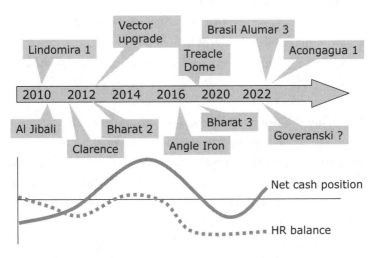

Figure 12.1 Road maps connect events and resources

Tool: Back casting

Another approach, much used in technology companies, consists of identifying a future state for the industry, or perhaps for a key technology within it, and working backwards in order to say what needs to happen for this to be delivered on time. Thus, if an aeronautical company targeted to double the energy efficiency of their jet engines in the next 20 years that requires – let's say – ceramic blades capable of working at white heat. And the injector nozzles will need to ... And the bearings ...

This exercise is usually more useful in exploring the perceptions of the participants than it is in giving a true estimate. However, it is valuable for two additional reasons; first, because it enforces a complete analysis and second, because it provides a discussion tool around which people can look for better ways forward. It provides a spur to innovation: 'if we could bypass that roadblock ...' Road maps work well in well-specified domains, once the initiative is scoped.

Managing the results of innovation into the portfolio

Geoffrey Moore[137] points out that the established organisation is set up to support the current year operations and the areas of research that are the domain of market research and R&D, whilst developing the next generation of opportunities often falls into a kind of 'no-man's-land', called Horizon 2.

Moore states,

> These [Horizon 2] projects fail to be embraced because they cannot deliver current year returns but are nevertheless held to the same yardstick ... Thus the advantages of in-house innovation at asset-rich corporations turn out for the most part to be illusory.

Innovations are better off in bootstrapped start-ups, because at least there they can get access to the market and suppliers, and their investors will use fairer standards of measurement.

He suggests a number of guidelines to growing innovative products and services within established organisations:

- Isolate and insulate current revenue Horizon 2 units, with different structures, processes and reward systems.
- Use acquisitions in the short term to help fill the Horizon 2 gap.
- For the long term, incubate businesses not products − create separate business units with a focus on a single high-value segment and adapt 'crossing the chasm'[138] thinking to the dynamics of operating inside a major enterprise.

Moore writes,

For some time the venture community has known that the fastest way to grow a disruptive innovation into something really profitable is to focus on dominating a niche market where the new technology solves a mission critical problem. Established enterprises, however, cannot afford to be so precise on their focus. The challenge of achieving growth atop an already huge revenue base requires them to operate on a grander scale, and all their processes, metrics and targets reflect this fact.

Since the processes of established enterprises are toxic to Horizon 2 ventures, exceptions must be agreed for them during the duration of Horizon 2. This is difficult in established organisations. He identifies two measures that will increase the chances of success:

- Focus on leaders, *not* funding − the scarcest resource in growing innovative businesses is effective, entrepreneurial leaders, not funding. The organisation and role must be structured to make this a challenging and rewarding career opportunity for the organisation's best executives, otherwise they will go elsewhere.

- Block resource migrations across horizon boundaries – i.e. make sure the current revenue streams don't cannibalise the Horizon 2 developments by attempting to develop and launch Horizon 2 products and services within the structure used in the specified, or upper cone of a PS-RO.

Changing the portfolio

Active portfolio management

A formal assessment of the organisation's assets is the basis of active management of the portfolio. Getting this in place involves a review of the current position, e.g.

- The audits described in Chapter 11.
- Analysis of the current portfolio.
- Review of fixed and financial assets.
- Analysis of potential investments, looking forward 1½ life cycles, and asking whether there is cash to pay for the required investment.

Looking forward, there are three relevant questions. First, what views does the organisation have about the future – is activity robust enough for the expected volatility? The second question relates to potential investments and whether they take the organisation in the desired direction (linking into the narrative). In other words, are we getting the right kinds of project? Finally, what are the decision points, how far can we stay 'open', avoid premature commitment?

Requests for investment arrive from three sources:

- Support for extant activities, current logic, including legal and other fixed requirements. There are scale effects here: the biggest revenue streams and budgets get most of the investment cake, because politically inside the organisation they are best represented.
- Expansion beyond current activities: this may be new markets, with new or existing partners, acquisitions and other purchases – as discussed in Chapter 5 – and new projects in traditional areas. These incremental initiatives may well be centred in the upper or specified cone, and use well-calibrated evaluation tools, focused mostly around financial measures.
- New things – new products, places, styles – always have to battle for acceptance, as discussed above. This is partly investment pressure from the first two sources, but also the very real Horizon 2 concerns discussed above.

It is clear that portfolios 'on autopilot' don't change significantly, though they may drift – usually to decay as markets move away from existing products. Portfolios under active management achieve focus, reflecting the organisation's Narrative (see Chapter 13).

New projects must meet strategic criteria in a PS-RO, for example:

- Are they clear winners in each one of the scenarios? (In other words, if one scenario were certain to occur, what would be the winning strategic moves?)
- Do they contribute to resolving current competitive issues of the business?
- What initiatives would allow building the required capabilities identified?

PS-RO processes for active management

The core process for active management of the portfolio is active conversation and dialogue, within the Board and across the organisation.

In a PS-RO, the approach tends to be 'we can solve this'. The solution is found in the context of the organisation Narrative, within a culture which is open to new ideas, unfiltered by the system. Aspects that are considered important are:[139]

- Skilled people with a range of styles, highlighting the importance of recruitment, training and development.
- Co-operation between people across the organisation, an essential aspect of a PS-RO culture.
- Management support, through processes and allocation of time.
- Checkpoints to provide focus, hence the importance of the peer review (first and second screening as in Chapter 14) and senior panels.
- Groups working together, within core Values and Narrative, the source of extraordinary competence.

Areas which organisations often find to be particularly difficult are:

- Linking procurement to new strategies or priorities.
- Linking recruitment to new strategies or priorities.

Linking into budgeting and action

The oil and gas group StatoilHydro in Scandinavia has rethought budgeting with an approach which has caused a number of changes in management and leadership. The new model is based on the approach that, as people are very responsible in their daily life, they can be expected to take a similarly responsible approach at work if enabled to do so. The model aligns financial and HR measures, and specifically asks budget holders to distinguish between:

- Target revenues, front-loaded and ambitious, relative to competition where relevant and
- Forecasts, business not calendar driven, containing expected outcomes and early warning of disruptive events, with limited detail.

Resource allocation is dynamic, with no pre-allocation, using a transparent process with project gates and decision criteria, and intervention occurs only if seen to be needed through the monitoring system.

By separating these concepts, the company has pioneered an approach which takes investment requests at any point in the annual cycle, significantly enhancing adaptability.[140] This approach is very supportive of a PS-RO.

Assessing Options

Given an often long list of potential initiatives, how can these be turned into Options?

The full analysis of strategic options will typically include:

- Financial aspects: what is the full value of the option – discounted cash flow plus option value – and required level of investments? Most organisations have standard tools for financial evaluation of investments.
- Strategic: what is the fit with the core Values and Narrative? Does it build any of the required capabilities? This is where the skills audit in Chapter 12 is valuable.
- Risk: what risks surround the options in light of the different scenarios? Do the options become more or less attractive over time? Do some options which fail the financial tests above pass in different scenarios? What does the future portfolio look like? A tool for evaluating this is described below.
- Organisational analyses: how well does the Option fit with the firm's culture, competences and Narrative?

Tool: Viewing the initiatives

A framework for viewing a portfolio of initiatives was developed by Lowell Bryan,[141] combining three horizons of planning with levels of uncertainty. Uncertainty is seen as related to the level of familiarity of the organisation, ranging from familiar, where the organisation has distinctive competences in that area, to uncertain, where the organisation does not have skills to determine the probability of success. Initiatives are plotted, the size of the circle showing the size of opportunity, as in Figure 12.2.

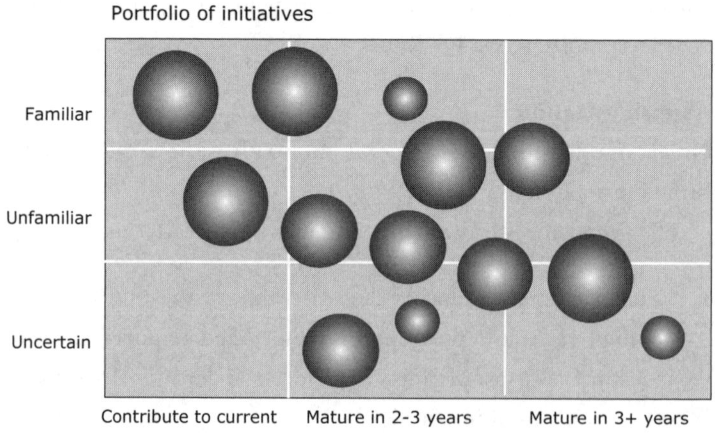

Portfolio of initiatives

Familiar

Unfamiliar

Uncertain

Contribute to current   Mature in 2-3 years   Mature in 3+ years

Figure 12.2 Portfolio of initiatives

Tool: Assessing the portfolio

A tool which can be used to evaluate the portfolio is based on the MA/C matrix, derived from the directional policy matrix, developed independently by Shell and by GE.[142] This matrix uses market attractiveness and organisation capabilities as the two main axes, based on a weighted sum of a number of variables. Using these measures, businesses are classified into one of nine cells in a 3 × 3 matrix, as shown in Figure 12.3. So that, for instance, if a business was assessed to be in a highly attractive market but the organisation's capability to be weak, the diagnostic is 'Double or quits', i.e. unless the organisation can improve its capability, it should get out of that business.

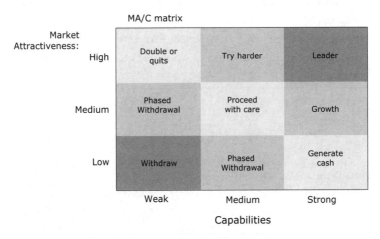

Figure 12.3 Market attractiveness/capability matrix

Case study – analysis of the future portfolio

At a computer company, a portfolio of potential new business options had been developed. For each option in the portfolio, the effect of a set of scenarios A and B developed earlier was assessed to see what its position would be in 10 years' time. A very simple scoring method based on up to 20 descriptors of the scenarios gave good discrimination. Some were trends common to all scenarios and others were scenario specific.

As an example, consider the three Options (P1 to P3 in Figure 12.4) and the diagnostic position currently (e.g. P1) and under each of two scenarios A (e.g. A-P1) and B (e.g. B-P1). It was found that movement was by no means in the same direction for all Options.

P1 remains an attractive market, but under scenario A the capabilities became less suitable.

P2 became more attractive and stayed oriented to the organisation's capabilities under both scenarios.

P3 became part of an unattractive market in scenario A, although it fitted with the organisation's capabilities. It remained a 'Phased Withdrawal' business under both scenarios – not a candidate for investment!

The options chosen for investment became successful businesses and the idea champions for the other options recognised the validity of the choice.

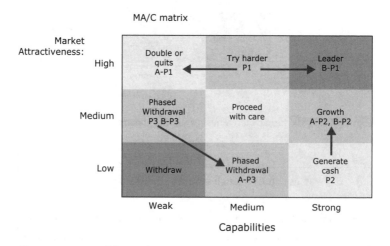

Figure 12.4 Portfolio under two scenarios

A representation similar to Lowell Bryan's can be used to analyse an optimal portfolio of initiatives using three types of potential investment – robust initiatives, flexible options and bets; and a vertical axis relating to positive, neutral or negative value creation. This can then support calculations of the payoff under each scenario and the risk return of each portfolio.

Executive Summary

- Options take the information generated by Insight and identify the choices open to the organisation.
- Innovation is not one thing, but many and it is a key extraordinary competence of a PS-RO.
- The ability to identify and engage idea champions in generating and selling ideas across an organisation is an extraordinary competence of a PS-RO.
- A research management toolkit consists of:
  1. Management of research material.
  2. Management of the research process.
  3. Management and development of people.
  4. Roadmaps for exploitation of innovation.
- Tools to help senior managers visualise a portfolio of Options are important to the discussion and decision process.

Chapter 13

Narrative

Narrative is the glue that holds the organisation together – it connects the core Values, Insights and Options. In doing so, it enables you, whatever your level of seniority, to identify the Machinery and tools you need to get the output you want. It helps to begin to specify what was unspecified, and in the lower cone. Narrative helps people to work with what was previously more uncertain and ambiguous, and encourages innovation aligned to the organisation's direction and strategy, thereby facilitating renewal. It saves the time of senior managers by ensuring that projects presented to them for investment are aligned to the organisation's direction, and allows for effective communication between senior managers and with shareholders.

An organisation has an over-arching Narrative, based on its core Values and purpose, which is likely to change only slowly. This acts as a filter for complexities, allowing the hearer to take in relevant information. Narrative allows stakeholders and senior managers to discuss structural issues and strike a measured balance between Options. In some fields like education policy, Options can take a generation to mature: over such a time frame a continuous Narrative provides cohesion of delivery. However, a Narrative also needs to be able to accommodate renewal. Each group will also have a Narrative that fits into the over-arching organisational Narrative. The difference may be in the stories that are told which have direct meaning for the particular group.

The organisation's Narrative sets a context for discussion of which 'wars' to fight; where it should put its resources. It connects bright people together to provide extraordinary competence, an engine for change. It allows outsiders such as suppliers to connect to the organisation.

Different parts of the organisation may exhibit different behaviours. And different generations may have different Values and Narratives. In Chapter 14 we use the example of communicating scenarios to explore ways of reaching different audiences. It is also worth noting the significant differences between Generation Y, Generation X and Baby Boomers.

Two large surveys of college graduates[143] show remarkable similarities between Baby Boomers (approaching the traditional retirement age) and Generation Y (born in the 1980s and 1990s).

Both groups ranked in the top 7 of rewards for working:

- High-quality colleagues.
- Flexible work arrangements.
- Recognition from the organisation or one's boss.
- Access to new experiences and challenges.

Generation Y were also concerned with advancement, whereas the Boomers looked for intellectual stimulation, autonomy and being able to give back to the world through work. Another study showed up differences across the three main cohorts (including Generation X) but emphasised the strong similarities in needs of people in the workplace.[144]

As a leader, you begin with understanding Narrative on an individual basis before going on to develop the group Narrative. The group Narrative is something that is created by the group, together;

therefore, if you don't understand how your own personal Narrative contributes, you could end up with an organisational Narrative to which you don't know how to contribute.

The Narrative processes have three key aspects:

- Processes for the individual.
- Processes for the organisation.
- Creating a Narrative for the organisation.

As with many PS-RO processes, these are emerging continuously, they must be regularly revisited to ensure an organisational Narrative that is fit for purpose.

In this chapter we introduce you to tools:

- Ladder of Inference.
- Background Narrative.
- Lifeline/Hero's Journey.
- Questions for Uncovering Narrative.
- Getting Narrative into an Organisation.
- Organisational Narrative.

What is a Narrative?

Stories – or narratives – are part of what being human is about. We make sense of the world around us through stories. They help us to build a shared culture, help us to survive in turbulent, ambiguous, uncertain times and make sense of what we experience. They can help to frame the organisation's response to ethical issues in a more memorable manner than guidelines or bland statements.

In Chapter 7 we talked about what was important to understand about Narratives:

- A Narrative is not imposed from outside a group but arises from within it. It is constructed as needed in experiential threads. Hedgehogs like to cling to their Narrative and resist changing it.

- A Narrative can be strong and wrong, as well as right. It can be 'sold' or pushed by interest groups. Therefore, it needs to be continually questioned and tested.

- An organisational Narrative is needed to ensure that different audiences receive and understand the same message. The core Values, purpose and Options must be in harmony regardless of the language used to express it to different listeners.

A Narrative can be largely invisible – containing the behaviours and stories that are part of the social system; regular, obvious and acceptable. Narratives only become visible when either they fail or we choose to reflect upon them. They are important because it is through Narratives that organisations move and change – they address the emotional and rational levers which not only allow change to occur, but uncover where the energy is, the drive that will make changes happen. It is through Narrative that an organisation's culture is defined and shared. A Narrative helps to define the playing field for innovation; without a supportive Narrative, innovation will not happen. For these reasons a PS-RO works consciously and purposefully with its Narrative.

Sense making – making meaning out of incoming information
There is so much information in our environment that we cannot process it all. Human beings need to find a way to filter what they work with. There are two main ways we do this. An analytical approach depends on 'declarative' knowledge – that is, facts and things that are quantifiable. In general, we can easily validate this type of information, and sharing it is not complex.

The Narrative approach connects strongly with 'procedural' knowledge, which is likely to be more qualitative and more difficult to describe and share. Narrative helps us to recognise patterns. These patterns help us identify our individual views of reality; Narrative provides a framework/process in which we can share our own views and learn from the views of others. Narrative forms an important part of corporate memory.

Language: creator of reality

Language is not a tool to describe our reality – it creates our reality. Language is a *doer*, it is active, it moves people and creates life. We construct both reality and our future based on our knowledge of the past, and we use language to do this. What we say and *how we construct* what we say is a key part of creating our reality, and as such is the keystone of evidence-based policy.

The way we see the world – and describe it to ourselves – is a Narrative and our actions are based on this. Our *perception*, however, is not necessarily reality as others experience it.

Anything that happens in a system or organisation has coherence, fit and logic according to that system. Each system has its own 'grammar'. If we want to change the system or organisation we need to join the 'grammar' and speak the same language. We do this by focusing on stories and behaviours – the organisational Narrative. We can then explore the beliefs people have about their own position in the system, about the logic of the system – how it works – and so on.

Often we make the mistake of thinking that our opinion about something (the description, story or interpretation) is actually the experience of the event itself. Organisations frequently do not know the difference, perhaps because they are unaware that there *is* a difference. It is as if they mistake the photograph or description of the pudding on a menu for the pudding itself. This can be very costly for an organisation. If they accept someone's story or presentation as fact when it contains opinion, any decision they make based on it will not be objective and has the potential to be harmful to the organisation.

If you ask 'Why?' you are more likely to get an unthinking or defensive answer from the menu (an interpretation or opinion). If you ask 'What happened?' you are more likely to end up with the facts and a description of the event itself.

Mental models

Mental models are a type of Narrative we use as a filter to view the world around us. They help us to discern patterns, make sense of – and order – what we see 'out there'. They are usually tacit and we aren't aware of them unless we look for them. The Man Group case study, in Chapter 11, shows how scenarios can be used to expose mental models.

Mental models shape our behaviour and define our approach to solving problems. In effect, they are a way that we map what we see so that we can make sense of it. Many people assume that the mental models they use are somehow the right ones, or the ones that everyone else uses too. It is useful to uncover what mental models are in use because it then gives us more possibilities to work through uncertainty, to work together and to solve problems. Not to mention working from the same, agreed model!

Chris Argyris[145] speaks about the 'ladder of inference' (Figure 13.1) – a way that we construct a Narrative. You first observe or experience something. Then you choose the data from that observation that is important to you – this is usually done unconsciously. From that data, you make sense by starting to build a mental model. You add meaning to it. Then you make assumptions based on that

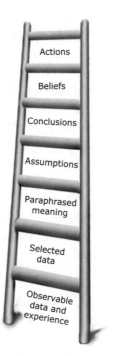

Figure 13.1 Ladder of inference

meaning (a 'truth') followed by drawing conclusions based on those assumptions. Finally, you take on beliefs based on the conclusions and your actions follow from these beliefs. It is a cycle – these beliefs will affect your choice of data for the next experience. There are other ways to construct a Narrative, such as the DiaLogos Flame Model,[146] which looks at different kinds of perspective. What is important is to find a model that helps you to uncover assumptions and opinions.

Tool: Using the ladder of inference

Think about a time in your life when you 'jumped to conclusions'. What was the cost of that to you? Think about this in terms of relationship(s), communications and trust.

As you can see, it often isn't easy to uncover your Narrative(s). Developing them is something you do without conscious thought. However, it is very important in a PS-RO to be aware of Narratives, both on an individual and an organisational basis. It is important to keep questioning your personal Narrative if it is something that is dysfunctional which you want to change, perhaps with the help of a mentor or coach as in the case study below. To uncover Narratives we use the tools of enquiry and reflection.

Case study – individual Narrative

A production manager was quite despondent after a meeting of senior staff. He felt that he hadn't understood things properly and had needed to ask too many questions. Yet he was a senior leader in the organisation, was well respected by the directors and had clearly achieved a great deal.

His peer mentor was present at one of the meetings and was surprised to hear that the manager felt he had shown up particularly badly during the meeting. The mentor shared his experience with the manager; the questions had, in fact, proved helpful to everyone in the meeting, in getting everyone to understand what was needed, clarifying other issues which arose around the original uncertainties, and moving the group forward. The perception that the CEO was annoyed was cleared up when the mentor pointed out that there were difficult contract negotiations around a different project which were pre-occupying the CEO.

The manager realised that he was listening to his own Narrative of 'not good enough' rather than checking his assumptions with others.

The individual Narrative

You need to work on your own Narrative first before you can begin work on the organisational Narrative. You need to understand your own 'filters' before you can see what others' Narratives might be, what an organisational Narrative might be. Understanding how to work with and change your own Narrative then helps you to see how you might encourage change in others' (or the organisation's) Narratives.

Tool: Background Narratives

To start uncovering personal Narrative, you need to look at your own 'background Narrative' or 'conversation'. We all have these in our heads. Frequently they are negative, limiting Narratives. Consider the following background conversations that we all have from time to time. You can then agree to suspend them while you work through the rest of this section.

1. *Find the Flaw.* This means that whatever anyone mentions or brings up in a discussion is immediately examined for flaws. 'Find the Flaw' crushes creativity. In our fear and problem-solving mentality, we are always looking to avoid problems; to cover ourselves and avoid blame. And this stops us from breaking out of the box and trying something totally different! The cost of 'Find the Flaw' is lost motivation, creativity and efficiency.

2. *Not Responsible* (also known as the 'Tragedy of the Commons'). If we are all responsible for something, then I don't really need to worry about it because I know you (or someone else) will take care of it. So no one takes responsibility or does anything. The cost of this conversation is that there are no results, only reasons why something didn't get done.

3. *Us vs. Them.* This gets Us thinking about and behaving differently towards and in competition with Them. If we are *against* them, we

---

cannot work *with* them. The cost of this is loss of trust between groups, competition between groups (instead of co-operation) and we all end up in a lose/lose situation.

4. *Either/Or.* When we are listening to the either/or conversation, we are in binary mode, as if there are only two possibilities. We don't see other alternatives. In today's world with the growing amount of uncertainty, ambiguity and complexity, it is useful to start thinking in terms of *Both/And.*

5. *Scarcity.* This conversation tells us that there isn't enough to go around and that if we don't get some, someone else will get it and we will have nothing. If we believe that there is scarcity, there will be and if we believe in plenty, there will be. Scarcity conversations force us to think *Win/Lose.* They force us to defend what we have. They restrict our ability to see other alternatives or opportunities. People find what they search for, so it is far better to search for abundance than scarcity. We believe that this perception is, without a doubt, the single greatest constraint on human imagination, vision, creativity and enterprise.

Tool: Lifeline/Hero's Journey

This exercise helps you to see what some of your Narratives may be. By looking at what has happened in your life and reflecting upon it, you will become clearer on what your own Narratives are. You tell the story of your life by drawing a line, including the highs/lows and choices that you made or that were imposed upon you. It is an opportunity for you to gain understanding of your life so far and reflect upon the decisions you made and the meaning that you give to the events in your life.

Start with the matrix as shown in the example in Figure 13.2. Plot what has happened to you in the correct quadrant. It is helpful to note those things that were significant choices you made and those that happened to you by putting them into the correct quadrant. Then draw a line which connects them in chronological order. This is for you and there is no right or wrong way to do it. When you have finished, look at the line and ask yourself any or all of the following:

- Of what are you most proud?
- What is the best learning you had?
- What is your USP (Unique Selling Proposition); that which makes you distinctive?
- When did you feel most alive, enthusiastic and energetic? Why?
- What events were particularly significant?
- What values shaped your lifeline?
- How have events from your life shaped your values?
- What recurring themes or patterns do you notice?
- How has your behaviour shifted over time?
- How has learning shaped your lifeline?
- Have you been active or passive in shaping your life?
- What have you learned about yourself?
- What are your Narrative themes?

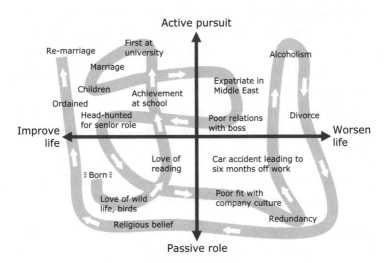

Figure 13.2 The Hero's Journey

Take some more time for reflection: examine your lifeline by looking at your journey and concentrating on leadership – where you led yourself and others. What core leadership skills do you see? Step outside your own day-to-day life for a moment and assess where you are and where you would like to go from here. Good leaders spend time in regular reflection – they look at whether or not they need to correct their course and by how much.

In fact, you are the hero and leader in your own life. It can be useful to reflect upon how your life follows the Hero's Journey, based on Joseph Campbell's research[147] into the *monomyth* – the story or tale that is the same across all recorded stories and myths of humankind. Few stories have all of the 17 steps that Campbell identified, but most will have at least the three main parts: Departure, Initiation and Return.

In Departure, the hero receives the call to adventure but initially refuses it. However, he then changes his mind or receives help to cross the threshold into that adventure and moves out of his comfort zone and into the new world on his quest.

In Initiation, there are trials to overcome and tests to pass while on the quest. The hero may find a helper or teacher and a meeting with true, unconditional love (for our purposes, this could be accepting him as he is, or our hero aligning a part of himself that wasn't aligned before), followed by achieving the goal or attaining the prize.

Finally in the Return, the hero decides to bring the gift or elixir back to his own reality, making it part of himself and sharing it with the rest of humankind.

Tool: The Hero's Journey – continued

- How does this fit in with your life story?
- Are there places where you can find a match?
- What are your gifts that you bring back from your quest?

- What did you learn?
- How does this relate to the values that you have uncovered?
- Are you lacking a particular value? What do you need to do to correct that?
- Is your preferred leadership style Hedgehog or Fox? What do you think it needs to be?

Figure 13.3 Developing narratives

Self-awareness – the first step in developing Narratives

To work with Narrative, you need to be self-aware. From your own awareness, you can start to manage yourself. Once you have done that, you can become aware of others and then manage the relationship which is part of working with Narrative. *Self-awareness* helps you to recognise and uncover your own Narrative, *managing yourself* allows you to change your own Narrative consciously, *other awareness* helps you to be aware of the Narratives of others and of organisational Narrative and *managing your relationship with others* helps you to influence those Narratives.

The organisational Narrative

Organisations were first seen as a type of machine, and so many of the models we use are mechanistic. However, experience shows that actually they behave more like organisms – complex adaptive systems. This change of focus has a profound impact on our mental

models; we need to be able to change our Narrative as the organisation – the organism – evolves. The tools we use will also be affected.
For many, this will be a different approach. But it is the approach
used by PS-ROs; the model needed for organisations to survive in
uncertain times.

Organisations exist as a network of processes and organising
activities, undertaken by people interacting socially each with
their own mental models. Each person's Narrative affects the
organisation and also each other. Organising is a continuous,
ongoing and emergent activity in the non-specified, lower cone.
It is self-organising and dynamic, both personal (it affects us
individually) and social, affecting the organisation. This means that
we need to keep the bigger picture in mind when working with
and across organisations or when discussing Options or when
working within the senior management team.

In a PS-RO, a leader's focus should be able to shift, as and when
needed, to the facilitation of structures, processes and procedures.
A PS-RO's Narrative is likely to be different from those that people
are used to and therefore different behaviours and ways of working
will arise. As the context and circumstances change, this Narrative
helps the organisation to adapt quickly, and prevent the decay
which comes without purposeful self-renewal. Narrative provides
the framework for useful analysis, for discussing the right internal
and external balances.

How the organisation's Narrative emerges

To start identifying an organisation's Narrative, you will need to
begin from a position of not knowing. Acknowledge this by asking
questions to create connections. Once you begin to understand,
you can influence things by joining the grammar of the system,
by joining the beliefs and by affirming, not criticising. You can
begin to contribute to – and build upon – the Narrative. Through

questioning, you can build change by creating the possibility for reflection.

To find out what the organisational context is – which means how people use words and what they do as they use them – ask more questions. This can change the framework or context around the issues. To do so, you need to be neutral and suspend your own beliefs and judgements in order to enter into another person's story and organisational context, making sure you understand it to *their* satisfaction and then bridging from where they are to your own ideas.

Brand

Brand is the part of the organisational Narrative which is visible externally. When people work on branding, they work on influencing the Narrative – the stories told about the brand, the ideas and experiences associated with it.

What does your brand say about your organisation? What stories do people tell outside the organisation about your organisation and about its products and services?

Stories the organisation tells itself

PS-ROs consider these Narratives carefully to make sure that they tell the right stories. They have induction programmes to help the new person transition in and to help them join the 'grammar' of the system and learn the new Narratives. PS-ROs test the Narratives, too, by asking new recruits for feedback.

Think back to when you first joined the organisation. You will already have had ideas about it from the outside. What stories did you hear from the inside? What stories were told so that you learned 'how things are done around here'? Remember, Narratives can be strong and wrong. Narratives are presented as 'truth'. When you come in fresh, you can see them and potentially question whether or not they are true. They are, nonetheless, extremely powerful.

Case study – organisational Narrative

In an energy company, one of the first Narratives all new staff learned was 'It is better to ask forgiveness than permission'. This yielded an entrepreneurial culture with people stepping up to take responsibility.

Conversely, in a global division of a high-tech manufacturing company new staff learned the organisational Narrative through the many apocryphal tales about one of the leaders – he was a 'macho man', who swore at people and dressed them down in front of others. This Narrative led to a blame culture where people were risk-averse to the point of making sure that they covered up any bad news.

Uncovering the organisational Narrative

There is one incredibly powerful tool that we all have for uncovering the organisation's Narrative(s) that we frequently don't use or don't use as effectively as we could. That is enquiry. Not only simple questions, but well thought out enquiry. Questions are part of communications, but they are also part of our thinking and come from our mental models. New and different questions can help you to change your perspective as well as helping others to change theirs. The questions we ask drive the results we see. They direct our attention. They can release energy. Are you asking questions that focus your attention on the right place? Do you know the right place? And how would you know if it were the right place to focus? What would you see and feel? Does your question enable movement or does it inflict inertia?

The power of questions is that they can lead us to failure or success. As noted earlier, the language we use helps to create our reality. It is important to be aware of this because it can often get in the way if used without thought.

Tool: Questions for uncovering Narrative

- What Narratives are you aware of? What possible consequences could there be to those Narratives?
- What assumptions are you making? What assumptions are others making? How else can you think about this situation? What are others thinking, feeling, needing, wanting?
- What is working?
- What can I learn from this?
- What are my choices?
- What am I responsible for? What do others need to be responsible for?
- What else is possible?
- Who is the client for change?
- What is changing? What will be different because of the change? Who's going to lose what? Who's going to gain what?

It is important to pay attention to the way that language is used. Look at the attitudes that you see, the aspirations and criticisms that you hear. Look for the knowledge that people share and the way it is shared. What is working well and what isn't? How do people talk about this? Are the Narratives around structure, control and bureaucracy or are they around letting things emerge, be created anew and change?

How do you know when a conversation is strategic? What happens after such conversations? How do people participate? What stories are told afterwards?

It is particularly important to identify where there is dissonance; where you notice non-alignment. Perhaps there are places where information falls through the cracks or things don't work so well. What is happening here? What stories are being told about it? If things are muddled, what kind of Narrative is needed to help?

Paradigms

We use the word 'paradigm' to mean what is inside the 'box'. 'Thinking outside the box' is thinking outside the paradigm. Paradigms are all but impossible to see for someone who is part of the paradigm or organisational system. New people coming in can often see the paradigm but it may be difficult to articulate what they see. Paradigms make up organisational culture and are part of the Narratives in the organisation. Examining the Narrative closely will help you to see the paradigms – and the hidden assumptions connected to them – that are in operation, which in turn allows you to consider whether they need to change, and if so how.

The cultural paradigm for a PS-RO is that organisations are organisms, they adapt well to their environment. In order to do so, they embrace complexity and emergence; they expand their comfort zone to include the 'unspecified space' of the bottom cone, the area encompassing uncertainty and ambiguity.

Assumptions

We all make assumptions which can be good or bad. When something happens we all tell a story about it – for instance, someone says something to you and they are unusually short with you. One generally makes assumptions about why this has happened, but you cannot *know* the reason behind it without asking. What kind of reasons/stories might you come up with? Does that happen to you? It is very hard to stop yourself, but just being aware of the possibility that you are making assumptions can help you to stop and enquire. Use Figure 13.1 to see where you are on the ladder of inference and help yourself 'down' the ladder and away from assumptions.

Developing organisational Narrative

Creating organisational Narratives requires big-picture thinking and an awareness of the whole system. It will be used in a wide range of contexts – to anticipate problems in new areas – to help set the Board agenda by excluding items not coherent with the Narrative. So it needs to consider the organisation as a system, not just a divisional structure, and also the larger environment of which it is a part.

The organisational conversations we take part in shape our participation in the organisation, and shape the Narrative. The way we experience these and the learning that comes out of them leads to modifications of our beliefs and through beliefs, our behaviours. In a PS-RO, relationships matter and so the Narrative must support relationships – co-operation, respect and responsibility.

Creating Narratives requires communication, communication and communication – all the time, in many different ways.

Communication is two-way, so it means not just broadcasting, but far more importantly listening and checking that what people hear and understand is what you meant to convey. It is an ongoing conversation about the organisational environment and the shared sense of who we are as an organisation. It is an understanding that as the organisational Narrative changes, so too must the procedures, practices and behaviours change. The part that does not change is the underlying Values and purpose of the organisation – this is the bedrock upon which the Narrative is built.

To create an organisational Narrative requires not just large-group interventions, but also work with smaller groups and much iteration so that the Narrative grows to reflect the richness of the organisation. It means making sure that the right people are speaking to one another, and connecting people and groups.

Tool: Getting Narrative into an organisation

Methods for getting a story 'into' an organisation have been the result of much research.[148] We highlight here:

- Make explicit links to values, culture, myth.
- Motivation – why this will help you in your day job, and the consequences of not aligning.
- Facilitation skills, designing engagement to group needs (e.g. senior staff, outsiders) for workshops and for learning.
- Pre-release testing with focus groups.
- Repeated exposure, preferably in a format which allows the 'target' audience to explore the implications for themselves and to come up with new ideas, and makes it clear whether the communication is merely raising awareness, or is actively seeking solutions.
- Written communications should be short and used sparingly, use instead interactive engagement in the form of briefing presentations to encourage 'so what?' discussions, intranet blogs, software games, with paper backup reference documents.
- Finally, follow up to learn what worked, through surveys, blogs, etc. It is important to test people's perceptions before a message, to define the target, and after the message, to see if they understood what you wanted them to. This is a professional process which demands specialists and experience, and is considerably resource-intensive.

Clarity about what you want to achieve

What kind of Narrative or story would you tell that would encourage behaviours aligned with the core PS-RO Values of co-operation, respect and responsibility? If you look at responsibility, a PS-RO Narrative would be one such as in the example about the energy company – 'ask forgiveness, not permission': not a blame Narrative, but about people taking initiative, supporting one another (this links into respect and co-operation) and going the extra mile. Then you can start to look for examples of this behaviour so that the stories that should be part of your Narrative are shared widely.

Here are some questions that might help you to think about what kind of Narratives you would like to encourage the organisation to have. Look at the Narratives you are aware of at the moment and then think of how it ought to be for the organisation to live up to its purpose and core Values.

Tool: Organisational Narrative

- What kind of Narratives does your organisation have around the way people are treated?
- The way you get things done? How easy is it to figure out how to get things done – is there a structured handbook to follow? Is it bureaucratic? Or is it via networking and knowing the right people to ask? How do you find the right people to ask?
- Where is creativity and innovation in the organisation and to what are they applied? Are they only for product development? Or can people be creative in any area? Is creating expected of certain people only or is it expected that everyone applies creativity to whatever they do? Narrative around innovation and creativity is key to an organisation's success and sustainability.
- What Narratives are there around the way senior management communicate? Around how well they listen? Around how upward feedback works? Around peer feedback?
- What Narratives are there around development for people in the organisation? Around learning? Around how learning and knowledge are shared?

- What Narratives are there around how people get promoted? Around the kind of behaviours that leaders in the organisation should exhibit? Around how managers treat their staff?
- What Narratives are there around how customers are treated? How are customers viewed?
- What Narratives are there around the environment? CSR? Carbon footprint and energy usage? Procurement? How are suppliers treated?

Designing a better Narrative architecture

Your Narrative will be unique to your organisation. Based on your core Values and purpose, it yields the behaviours that you need to fulfil those. A PS-RO will have a considered Narrative supporting co-operation, responsibility and respect.

To create the Narrative that you want, you need to let go of the past to make room for the new. To do this, you and your team need to be clear about what success looks like from every angle. What will it look and feel like? Who is talking to whom? How are you working? What is different? What is the same? What have you stopped doing?

Working together, describe in as much detail as possible what it will look like from each person's perspective. A reality check is accomplished through the discussion, but also when you make sure to check your vision of future success against the organisation's core Values and purpose.

This view of success should be energising for the team and this helps them to start creating it. Create a journey of discovery to move from where you are to the new place of success. Make sure that you celebrate success and celebrate the early wins, the first stations on your journey. When people know what success looks like, they are more likely to achieve it and it is easier to correct their course.

The right Narrative can transform an organisation. The leaders in PS-ROs step off the hierarchical merry-go-round and put their organisation and the people in it at the centre, enabling a supportive space for all to create value for the benefit of the customers and stakeholders, the organisational purpose and the wider community of which it is a part. These leaders understand that PS-RO leadership is about inclusiveness and creating the renewed organisation together.

What to do when Narratives clash
A dissonance can occur when parts of the organisation interpret the Narrative in a different way so that the behaviour which arises is not in alignment. An example might be the tension between the 'day job' in the 95% or 99%, and contributing to renewal. Using the 'ladder of inference' tool, you can help to make clear exactly what is happening and where assumptions are being made and the communication is going wrong.

When you are working with Narrative clash, it is especially important that you explicitly recognise that teams and the people in them are heroes of their own narrative and have positive intent. Treat them with respect, one of the key PS-RO values. To address Narrative clash, you need people to listen to you. The best way to do that is to acknowledge and validate their experience. Create a positive platform from which to move forward. Focus on the positive intention people have – ask them what it is. Even when someone thinks that everything is wrong, they clearly hold a vision of what 'right' is. Ask about it. Hear them out. Ask what can be done to get there.

Sometimes the Narrative has been around so long and is so deeply ingrained that people are unwilling to shift their stories. If people are unwilling to change – if there is no 'client' for change – then nothing can be done. Remember that change must begin with the individual, who must choose and want to change.

Scenarios as Narrative

Scenarios can be used in groups to uncover organisational mental models, as described in Chapter 11. They can become shared memories of different futures, helping the organisation to create a common Narrative around itself in the future, and creating new mental models linking imagination to action.

Case study – when Narratives clash

An organisational audit was performed for a manufacturing company that assembled computer boards with tiny components on them. There were assembly lines with machine and hand placement stations on them. Morale was very low and there were quality problems with the product.

The managers had a Narrative that the workforce was crap, while the workforce's Narrative was that their management was useless. The audit team identified the Narrative dissonance and defused it by asking, 'What actually happened?' They wanted facts, not opinions or judgements. They wanted to move down the ladder of inference.

The managers had told them that operators were damaging work in progress. So they asked, 'Which operators were causing the damage? Which lines?' They asked questions that would help them to understand exactly what was happening, rather than jumping to conclusions or making assumptions (as the managers had), which led to judgement and blame.

This helped them to find the two lines where the problems were occurring. What these two lines had in common was a new automatic placement machine which – it turned out – had been incorrectly calibrated. If the organisation had continued down the line of judgement – asking the wrong question – the cost to the company would have been high indeed.

Executive Summary

- Narrative is the glue that holds the organisation together, it forms an important part of corporate memory.
- An over-arching Narrative is likely to be stable over decades.
- A Narrative can be strong and wrong as well as right.
- Creating and using Narratives requires communication, communication, communication.
- Enquiry is a powerful tool for uncovering Narratives.
- When people know what success looks like, from the organisation's Narrative, they are more likely to achieve it and it is easier to correct their course.

Chapter 14

Machinery

Machinery – the dynamic infrastructure of the organisation – plays a central role in a PS-RO. It supports and integrates the other four qualities to enable an organisation to be a PS-RO.

Overall, one of the key issues for an organisation in pursuing renewal is that most of its resources are committed to existing projects and enhancement plans are always well argued and defended. This applies in all scenarios! These issues are discussed below, where we describe the connection between the Three Ring Circus and the formal planning system.

Another issue is that of blame. In the public sector, if we succeed it is the politicians who won; but if we fail it is a civil service mistake. Or, in the private sector, the Board vs. the line units. This is hard to tackle, as it is characteristically human. But having recognised renewal processes, implementation of the Three Ring Circus can go a long way to putting the culture in place to reduce blame. Similarly, the Three Ring Circus provides a context for the Board to be able to have productive conversations about the options before them.

This chapter takes a more general look at the interlocking parts of the Machinery specific to a PS-RO, *over and above* those in any well-run organisation, under the headings of processes, ICT, communication, knowledge management and people, all of which are covered in greater detail below.

Then, we consider the Machinery specific to two types of organisation which we introduced in Chapter 5, the '95' organisation and the '99' organisation. We also look at Machinery for groups. Along the way we introduce a number of tools:

- Portfolio management.
- Processes for evaluating ideas.
- Enabling dialogue.
- Methods for communicating scenarios.
- The WonderWeb of Possibility.

Renewal

As chaos theory suggests, an organisation will decay if left to respond randomly to the environment.[149] In a PS-RO, processes need to be tied to an outcome in order to achieve purposeful self-renewal; at the same time, the need for course correction is recognised. The desired outcome needs to be visible and discussed before engaging with full force.

We identified the attributes of PS-RO processes in Chapter 7. But the terms of reference of processes for renewal are also different from those in the specified cone. While the specified cone deals with tangibles such as sales and sales targets, the unspecified cone deals with intangible factors such as:

- A desire to explore new things, openness to possibility, curiosity.
- Creativity, linked to a sense of purpose.
- The desire to understand and learn.
- The ability to accept ambiguity and the fuzziness of the future.

These differences mean that renewal activities need to be visibly professional in their planning and delivery in order to be respected.

The formal planning system: the role of the Three Ring Circus

Setting up these structures

Operations, the inner ring
The operational processes are assumed to be in place. They will differ in detail between organisations, but will generally involve the activities shown in Figure 14.1.

Portfolio management, the middle ring
Successful assessment combines scrutiny of individual plans using, for instance, a one-page business review, combining intuition with the numbers, knowing the people and having credible staff involved.

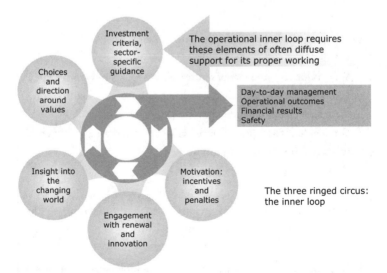

Figure 14.1 Inner ring of the Three Ring Circus

Tool: Portfolio management

The cycle for portfolio management may be annual or biennial, the output may contribute to the Annual Report, and it has a major formal financial element.

Role and responsibilities
This part of the organisation also often takes responsibility for assessing other assets and liabilities:

- Intangibles, such as corporate and product brands.
- Knowledge and capability, covering IT and knowledge management, patents and intellectual property.
- Human resources both extant and in prospect, their motivation and geographical spread, talent management.
- Partnerships and external relations.
- Regulatory position.

It also often critiques performance, e.g.

- Do sectors meet hurdle targets? Are these reasonable? Is the sector volatile?
- What is the required rate of return? What appears to govern Capex? Is it dominated by scale and past habits, profitability and risk, or is there an element of randomness?
- Do the functions (e.g. finance, HR, IT, purchasing) deliver as required? Are they fit for purpose?
- Do intangibles have 'owners'?

This means that there is an opportunity to assess – and reset – the direction of the organisation by asking:

- Does the foreseen position meet the organisation's goals? Is it coherent? What is the 3- to 5-year target?

- What needs to change? How can it be changed? How quickly? At what cost? What levers to apply?
- What are the project selection criteria? Are we getting serious innovation projects around our Narrative?
- What resource can we allocate to exploration of options for renewal?
- Do we communicate effectively?

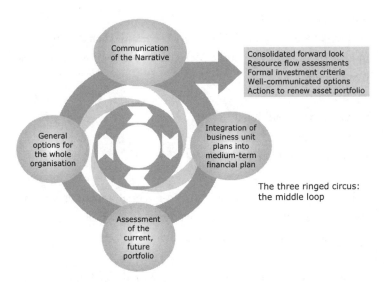

Figure 14.2 Middle ring of the Three Ring Circus

Some dangers of assessment are that it can be seen as a critique of the Board or it may unduly claim power, or it may impede the plans of powerful people. It is easy for it to become focused on numbers while it ignores the qualitative data. It often displays long-range over-optimism and suggests a spurious cash surplus in the long term (see Figure 14.2).

Generation of Insight: the outer ring
Processes for Insight were covered in more detail in Chapter 11. Here we focus on the connection to the other rings of the Three

Ring Circus. An important aspect of this is continuity of staff assignment: this needs to be combined with rotation of staff into the unit charged with Insight. The Insight unit needs to be firmly connected to operations and recognised by them to be useful both before, and after, any major analysis. Connection to operations ensures that think-tank discussions are more purposeful.

The role of models in Insight

Numeric modelling should be rarely used, and when it is used, the models should be transparent. More useful are contrasting qualitative models, e.g.

- Green vs. Traditional
- Communism vs. Capitalism
- Network vs. Hierarchy

People relate to images and giving a model a name is a useful way of ensuring that people connect with and remember it.

The configurations of the model should include:

- Key dimensionality – what drives the model and differentiates it from other models? What are the possible configurations?
- The model should provide 'useful' stories, with implied major changes, but also credible, 'probable' stories, with relative likelihood – extremes diffuse credibility.
- The trajectory of the key dimensions of the model is central.
- Useful models provide a framework for discussing policy.

The activities of the outer ring are captured in Figure 14.3.

Working with the portfolio management team

While some people may work in both the portfolio management team and the Insight team, the key differences are:

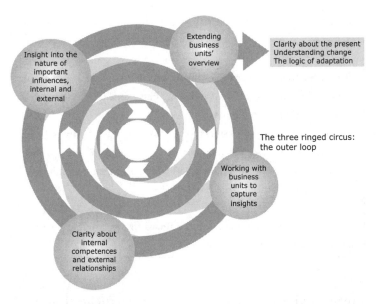

Figure 14.3 Outer ring of the Three Ring Circus

- The portfolio is about what matters now.
- The portfolio will be modified by the next round of Insight.
- Insight draws from the portfolio in setting targets.
- Insight is about what is going to matter and the tools to address this.
- Key messages from Insight need to be fed back quickly to the portfolio team.
- The Insight team are concerned with novel ideas and insights, within agreed ranges for uncertainties, and within agreed and qualitative trend time scales.

Tool: Processes for evaluating ideas

The processes for taking ideas towards adoption need to be visible throughout the organisation. They should be accessible to all and offer concrete rewards to offset the risk for any proponent. A typical process might be:

First screening – a peer review by a panel, e.g. exploiting knowledge pools, covering the concept and providing a qualitative approach to the magnitude of the impact.

Second screening – a business idea, a formal project proposal, to a formally constituted body – probably not to the Board but to a Panel with discretion for small proposals and endorsement/recommendation to the Board for large proposals.

This two-stage process allows the Board to focus on big decisions and have adequate background for these.

Product retirals and new products mean portfolio changes

The issue faced by many organisations is: how to change purposefully and rationally? It is often harder to stop doing things or to do things differently than to start new initiatives. But unless as much focus is put on walking away from parts of the portfolio as on enhancing it, all parts of the business will be starved of investment, as discussed in Chapter 6. And battles for budget are often interlaced with ostensibly strategic discussions.

Old activities must justify themselves anew. A useful question is, 'If we were starting from scratch, would we choose this business?' This question is often the hardest for a Board or senior management group to answer honestly. Setting the discussion in the context of future scenarios as below changes the focus and allows for less defensive behaviour.

In the public sector in particular, the decade 2010–2020 will see shrinkage of budgets and staff, though with greater roles in some areas (e.g. regulation). This can be seen as a problem or an opportunity to rethink the processes, as in the public sector case study in Chapter 12.

Multi-skilled workforce

A project to develop a new idea and take it through to a formal proposal will require a range of skills, covering:

- People who are good at seeing a business concept – mapping a technical or process idea into the organisation.
- The ability to sell the idea using communication tools to suit the intended audience, from spreadsheet to scenarios to graphics.
- Finance skills to provide the link into the portfolio management team in terms of hurdle rates, etc.
- It may be relevant to consult with experts on competition, brand, legal, regulatory or IP.

The development project team usefully combines staff people with operational people on assignment.

A team to deliver and implement specific changes, once agreed, is outside the scope of this book, but the principles are well covered in Lawler and Worley's book, *Built to Change*.[150]

A PS-RO: beyond the Three Ring Circus

The Three Ring Circus architecture exists in all organisations – though the outer ring activities may not be systematically planned and managed. What a PS-RO adds is capability to quickly sense change occurring around it and to respond to that change, through enabling dialogue.

Tool: Enabling dialogue

There are practical levers to encourage dialogue, such as:

- Setting the ethos, values, expectations.
- Wide understanding of the quest.

- Rewards, which can be recognition or money (or both!) and targets.
- Training and development in – for instance – skills in dialogue, strategic thinking or working collaboratively.
- Capturing learning; it is not failure – it is feedback.
- Active mechanisms to generate useful ideas, where 'useful' equals assisting the 'journey' and the expectation that ideas will be considered.

There may be good reasons why people do not debate and engage in dialogue. Hurdles to dialogue include:

- Board-level baronies vs. teams working across divisions, discouragement by lack of allocation of resources, by forbidding engagement by subordinates, or by discouraging innovation.
- Line managers from the specified part of the organisation may not have been exposed to debate and dialogue, have no training, and/or no examples.
- People often have a tendency to revert to their comfort zone and role play, as shareholders' representative, or defender of the fiefdom.
- 'Information is power' culture; 'access', which negates the value of knowledge flows, links status to 'need to know' and access to senior staff.

We discuss below, under Communication, how to create an atmosphere of open discussion and dialogue.

Cultural aspects

Once a problem has been defined and skills brought to bear, one difficulty that can be encountered is the need for a culture of gradual change, for there will be many course corrections during the journey. Most improvements are incremental, and developed by iteration around a subject in a culture which allows for physical or virtual 'water cooler' discussions.

A PS-RO's culture is pragmatic and aware of the value of debate, recognising the need for conceptual discussions and willing to tame and temper it to go from divergence to convergence. It requires self-discipline from staff and is critical of meetings for meetings' sake and 'busy work'.

The role of challenge

Challenge needs to carry legitimacy, which implies that it is within the core Values and purpose of the organisation and is both:

- Relevant, i.e. connected to the relevant Narrative; addresses perceived issues; and is pitched at the right archetype of organisation.
- 'Practical', implying that the issue is within the organisation's grasp, is timely, seemingly important and tractable, and that measures exist or could be put in place that would allow the impact to be monitored.

Five interlocking parts in the Machinery

We discussed above the *processes* of a PS-RO relating to renewal and connecting to the portfolio. Now we identify processes specifically underpinning a PS-RO.

Most organisations have not yet incorporated *ICT* into their unspecified processes – we identify some emerging technologies and their potential impact.

Communications – we discuss communications between the specified and unspecified cones, between both and the portfolio ring, and across the unspecified space. Good communication is needed for Insight, for exploring Options and for implementing change. Communications take as their basis the organisational Narrative and the Values.

Knowledge management is about more than ICT and communications – and is one of the basic capabilities of a PS-RO.

Organisations are contexts for *people* to become parts of extraordinarily competent groups – some of the tools to do this are discussed below.

Processes

Processes for connecting the three rings are needed in a PS-RO. For example:

- Processes for sharing innovation across line units, for harnessing Insights from the specified cone, for learning from innovation; for creating a shared view of Options and for communicating between the upper and lower cone.
- Audit processes – skills, knowledge, reputation, IT and organisational audits were discussed in Chapter 11.
- Processes which feed senior management with adequate information to make decisions, based on the knowledge and Insights of the organisation.
- Processes which ensure that functions such as procurement, HR, IT and finance are aligned to the PS-RO and not to the past.

A PS-RO needs these processes *in addition to* well-specified and executed planning processes. The importance of effective planning and implementation was emphasised by a study[151] that compared planning in 886 organisations globally. They found that there were four types of planning:

- Symbolic planning, which articulates the mission, vision and strategic intent of the firm.
- Rational planning, a hierarchical planning system with budgets and tight operational controls.

- Transactive planning, which allows for plans to develop iteratively.
- Generative planning, in which both product or service and internal process innovation are encouraged.

They found that symbolic planning was negatively correlated with performance. Generative planning was most strongly positively correlated with performance, followed closely by transactive and rational planning. This emphasises that the output of analysis needs to be aligned to the innovative needs of the organisation, either currently in the specified cone, or for new activities through the lower, unspecified cone.

The role of ICT

Since the 1990s the role of ICT has changed radically in both private and organisational life. In private life, the Internet is actively used by consumers and citizens worldwide, and many industries have been turned upside down by consumers' ability to make comparisons and choices through the Internet.

Inside organisations, the roll-out of enterprise-wide software is mostly complete, automating many middle manager tasks.[152] Intranets are in wide use[153] and used mostly for employees to find information rather than to share it. Wikis provide a format for gathering information from a number of sources and sharing it. Blogs are used by technical communities with a fairly specific focus, such as IT consultancies, and by critics of organisations to share critiques.[154] Many employees find that they have access to more software and tools at home than in the office.[155]

The comments below apply to organisations of all types, as ICT is ubiquitous and scalable.

Metcalfe's law

Metcalfe's law[156] states that the usefulness of a social or electronic network rises with the square of the number of entities connected to it. For example, when faxes were first introduced they were largely useless, until a critical mass was achieved, when it was possible to assume that there was one in every office. However, the caveats to Metcalfe's law are in many ways more interesting than the law itself:

- It is not enough for the nodes to be connected; they have to be interacting.
- The quality of the interaction is of central importance to the value that the group creates.
- Unfocused traffic across a network can choke it, and destroy its usefulness.

The implications of this are twofold:

- First, Metcalfe's law promises extremely large returns if we can extend our network without compromising quality.
- The second is that managing the quality of discussion is of extreme importance for a good outcome; the network cannot make up for deficiencies in the correspondents. What it does do is provide open access (unless controlled), unlike physical meetings or discussions.

Early US-based bulletin boards found this out the hard way. Clay Shirky[157] observes that groups are also poor at learning from failures of this sort.

Social networking

Web 2.0 applications have an extremely uneven success rate. For example, Yahoo discussion groups mostly fail, though a few show striking success. The success of the durable groups is, in part, due to the innate popularity of a particular topic – although there are nearly always many other spaces in which the same topic is under debate – but also to the tone and style with which the early posts set the debate in motion.

However, something else has emerged from the online world – as well as from software co-operatives – which is a form of crowd management through self-selecting elites. Technically capable people – or those who sound capable online – enter into a dense conversation which ignores the contributions of those beyond the charmed circle.

The positive side of this phenomenon is that the core group becomes what Art Kleiner[158] described as 'the key group within the group'. Within an organisation this constitutes an empowered elite, people who are not necessarily highly ranked in the corporate hierarchy, but who assert power through their collective influence. Such groups can begin as a source of challenge and innovation. The problem is that because they are aligned primarily through habit and values, they can also become a drag on decision making when events move on.

These expert communities can become prone to the evolution of in-groups, elites who talk a specialist language and turn their backs on the crowd that could, perhaps, help them in their tasks. Metcalfe's law demands numbers but it also demands high-quality interactions. Elites are not the answer. Neither are unstructured discussions with open access. What is needed in a PS-RO is something quite different: systems that manage such debate in a structured manner and allow the key group to emerge and be effective – with extraordinary competence.

Communications

An atmosphere of open discussion supports renewal, insight and risk containment by:

- Improved ability of senior management to discuss things outside the scheduled meetings.

- The ability to explain things to stakeholders.
- The harnessing and alignment of energy to teams, reducing aggression and opening them to possibility and to change.
- Reducing the likelihood of trivial politics getting out of hand.

Within a PS-RO the desired result of all activities and processes is a win for all concerned; the core Values help to define how we interact and how to allocate time and resources.

Rational change is relatively easy, using the tools discussed below. However, culture clashes are less rational and can cause serious dissonance/disruption (for instance, after organisations merge), which can last for up to 20 years.[159]

Tools and methods to encourage a culture of open discussion include:

- Induction and training.
- Leadership styles and behaviours.
- Communications Machinery, as below.
- KPIs based on subjective as well as objective items, team as well as individual.
- 360° assessment, including assessing for the behaviours that support the core Values of co-operation, respect and responsibility.
- Rewards aligned to core Values.
- Time allocated to processes for Insight and innovation.

Although open debate is to be encouraged, there is a danger that louder voices will talk more; this can be a licence for those who like the sound of their own voice. The role of leaders is to bring out the silent but potentially knowledgeable, to hear the small voices which may be the first with a particular insight, to assess and filter ideas. The process should allow pauses to reflect and echo back. This requires quite skilled facilitation, either by the leaders themselves or using an external facilitator, for physical groups or for participation in online media.

Good communications structure

The basic triple structure of good communications is:

- Tell why this matters: the context.
- Tell what it says: the content.
- Tell what to do about this: the action.

Targeted communications work best, so it is useful to remember that groups differ in many ways, for instance:

- Implicit values: scientists and sales people typically differ in their preferred rewards.[160]
- Implicit context: the complaints department has a different view of customers from the sales people.
- Educational attainment, fluency in the language of the organisation (at Electrolux, a Swedish–Italian company, they all speak 'bad English'[161]).
- Different learning styles.[162]
- National cultural differences.[163]
- Generational differences, with the digital generation having different attention spans and ability to multi-task.[164]

These groups need different support, distinct contexts and framing of the message using different words and metaphors. Communication of the outcomes of scenario projects is worth taking as an example.

Options for scenario visualisation

Schematic diagrams are widely used, both in developing scenarios and communicating them. They expose the underlying structure

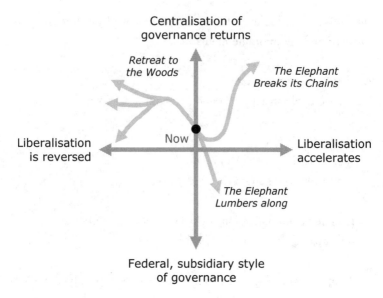

Figure 14.4 Three scenarios for India, example of a scenario cross

of the scenarios and ensure that the scenario space is covered. The schematic may be based on a 2 × 2 matrix or scenario cross (as in Figure 14.4), a cube (as in Figure 14.5) or a radar diagram (as in Figure 14.6). From the many different ways of depicting scenarios, the important thing is to use something which can help people to visualise them. The scenario cross is often used within the team, whereas the two representations that can show more than two dimensions below are often used to communicate to stakeholders. Other, non-graphic, representations are discussed further below.

A scenario with three dimensions of uncertainty is hard to visualise. We have found that a cube is quite useful because we can show positions inside a cube at various points along the axes.

A radar diagram, on the other hand, has the advantage of contrasting different scenarios according to the strength of their

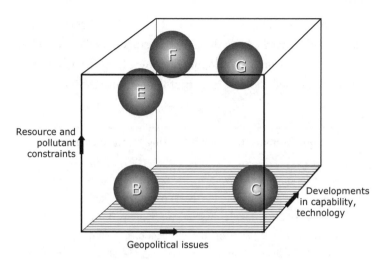

Figure 14.5 Representing three-dimensional scenarios

Environmental pressures:
The logarithm of the ratio of the current situation to the probable long-term sustainable limit

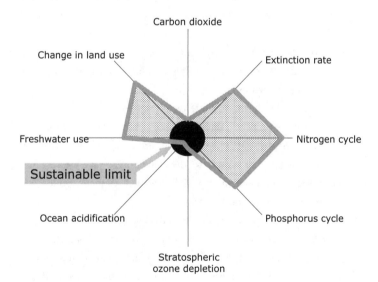

Figure 14.6 Radar diagram[165]

capability on any number of axes, as displayed in Figure 14.6. All graphical plots need care in defining and explaining the axes. They are useful for a team in developing their own Insight, and for communication to stakeholders as part of a longer discussion.

Tool: Methods for communicating future scenarios

- A conventional *PowerPoint presentation*, even if dressed up with images, is not particularly effective at communicating a scenario set. It can be used to provide the analytic framework which will set a context for a discussion on the implications, preferably with the stories also in hand. Many scenario sets include tabular descriptions, more detailed than fit on a PowerPoint slide. These may be focused around qualitative descriptions or numeric data extracted from models, either computer-based or 'back of the envelope'. Scientists and engineers like tabular formats.
- *Stories* may be communicated via the written word, or images, or a combination. The essential is that the stories be plausible and internally consistent. They should allow readers or viewers to extrapolate from the story to the implications for their domain. Written and multi-media stories support testing/refining workshops and public involvement activities.
- *Videos* of 'talking heads' are often used to describe scenario stories. This allows several characters to discuss, for instance, why a scenario evolved as it did. The difficulties are in providing a backdrop which is imaginative and allows the characters to take viewers into the future. It has been successful, however, with focus groups as a way of briefing them on scenarios.
- *Multi-media presentations* are designed to engage the emotions as well as a cerebral understanding of the futures, by combining images and sounds with text and/or voices. Images, text and sounds can be stored electronically, transmitted and re-used and so have advantages for a series of workshops with a substantially common agenda. Multi-media presentations can also be accessed via the Web.

- Capturing *graphic images* on paper during a workshop or creating a timeline gives a sense of difference to an event and can stimulate people to think more imaginatively. It also increases participants' sense of involvement if their ideas are captured immediately 'on the wall'. However, the storage and re-use of images captured on paper can be problematic.
- Play-lets with actors (*Forum Theatre*) work well with a 'one-off' event, e.g. after a dinner during a seminar, or as part of a scenario creation workshop, when actors interactively develop a story line with the group. In the first case, actors work from a jointly agreed script developed with the scenario team. In the second case, actors work with the team to interactively think through the characters and timeline to populate the scenarios. It can be set up as a one-day workshop, with groups working on the different scenarios in the morning and presenting their plays in the afternoon, followed by discussion of the implications for the organisation. The use of actors generally creates a high level of energy and engagement in the process. It also creates a very different impression, which scores highly on the 'water cooler' test, i.e. it is talked about afterwards.
- *Computer models* can be divided into two categories: 'serious' models, used to explore inter-related scientific effects, such as the climate change models, and models intended to be used interactively to help people understand their environment, such as 'Fishbanks' (developed by Dennis Meadows, co-author of *Limits to Growth*). Dennis Meadows is now involved with the Browne Centre, which appears to have developed similar games.[166] These are all models which explore the implications of decisions, for instance over-fishing.
- Historically, *simulations* have been based on system dynamics, or agent-based models. The processing power needed and the programming requirements have in the past resulted in high costs. This has meant that relatively few organisations have been able to exploit the opportunities of simulation. In parallel with the computer games industry, there have been major advances in simulation science that make real-time simulation, often linked to business systems, a cost-effective option for a wide range of organisations.

Knowledge management

We defined knowledge management in Chapter 11 as 'systems to support the creation, transfer and application of knowledge in organisations'. How can the knowledge in organisations be identified? What is clear is that centralised views of what is known throughout the organisation are often wrong.

Many organisations undertake regular – e.g. annual – surveys. These may have an implicit agenda, for instance the questions are asked from a central office perspective, and these questions may seem abstract and/or pointless to those replying from outside the centre. The style is often a closed questionnaire, with 'score us 1–10 on X', rather than an open questionnaire: 'why do you think X matters?' The tendency is for the replies to be bland and not contentious, and the results presented as 'average percentage' with all richness inhibited or filtered out and no unexpected answers permitted. The survey agents typically ask and learn nothing about the unspecified, lower cone.

People are remarkably ignorant of their organisation. In one company, the new CEO decided to send a personal email to all staff wishing them a Happy Christmas. He got back a reply from an employee in New Zealand which was in its entirety 'and a happy Christmas to you too but who the hell are you?' Employees may not know such things as which parts are profitable; which spend money; the history of the organisation; the owners and their aims; the major competitors; how the technology works; where the organisation is going.

Many organisations find out too late that wheels have been reinvented partly due to either not knowing how to find the original, or indeed if it exists. And even senior managers find it impossible to keep up with what is happening.

While no organisation would want all of its people to 'speak MBA', in a PS-RO people do need to know and align with:

- the core Values and organisational purpose;
- the organisational Narrative;
- the unit Narrative.

In the sections below we discuss specific knowledge management approaches for '95'-type and '99'-type organisations and for groups.

People: staffing a PS-RO
The specified parts of organisations (upper cone) work by specialisation, with:

- Silo black boxes – that is, functions and groups of people with a clearly delineated work area. They are clear what is part of their remit and what is not and do not work with what falls outside their remit.
- Tightly defined work roles, allowing people to focus only on that which falls within their defined role, the rest being someone else's responsibility.
- Accountability, budgets, targets.
- Outsource anything not 'core'.

People are mostly directly replaceable and job roles are focused on the ability to deliver the specified outcomes. Only senior management 'think strategically', and not very often, as in Chapter 11. Training for the transition from a specified role to a senior role with responsibilities for the unspecified, lower cone is hard to define and often neglected.

Additional roles in a PS-RO
Most people in a PS-RO will work in the specified parts of the organisation, the upper cone. But their job becomes different in a PS-RO, in that:

- People work in a semi-permeable world where change is visible and responsibilities to the organisation as well as the group or unit are recognised.
- Partnerships are very important; partnering and collaboration are key to a PS-RO's success, at Board level and all the way through the organisation.
- Stakeholders find that they connect at all levels, and the organisation is able to learn from outsiders such as suppliers.
- The ability to discuss and recognise patterns is a valuable skill.
- The ability to explore options is important, and this is recognised in setting 'specified job' targets.
- Quite junior staff have to learn to 'think strategically'.

Career paths – skills and competences in a PS-RO

Careers in a PS-RO may well involve job enrichment rather than purely promotion as a development mechanism. People in a PS-RO require skills and competences including:

- Continual learning, reassessment of insight.
- Reflection and course correction.
- Social skills and networking are important at much more junior levels to form or contribute to groups.
- Disciplined multi-tasking is at a premium.
- Self-discipline replaces part of the line manager's role.
- For some staff (the '1%' or '5%'), the line is augmented by a net of peers, with emergent authority associated with capability.
- Peer coaching.
- Ability to operate in a culture which understands rapid prototyping, where failure is useful because it provides feedback and learning.

The '95' organisation

Knowledge management

Knowledge management (KM) in the '95' organisation is complex because 'water cooler' conversations, where people bump into each other, are rare or non-existent, due to multiple locations and few shared events. In this environment, how do you ensure that knowledge is shared? That people can find what they need? That they don't reinvent the wheel?

A PS-RO regards KM as an important part of its strategy and competitive advantage; the better it is able to share learning across the organisation the greater the benefit to the organisation and the greater the benefit to its bottom line.

There is no magic bullet for organising knowledge and learning to be shared; the important things to think about are:

- How to make people aware knowledge exists?
- How to reward people for posting information and handling queries?
- How to make knowledge easy to access?
- How to reward people for re-use rather than invention?

PS-ROs use combinations of tools to provide structure for what they want to share, such as Sharepoint, Wikis, blogs and social networking and communities of practice (CoPs), as well as networking within the organisation to share information and learning from projects. They share learning through methods such as action learning groups, CoPs and after-action reviews.

Because the Machinery of a PS-RO values and rewards co-operation, people partner together and collaborate readily – there is no need to force people to work win/win when they already have an attitude of supporting one another and sharing what they know. Such an attitude and way of working is contagious. It develops its own energy. It cannot be forced, only encouraged. It enables people to ask for help when they need it and share both what worked and what did not, as well as the context in which it took place.

Tool for working with partners

One of the key aspects of a PS-RO is the ability to work with partners and to harness innovation. An interesting tool that we have developed is called the WonderWeb of Possibility.[166] See Figure 14.7.

Tool: The WonderWeb of Possibility

A WonderWeb is a particular sort of mind map. A mind map is a diagram used to represent ideas around a central key word or idea, used as an aid in decision making.

A WonderWeb uses Possibility as its focal point. You focus and brainstorm around the possibilities you see around you: which partners or other groups might have expertise that could help tackle the issue you face.

It usually takes up one or more flipchart sheets and up to an hour to get the first cut. After that, divide the map into different areas. They may be partners, internal groups, academic research centres.

Then write down the different possibilities you see in each area. This could be the name of a contact, or the organisation, or the organisation type (or need that it would meet). Frequently that connects to another and another and so on. What you write doesn't matter; it's the *possibilities* – usually around a relationship that you already have with someone in an organisation – which reveal themselves clearly and provide you with an enlarged universe of possibilities.

Outcomes of creating a WonderWeb.

You will find yourself re-energised, more focused, motivated and connected. When you revisit your WonderWeb, you will usually see another connection that you can follow up. It can also be clear when you need to stop doing something because it is no longer important to you or connected to the other things that you are doing.

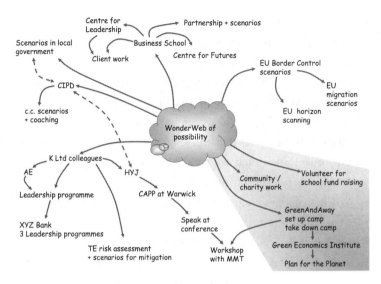

Figure 14.7 The WonderWeb of Possibility

The '99' organisation

Large-scale interventions (100+ people)

Large-scale interventions or groups sessions are powerful tools which enable individuals to make new connections, to hear a common Narrative and to co-create a self-renewing organisation. It means that all voices are in the room and real progress can be made. Conversations are part of what makes organisations work – large-group interventions enable them to take place and to be captured and immediately fed back into what the organisation is becoming.

Large-scale interventions need clearly defined success criteria and outputs, with a small organising team which includes expert facilitators as well as people from across the organisation. Together they can design and orchestrate the sessions. There are many different methods that can be used. For example:

- Future Search[168] is a three-day meeting process that is task-focused, brings together 60 to 80 people in one room or hundreds in parallel rooms. People tell stories about their past, present and desired future. Through dialogue they discover their common ground. Only then do they make concrete action plans.
- Appreciative Inquiry[169] is an organisational development method that assumes that whatever is needed, already exists in the organisation, and so harnesses the images of success to provide energy for purposeful change.
- World Café[170] is a simple process for creating quality conversations about important issues.
- Open Space[171] is a generic term describing a wide variety of different styles of meeting in which participants define the agenda with a relatively rigorous process, and may adjust it as the meeting proceeds. A large meeting of this sort is called an open space conference or unconference.

To get the best out of the intervention, a variety of experiences should be used, from plenary sessions to small-group break-out sessions to working in pairs. It is also important to allow time for reflection in whatever way that people find useful – again this could be in pairs or small groups, but it can also be on an individual basis as some people find writing about their experience to be a learning-rich method.

Finally, it is important not just to capture the outputs of the intervention but also to be very clear about the place it holds in the ongoing process of renewal. A large-group intervention is one station along the journey. People need to be clear where on the journey it is and what other stations there will be on the way. There should be opportunity for commitment to action and follow-up.

While large-group interventions are a complex process, the results are gratifying. You can identify where there is energy for change and launch initiatives that are on target using that energy.

You get immediate feedback to ideas and can tweak those that aren't quite right, on the spot. You identify where there are blockages and have the right people in the room to innovate your way around them. A good guide to large-group interventions can be found in the *Guide to Organisation Design* by Naomi Stanford.[172]

Connecting market and customer data to the lower cone

One of the key methods of moving from the lower cone's uncertainty and ambiguity to the upper cone's structure and specificity is through horizon scanning (Chapter 11) and enquiry. We don't know what we don't know, but if we don't ask we will never learn. It requires active listening and asking for feedback. There are many ways to do this, from face-to-face visits with clients, desk research and market surveys to surveys on the Web using special survey tools such as SurveyMonkey or Rypple.[173]

The data that is gathered needs to be distilled into useful information which in turn needs to be shared, assimilated and fed into the Insight and Options processes.

Joining up silos

PS-ROs know that organisational silos slow them down and damage their competitive advantage, the working relationships within the organisation and ultimately limit their effectiveness and profitability. Their core Values of co-operation and respect are important in creating an environment of collaboration, but they also actively encourage cross-functional working and sharing through their reward system and their leadership.

A PS-RO uses any opportunity for people to work across silos, either face-to-face or virtually.

Knowledge management

Knowledge management for the '99' organisation is slightly easier than for the '95' organisation. There are fewer boundaries to cross, but they do exist nonetheless.

Larry Prusak of IBM talks about a continuum of knowledge[174] with 'capturing knowledge' at one end and 'connectivity' at the other. Captured knowledge is explicit knowledge; it is known and in the specified cone. At that end of the continuum, an organisation has lots of manuals and written documentation (which could be web-based) on the learning/knowledge. It is very structured. On the 'connectivity' end of the continuum it is about organising processes to enable tacit behaviour – knowledge in the heads of your people – to emerge into the organisation. It is about setting up and enabling opportunities for people to have conversations. A PS-RO knows where on the spectrum it needs to be and it plans and budgets accordingly.

Groups

In this section we describe briefly some of the Machinery for group effectiveness, valid for all organisations. Groups may be co-resident or dispersed, an SME or community of practice. Whatever they are, a PS-RO needs to have groups with extraordinary competence.

Workshops

There are many different ways to design and run workshops. Groups in PS-ROs are very clear about the desired outcome before they begin because this dictates the design of the workshop itself, whether or not they need an external facilitator, and who they need to invite. The ability to design and run workshops is an under-rated art: we recommend reading a well-established guide such as Peter Senge's *The Fifth Discipline Fieldbook*.[175]

Facilitation

A facilitator helps a group accomplish its goals and encourages progress by paying attention to and controlling the process, actions and interaction. Facilitation ensures that there is 'safe space' so that possibilities, ideas, change, innovation and best decisions can emerge. A facilitator helps to find the appropriate path – for instance between structured and emergent – to deal with relations and to achieve goals more quickly and effectively.

The outcomes of a well-facilitated group exercise can be significant and substantial; organisations improve their competitive advantage by:[176]

- Making better decisions.
- Improving productivity of the group.
- Improving group motivation: as the group all have a part in making the decision, they are more committed to implementing it.
- Increasing group confidence, self-esteem, creativity and innovation.
- Enabling radical change.
- Improving organisational learning and capturing of learning.
- Improving working relationships between group members.

Case study – facilitation

As part of its 'Renewal' programme, Dow Corning implemented a programme that they called 'Facilitative Leadership' – which was teaching their senior leaders some of the skills and competences needed to be a facilitator. It was about enabling and developing their people. They saw it as one of the key skills all their leaders needed.

Their leaders were amazed at how differently and more productively their meetings ran once they had learned the new skills. They reported a huge reduction of disruptive behaviour once they and their teams had the tools to identify it and 'name the game', uncovering assumptions and finding out what worked best in order to do more of it.

As one CEO said about learning facilitation skills, 'it helps you when you need to work IN the business not ON the business'.[177]

Brainstorming

There are many ways to brainstorm and most people have tried at least some of them. The purpose of brainstorming is to allow creative thinking without any worries about criticism – in fact, the crazier the thinking/ideas the better.

Case study – one idea leads to another

During a bad winter, when there was lots of snow, the Belgian Airport Authority were snowed in and trying to figure out how to clear the runway. In a brainstorming session, someone made the crazy suggestion of putting a big frog on top of the control tower so that its tongue could push the snow away. From this crazy idea emerged the one that worked: they used jet engines to blow the snow away.

PS-ROs are creative in their use of this tool; they recognise when they need to be 'crazy' and open things up, they support the (sometimes mad) ideas that are generated and build upon each other's ideas.

Some other types of brainstorming are:

- Reverse brainstorming – limber up the creativity muscles – 'brainstorm' how NOT to do something. For instance, brainstorm something that won't carry water …
- Edward De Bono's *Six Thinking Hats*[178] – this provides a structure to help you think about an issue or challenge from different perspectives.

- Mind mapping[179] – looks at the connections to an idea or challenge. Visualise what it looks like and expand your thinking.

Brainstorming is important in a PS-RO as part of innovation.

Rapid prototyping

As Collins and Porras said in *Built to Last*,[180] 'try a lot of stuff and keep what works'. PS-ROs go around the Plan–Do cycle often (see Figure 14.8) and build such thinking into their organisations; they accept that mistakes will be made and learned from. They Plan what they want to try out, they Do it, they Assess how it worked, make Adjustments and Redefine before repeating the cycle. This rapid prototyping is applied not just to physical products but also to processes and organisation design. Often we don't know how things will work out due to the ambiguity and uncertainty

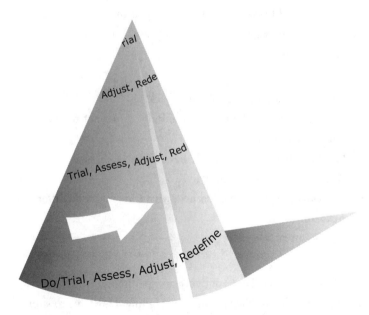

Figure 14.8 The Plan–Do cycle

surrounding us. A PS-RO will start small and try something. It will quickly get feedback so that it can adjust and try again.

Knowledge management in groups
Knowledge management for an individual group is much easier to get a picture of than that between different groups or an entire organisation. In a co-located PS-RO, it is likely to happen by itself because of the type of organisation it is. In a virtual or dispersed group, the need and the processes are similar to those in a '99' or '95' organisation.

Leadership development
In groups, leadership development is around developing the team members and managing their performance. PS-ROs need people who are motivated, creative and bring their energy and enthusiasm to their work. This is – of course – helped by the Values that all PS-ROs have – respect, responsibility and co-operation. PS-RO leaders know how to give feedback:

- Check that it is OK to give feedback.
- Keep the hero in the person in mind – you want to encourage people to bloom.
- Give feedback on observable behaviour.
- Ask what happened, not 'why?'
- Ask what the person has learned, what they might do differently next time.
- Ask how you can help.

A PS-RO leader listens actively and perceptively, summarising and paraphrasing to check his understanding. He wants to support his team members and to enable and encourage creative, sharing behaviour.

Getting around blocking influences

It would be an unusual organisation where there are no blocking influences. These usually boil down to an individual or group of individuals. The first step is to identify where the blockages are, and to do this you map the stakeholders to see who might be involved with or affected by your project. You need to identify where you want them to be with respect to the project – do they need to have knowledge of it? Do they need to support it? How actively? What do you need to do to ensure this? A useful tool is a Key Stakeholder List (see Figure 14.9). Each person is listed and by the 'traffic lights' you can immediately see where work is needed; those with red or yellow 'lights' are not where you need them to be and require effort to get them to the necessary level of involvement. What that work might be is identified under the action list. In complex projects it is useful to be able to quickly identify where there are blockages.

Then you will need to work with them on an individual basis, identifying why they are against the project. In Chapter 13 we discussed how knowing and managing yourself would enable you

Key Stakeholder List -Ongoing Updates						
				Involvement		Action: when and whom
Stakeholder group	Name	Function	Role	Target Level	Current Level	Action Required
Executive Team	Harry Smith	EXEC	CEO	Buy-in	Awareness	Briefing session
Executive Assistant	Jeremy Little	EXEC	EA	Understand	Awareness	Follow up conversation
Steering Board	John Doe	Business devt	Director of Business Development	Ownership	Buy-in	Weekly 1 on 1 contact
Directors	Mary Smith	Director	Financial Director	Buy-in	Awareness	1 on 1 briefing
Directors	Janet Clarke	Director	Technology	Buy-in	Awareness	Project communications
Advocate	David Jones	Divisional Head	Head of Europe	Advocate	??	Teleconference/ regular email
Advocate	Danielle Farar	Divisional Head	Head of Asia-Pacific	Advocate		1 on 1 briefing

Figure 14.9 Key Stakeholder List

to have awareness of others and manage the relationship. Approaching people with respect and co-operation – key Values of a PS-RO – you can then do what Stephen Covey recommends, 'seek first to understand, then to be understood'.[181] Even if there is what may seem to be a negative outburst, there is likely to be a positive motivation behind it if you can uncover it.

Executive Summary

- The Machinery of a PS-RO is what enables renewal: this Machinery links into the formal planning system through the Three Ring Circus.
- Machinery has five interlocking parts – processes, ICT, communication, knowledge management and people.
- PS-ROs understand the difference between failure and feedback and capture the learning which can result.
- Partnering and collaboration are key to a PS-RO's success, at Board level and all the way through the organisation.
- A PS-RO uses any opportunity for people to work across silos and functions, either face-to-face or virtually. The Machinery used may differ depending on the size and complexity of the organisation.

Conclusion: A Purposeful Self-Renewing Organisation

We hope that we have given you a strong sense of what your organisation would be able to achieve when transformed into a PS-RO. As we have said earlier, installing the component parts of a PS-RO is not particularly expensive. We believe the benefits are obvious, if not always directly quantifiable. However, our experience has shown that there are two main 'hurdles' which crop up frequently.

1. It seems difficult

What needs to be established can seem difficult, complicated. This is a concern which is familiar to anyone who has ever begun to assemble a piece of flat-pack furniture: will I be able to follow the blueprint? Will it all fit together and then work properly?

We can take the same view about an organisation, starting with the fundamental questions: how does an organisation settle on the right blueprint? And: how do we make it work?

Typically, this is done by trial and error. Organisations that face the need to change tend to look for small experiments, harmless areas where they can try an idea out and see if it is for them, for instance develop Insight processes. Activities to increase Insight or clarify Values, even if isolated, will certainly do the organisation no harm. They may, indeed, have the beneficial effect of averting surprises, for example, and any increase in overall clarity is always welcome.

However, without the integrated Machinery, they will not generate the great flood of ideas and potential which is found in a mature PS-RO. It is, therefore, better to set up a 'thin' version of the entire structure, and then adjust this to fit the organisation's needs, than to begin with piecemeal implementation of the component qualities of a PS-RO. Few things are more irritating than good analysis that is never used, for example.

2.   Impact on the rest of the organisation

The second area of concern revolves around what this new engine may do to the organisation. Can we control it, or will it run away with us? Do we really want to give our organisation a mind of its own? Indeed, is it possible to introduce this to sceptical colleagues, people who may view it as a diversion?

Anyone thinking of implementation needs to consider how a PS-RO structure will affect current systems of decision making. Its entire purpose is to deploy many more of the organisation's minds on issues that were previously confined to a small, elite group.

Naturally, this has its implications; it is a challenge to the existing powers. Also, it is quite impossible to anticipate the overall effect that such changes will have on the organisation. But PS-RO structures generate new potential, new ideas and new insights; that is precisely why they are needed, because new potential, new ideas and new insights are the only way to get strong, purposeful renewal. To state the obvious: if the organisation knew the correct options in advance, then it would not need the dispersed analysis and idea generation.

This unpredictability can make organisations resistant to the first steps into this new way of working. Authority may feel challenged. People who adhere to current ways of doing things may feel insecure. However, the changes that we propose are chiefly concerned with social transactions: with how people exchange information, and what they do with it. Creating a PS-RO is as much a social as an organisational task. For some, this may make the idea of moving towards a PS-RO less daunting, perhaps, less threatening.

Fact: Staying still is not a possible answer

This sounds like a challenge. It is a challenge. However, staying still is simply not a possible solution. The economic slow-down will leave many existing organisations in the West weak and outflanked. Renewal is the only way of avoiding this, and of thriving.

Let us recap finally and very briefly how you can help to ensure your organisation will be one to thrive:

- What you need is purposeful ingenuity, ideas that are bred from deep Insight, from strong Values and clear Options.
- To put this in place, you need formal Machinery.
- You also need a strong, universal Narrative, a way of shared thinking that allows your people to recognise a good thing when they see it in its embryonic form.

As we stated at the beginning of this book: the organisation of the future needs to be one with the desire and the will to create an environment which encourages and enables a whole organisation to take charge of its destiny.

Dear Reader: nothing less will do the job.

Additional sources of help

There are a number of sources which provide a core library for senior managers in developing their own PS-RO: our favourites are listed below.

Values

The Seven Habits of Highly Effective People, Stephen R. Covey, 1989.
The Eighth Habit, Stephen R. Covey, 2004.
Built to Last, Jim Collins and Jerry Porras, 2005.

Insight

The Art of the Long View, Peter Schwartz, 1991.
The Mind of a Fox: Scenario Planning in Action, Chantell Illbury and Clem Sunter, 2001.
The Living Company, Arie de Geus, 2002.
Scenario Planning: Managing for the Future, 2nd edn, Gill Ringland, 2006.
http://www.chforum.org

Options

Crossing the Chasm: Marketing and Selling High-tech Products to Mainstream Customers, Geoffrey Moore, 1991 (revised 1999).

10 Rules for Strategic Innovators, Vijay Govindarajan and Chris Trimble, 2005.

The Medici Effect, Frans Johansson, 2006.

Narrative

The Tree of Knowledge, Humberto R. Maturana and Francisco J. Varela, 1987.

Dialogue and the Art of Thinking Together, William Isaacs, 1999.

The Power of the Tale: Using narratives for organisational success, Julie Allan, Gerard Fairtlough and Barbara Heinzen, 2002.

Machinery

Leadership: The inner side of greatness, Peter Koestenbaum, 1991.

The Fifth Discipline Fieldbook: Strategies and tools for building a learning organization, Peter Senge, Richard Ross, Bryan Smith, Art Kleiner and Charlotte Roberts, 1994.

The Art of Possibility: Transforming professional and personal life, Rosamund Stone Zander and Benjamin Zander, 2000.

Learning to Fly: Practical knowledge management from leading and learning organizations, Chris Collison and Geoff Parcell, 2004.

Understanding the Knowledgeable Organization: Nurturing knowledge competence, Jane McKenzie and Christine van Winkelen, 2004.

Guide to Organisation Design: Creating high-performing and adaptable enterprises, Naomi Stanford, 2007.

The Five Literacies of Global Leadership: What authentic leaders know and you need to find out, Richard David Hames, 2007.

Good to Great, Jim Collins, 2001.

http://www.chforum.org/book/index.html is the website for the book.

The forum of the Challenge Network at http://www.chforum.org documents 15 years of public contributions to global scenario generation.

Endnotes

1. Berlin, Isaiah, *Hedgehog and Fox*, Simon and Schuster, 1953.
2. Gerstner, Louis V Jr, *Who Said Elephants Can't Dance*, Harper PaperBacks, 2004.
3. Tett, Gillian, *Fools Gold*, Little, Brown, 2009.
4. Sparrow, Oliver, 2009 (see http://www.chforum.org).
5. Sparrow, Oliver, 2009 (see http://www.chforum.org).
6. Corrado, C.A., Hulten, C.R. and Sichel, D.E., National Bureau for Economic Research, US Department of Labor, 2005.
7. Derived by one of the authors (OHGS) from data published by FTC & Thomson Financial Securities, 2009.
8. Derived by one of the authors (OHGS) from data published by *Financial Times*, 2009 and IMF, 2009.
9. Derived by one of the authors (OHGS) from data published by *Financial Times*, 2009.
10. Derived by one of the authors (OHGS) from data published by OECD, 2009.
11. Derived by one of the authors (OHGS) from data published by Challenge Network, 2009; Dow Jones, 2008; OECD, 2008.
12. Derived by one of the authors (OHGS) from data published by Barclays Capital Management, 2009.
13. Derived by one of the authors (OHGS) from data published by National Bureau of Economic Research, 2008.
14. Flatters, Paul and Willmott, Michael, 'Understanding the post-recession consumer', *Harvard Business Review*, **Jul/Aug**, 2009.

15. Derived by one of the authors (OHGS) from data published by Credit Suisse, 2009.

16. Reich, Robert B., 'Government in your business', *Harvard Business Review*, Jul/Aug, 2009.

17. World Bank, 'Youth and Unemployment in Africa: The Potential, The Problem, The Promise', 2009.

18. Challenge Network calculations based on World Bank data.

19. See http://www.archive.official-documents.co.uk/dti/dti-comp/chap6.htm

20. See http://www.archive.official-documents.co.uk/dti/dti-comp/chap6.htm

21. See the website, http://www.worldbank.org/reference

22. Haidt, Jonathan, 'The new synthesis in moral psychology', *Science*, **316**: 998–1002, 2007.

23. Carruthers, P., Laurence, S. and Stich, S. (eds), 'The moral mind: How 5 sets of innate moral intuitions guide the development of many culture-specific virtues, and perhaps even modules'. *The Innate Mind*, Vol. 3; see also http://www.moralfoundations.org

24. Herrmann, Benedikt, Christian, Thöni and Simon, Gächter, 'Antisocial punishment across societies', *Science*, **7**: 1362–1367, 2008.

25. http://ibm.com/uk/smarterplanet/topics/intelligence

26. See, for instance, the statement by President Molly Corbett Broad, American Council on Education, http://www.acenet.edu/AM/Template.cfm?Section=Home&TEMPLATE/CM/ContentDisplay.cfm&ContentID=30490

27. Edwards, Sebastian, Discussion Paper No. 4, 'Foundation for Research, Science and Technology', Wellington, 1996; see http://www.treasury.govt.nz/publications/media-speeches/guestlectures/edwards-mar06

28. Funding First, http://www.laskerfoundation.org/advocacy/pdf/exceptional.pdf, 2000.

29. Porter, Michael E., *The Competitive Advantage of Nations*, McMillan Business, 1998.

30. Scherngell, T., Fischer, M.M. and Reismann, M., 'Total factor productivity effects of interregional knowledge spillovers in

manufacturing industries across Europe', *Rumanian Journal of Regional Science*, 1, 2007 (http://www.rrsa.ro/rjrs/N1-FISCHER.pdf).

31. http://www.chforum.org

32. *The World in 2025*, European Commission, January 2009; obtainable via http://bookshop.europa.eu

33. Sparrow, Oliver, 'Open Horizons', Royal Institute of International Affairs, 10 St James Square, London SW1Y 4LE, 1998.

34. Ringland, Gill, *Scenario Planning*, 2nd edn, John Wiley & Sons, 2006.

35. http://www.chforum.org

36. Drucker, P.F., *Management: Tasks, Responsibilities, Practices*, Heinemann, 1974, p. 181.

37. Porter, M.E., *On Competition*, updated and expanded edition, Harvard Business School Press, 2008.

38. Hamel, Gary and Prahalad, C.K., *Competing for the Future*, Harvard Business School Press, 1996.

39. Corrado, C., Hulten, C. and Sichel, D., 'Measuring capital and technology, an expanded framework'. In *Measuring Capital and Technology: An Expanded Framework*, National Bureau of Economic Research, 2005.

40. From a conversation with R.D. Hames, 2009.

41. 'TQM, ISO 9000, and Six Sigma: Do Process Management Programs Discourage Innovation?', Knowledge@Wharton, 30 November 2005; http://knowledge.wharton.upenn.edu

42. Smith, Adam, *An Inquiry into the Nature and Causes of the Wealth of Nations*, first published 1776; republished as *Wealth of Nations: Books I–III*, Adam Smith and Adam Skinner, Penguin Classics, 2003.

43. Pisano, Gary B. and Shih, Willy C., 'Restoring American competitiveness', *Harvard Business Review*, Jul/Aug, 2009.

44. Rangan, V.K. and Bowman, G.T., 'Beating the commodity magnet', *Industrial Marketing Management*, 21, pp. 215–224, 1992; http://www.emeraldinsight.com

45. Holmes, Andrew, *Commoditisation and the Strategic Response*, Gower, 2008.

46. Emmons, Garry, 'The New International Style of Management', 2005; http://hbswk.hbs.edu/archive/4893.html

47. Emery, Fred and Trist, Eric, *Toward a Social Ecology*, Plenum, 1972.

48. *Tomorrow's Global Company: The Challenges and Choices*, 2005. Available from Tomorrow's Company, NIOC House, 4 Victoria St., London SWI ONE.

49. Miller, Danny and Friesen, Peter H. with Mintzberg, Henry, *Organizations: A Quantum View*, Prentice-Hall, 1984.

50. Ely, R.J. and Thomas, D.A., 'Cultural diversity at work: the effects of diversity perspectives on work group processes', *Administrative Science Quarterly*, 2001; http://www.jstor.org/pss/2667087

51. Reh, F.J., 'Matrix Management', http://management.about.com/od

52. Definition in Encarta World Dictionary, http://www.msn.com/encnet/features/dictionary.

53. A measure of volatility used widely in assessing the value of a stock.

54. *The Economist*, 19 September 2009.

55. A skunkworks is a group of people who, in order to achieve unusual results, work on a project in a way that is outside the usual rules.

56. Voss, Chris, 'Viewpoint', *International Journal of Operations & Production Management*, **18**, 2, pp. 114–130, 1998.

57. McKinsey, 'When to make India a manufacturing base', *McKinsey Quarterly*, June 1997.

58. 'Living Innovation', Design Council and dti, Admail 528, London SW1W 8YT, 2000.

59. Orihata, M. and Watanabe, C., 'Evolutional dynamics of product innovation: the case of consumer electronics', *Technovation*, **20**(8): 437–449, 2000.

60. Brody, A.L. and Lord, J.B., *Developing New Food Products for a Changing Marketplace*, CRC Press, 1999.

61. IBM, Global CEO Study, http://www.O3.ibm.com/press/US/en/pressrelease/19289.wss, 2006.

62. Rosnow, R.L., 'Hedgehogs, Foxes, and the evolving social contract in psychological science: Ethical challenges and methodological opportunities', *Psychological Methods*, **2**(4): 345–356, 1997.

63. Illbury, Chantell and Sunter, Clem, *The Mind of a Fox: Scenario Planning in Action*, Human & Rousseau (Pty) Ltd, 2001.

64. Ringland, Gill, 'Software engineering in a development group', *Software Practice and Experience*, 14 October 1984.

65. *McKinsey Quarterly*, September 2007.

66. Kostenbaum, Peter, *Leadership: The Inner Side of Greatness*, Jossey-Bass, 1991, p. 13.

67. Zander, R.S. and Zander, B., *The Art of Possibility: Transforming Professional and Personal Life*, Penguin, 2000.

68. Citation in Thomas, Martin, in *Business Planning for Turbulent Times*, Ramirez, R., Selsky, J.W. and van der Heijden, K. (eds), Earthscan Publications Ltd, 2008.

69. Rooke, D. and Torbert, W.R., 'Strategists and alchemists per seven transformations of leadership', *Harvard Business Review*, **Apr**, 2005.

70. Heifetz, R., Grashow, A. and Linsky, M., 'Leadership in a (permanent) crisis', *Harvard Business Review*, **Jul/Aug**, 2009.

71. Heifetz, R., Grashow, A. and Linsky, M., 'Leadership in a (permanent) crisis', *Harvard Business Review*, **Jul/Aug**, 2009.

72. Muir, H., 'Email traffic patterns can reveal ringleaders', *New Scientist*, 27 March 2003; http://www.newscientist.com/ article/dn3550-email-traffic-patterns-can-reveal-ringleaders.html

73. Zander, R.S. and Zander, B., *The Art of Possibility: Transforming Professional and Personal Life*, Penguin, 2000.

74. http://www.cipd.co.uk/subjects/perfmangmt/competences/ comptfrmwk.htm

75. Larson, C.E. and LaFasto, F.M.J., *TeamWork: What must go right/what can go wrong*, Sage, 1989; Hastings, C., Bixby, P. and Chaudry-Lawton, R., *Superteams: A Blueprint for Organisational Success*, Fontana, 1986.

76. Belbin, R. Meredith, *Management Teams: Why They Succeed or Fail*, 2nd edn, Butterworth-Heinemann, 2004.

77. Kanter, R.M., *Maintenance and Parallel Organisations*, Unwin, 1983.

78. Demers, M.A., 'A Question of Values'; http://www.mademers.com/ files/LivingValues.pdf, 2002.

79. Griffin, L.J., 'Narrative, event-structure analysis, and causal interpretation in historical sociology', *American Journal of Sociology*, **98**(5): 1094–1133, 1993.

80. Collins, J. and Porras, J.I., *Built to Last: Successful Habits of Visionary Companies*, Random House Business Books, 2005.

81. *The Economist*, 29 August 2009.

82. Ingvar, D.H., 'Memory of the future', *Human Neurobiology*, **4**: 127–136, 1985.

83. http://www.businessdictionary.com

84. Collins, J. and Porras, J.I., *Built to Last: Successful Habits of Visionary Companies*, Random House Business Books, 2005.

85. http://call.army.mil/products/thesaur/00007503.htm

86. Kaufman, H., 'Values as Foundation: The Role of Values in Leadership and Organizations'; http://www.leader-values.com/Content/detail.asp?ContentDetailID=909, 2005.

87. Demers, M.A., 'A Question of Values'; http://www.mademers.com/files/LivingValues.pdf, 2002.

88. Pedlar, M. (ed.), *Action Learning in Practice*, 2nd edn, Gower, 1991; Lustig, P.M. and Rai, D.R., 'Action learning in ActionAid Nepal: a case study', *Action Learning Research and Practice*, Vol. **6**, No. 2, Routledge, 2009.

89. Collins, J. and Porras, J.I., *Built to Last: Successful Habits of Visionary Companies*, Random House Business Books, 2005.

90. Holman, P., Devane, T., Cady, S. and Associates, *The Change Handbook*, Berrett-Koehler Publishers, Inc., 2006.

91. http://www.themanager.org/pdf/BostonBox

92. http://www.weforum.org

93. http://www.foresight.gov.uk

94. http://www.chforum.org

95. http://www.dni.gov/nic/NIC_2025_global_scenarios.html

96. Gladwell, Malcolm, *The Tipping Point: How Little Things can Make a Big Difference*, Abacus, 2002.

97. Schultz, Wendy, 'The cultural contradictions of managing change – using horizon scanning in an evidence-based policy context', *Foresight*, **8**(4), 2006.

98. *McKinsey Quarterly*, 'Cracking the Complexity Code', May 2007.

99. Martin, B.R. and Irvine, J., *Research Foresight: Priority Setting in Science*, Pinter, 1989, p. 154.

100. Taleb, N.N., *The Black Swan*, Random House, 2007.

101. Ringland, Gill, *Scenario Planning*, 2nd edn, John Wiley & Sons, 2006.

102. Ringland, Gill and Young, Laurie (eds), *Scenarios in Marketing*, John Wiley & Sons, 2006.

103. Ringland, Gill, 'Scenario planning: persuading operating managers to take ownership', *Strategy & Leadership*, **31**(6), 2003.

104. http://www.hse.gov.uk/research/rrpdf/rr600.pdf

105. Ringland, Gill, *Scenario Planning*, 2nd edn, John Wiley & Sons, 2006.

106. Porter, Michael, *On Competition*, Harvard Business Press, 2008.

107. Tata Nano; http://www.wikipedia.org/wiki/Tata_Nano

108. Kotler, P. and Keller, K., *Marketing Management*, Pearson, 2009.

109. Buzzell, R.D. and Gale, B.T., *The PIMS Principles: Linking Strategy to Performance*, Free Press, 1987.

110. Ministry of Foreign Affairs, Denmark, 2004.

111. Alavi, Maryam and Leidner, Dorothy E., 'Review: Knowledge management and knowledge management systems: conceptual foundations and research issues', *MIS Quarterly* **25**(1), 2001.

112. McKenzie, J. and van Winkelen, C., *Understanding the Knowledgeable Organization: Nurturing Knowledge Competence*, Thomson, 2007.

113. Christensen, C.M., Anthony, S.D. and Roth, E.A., *Seeing What is Next*, Harvard Business School Press, 2004.

114. A term used in the military, e.g. Echevarria, Antulio J., *Clausewitz's Center of Gravity: It's Not What We Thought*, Naval War College Press, 2003.

115. Gartner, Alan, Mary Conway, Kohler and Frank Riessman, Harper, *Children teach children. Learning by Teaching*, Harper & Row, New York, 1971.

116. Owen, H., *Open Space Technology: A User's Guide*, Berrett-Koehler, 2008.

117. Lustig, P.M., Rossi, K. and McKergow, M., 'A Comparison of Appreciative Inquiry (Ai) and Solutions Focus (SF)', Appreciative Inquiry Commons, 2003; found at http://appreciativeinquiry.case.edu/research/bibPapersDetail.cfm?coid=3231

118. Ringland, Gill, *Scenarios in Public Policy*, John Wiley & Sons, 2002.

119. From a conversation with Professor Peter McKiernan, University of St. Andrews.

120. Derek Wanless Report, 'Securing Our Future Health: Taking a Long-Term View', 2002; http://www.webarchive.nationalarchive. gov.uk

121. Bartlett, John, *Managing Risk for Projects and Programmes: A Risk Management Handbook*, Project Manager Today Publications, 2002.

122. http://www.scenariosforsustainability.org

123. There is a good discussion at http://en.wikipedia.org/wiki/Feedback

124. http://www.chforum.org

125. http://www.aidsscenarios.unaids.org/scenarios

126. Eve, Raymond A., Horsefall, Sara and Mary, E., *Chaos, Complexity and Sociology*, Sage, 1997.

127. Johansson, Frans, *The Medici Effect: What Elephants and Epidemics can Teach us about Innovation*, Harvard Business Press, 2006.

128. http://harvardbusiness.org/product/is-it-real-can-we-win-is-it-worth-doing-managing-r/an/R0712J-PDF-ENG?Ntt=george%2520day

129. Sichel, Bernardo, 'Strategic options: Transforming strategic insight into competitive advantage', http://www.thinkdsi.com/newsletter/2_1/

130. Chim, W. Kan and Mauborgne, Rene, *Harvard Business Review*, Reprint R0407P, 1997.

131. Zook, Chris, *Profit from the Core: Growth Strategy in an Era of Turbulence*, Harvard Business Press, 2004.

132. http://widstudio.wordpress.com

133. FutureMapping; see http://www.futuremap.com

134. Appelbaum, Eileen, 'High Performance Work Practices and Economic Recovery', 2008; http://lerablog.org/29/03/09/high-performance-work-practices-and-economic-recovery/

135. Harden, Erika, Krus, Douglas L. and Blasi, Joseph R., 'Who Has a Better Idea? Innovation, Shared Capitalism, and HR Policies', NBER Working Paper No. 14234, 2008; http://www.nber.org/papers/w14234.pdf

136. http://proceedings.esri.com/library/userconf/pug06/papers/en, Casey, 2006.

137. Moore, Geoffrey A., 'To succeed in the long term, focus on the middle term', *Harvard Business Review*, **Jul/Aug**, 2007.

138. Moore, Geoffrey A., *Crossing the Chasm: Marketing and Selling High-tech Products to Mainstream Customer*, First Collins Business Essentials Edition, 1991, revised 1999, 2006.

139. Rivas, Rio and Gobeli, David H., 'Accelerating innovation at Hewlett-Packard: a case study identifies significant enablers as well as barriers to innovation, along with management lessons for speeding the process', *Research-Technology Management*, **Jan/Feb**, 2005.

140. Bogsnes, Bjarte, *Implementing Beyond Budgeting: Unlocking the Performance Potential*, John Wiley & Sons, 2008.

141. Bryan, Lowell L. and Joyce, Claudia L., *Mobilizing Minds: Creating Wealth from Talent in the 21st Century Organization*, McGraw-Hill, 2007.

142. Kotler, Philip and Armstrong, Gary, *Principles of Marketing* (7th edition), Prentice-Hall, 1996.

143. Hewlett, Silvia Ann, *Top Talent: Keeping Performance up when Business is Down*, Harvard Business Press, 2009.

144. Cook, Niall and Tapscott, Don, *Enterprise 2.0: How Social Software Will Change the Future of Work*, Gower, 2008.

145. Argyris, C., *Overcoming Organizational Defences: Facilitating Organizational Learning*, Prentice-Hall, 1990, pp. 87–89.

146. DiaLogos Flame Model; see http://www.learninggroup.org/may05notes.doc, 2005.

147. Campbell, J., *The Hero with a Thousand Faces*, Fontana Press, 1949.

148. Allan, J., Fairtlough, G. and Heinzen, B., *The Power of the Tale: Using Narratives for Organisational Success*, John Wiley & Sons, 2001.

149. Artifex and Optifex, 'The Causes of Decay in a British Industry', Bibliolife 2009.

150. Lawler, E.E. and Worley, C.G., *Built to Change: How to Achieve Sustained Organizational Effectiveness*, Jossey-Bass, 2006.

151. Brews, Peter and Devravat, Purohit, 'Strategic planning in unstable environments', *Long Range Planning*, **40**: 64–83, 2007.

152. Moynagh, Michael and Worsley, Richard, 'Working in the Twentieth Century', Economic and Social Research Council, 2005.

153. 'Global Trends for intranets 2010'; http://www.netjmc.net/intranet-trends/

154. See http://www.cornucopia.org/2007/11/23-organizations-critique-wal-mart-sustainability-initiatives/ for an example of a consumer organisation critiquing a major company.

155. See, for instance, http://deals.venturebeat.com/2009/07/10/has-enterprise-software-has-always-been-terrible-gnips-eric-marcoullier-says-yes/

156. http://en.wikipedia.org/wiki/Metcalfe%27s_law

157. Shirky, Clay, 2009; http://www.shirky.com/writings/group_enemy.html

158. Kleiner, A., *Who Really Matters: The Core Group Theory of Power, Privilege, and Success*, Doubleday, 2003.

159. Lodorfos, Gorge and Boateng, A., 'The role of culture in the merger and acquisition process: evidence from the European chemical industry', *Management Decision*, **44**(10): 1405–1421, 2006.

160. Honig-Haftel, Sandra and Martin, Linda R., 'The effectiveness of reward systems on innovative output: an empirical analysis', *Small Business Economics*, **5**(4): 261–269, 1993.

161. Bartlett, Christopher A. and Ghoshal, Sumantra, *Transnational Management: Text, Cases and Readings in Cross-Border Management*, 2nd edn, Irwin McGraw-Hill, 1995, pp. 427–447.

162. Senge, Peter, *The Fifth Discipline*, Doubleday, 1990.

163. LeBaron, Michelle, *Bridging Cultural Conflicts: New Approaches for a Changing World*, Jossey-Bass, 2003.

164. Cook, N., *Enterprise 2.0: How Social Software will Change the Future of Work*, Gower, 2008.

165. Rockstrom, J., 'A safe operating space for hewarity', *Nature*, **461** pp. 472–475, September 2009.

166. http://www.brownecenter.com/dennis.html

167. Lustig, P.M., 2008; http://www.lasadev.com/newsletters/newsletter_13.htm

168. Stanford, Naomi, *Guide to Organisation Design*, Economist Books, 2007.

169. Lustig, P.M., 2003, 2008; see http://www.lasadev.com

170. Brown, Juanita and Isaacs, David, *The World Café: Shaping our Futures through Conversations that Matter*, Berrett-Koehler, 2005.

171. Stanford, Naomi, *Guide to Organisation Design*, Economist Books, 2007.

172. Stanford, Naomi, *Guide to Organisation Design*, Economist Books, 2007.

173. Survey Monkey; see http://www.surveymonkey.com

174. Davenport, Thomas R. and Prusak, Laurence, *Working Knowledge: How Organizations Manage What They Know*, Harvard Business School Press, 2000.

175. Senge, Peter, Ross, Richard, Smith, Bryan, Roberts, Charlotte, and Kleiner, Art, *The Fifth Discipline Fieldbook*, Nicholas Brealey, 1994.

176. Lustig, P.M., 'Leading Through Facilitation', http://www.lasadev.com/newsletters/newsletter_09.htm, 2008; Schwarz, R., Davidson, A., Cartson, P. and McKinney, S., *The Skilled Facilitator Fieldbook*, Jossey-Bass, 2005.

177. Gerber, Michael E., *The e-myth*, Harper Business, 1991.

178. De Bono, E., *Six Thinking Hats*, Penguin, 1999.

179. Buzan, T. and Buzan, B., *The Mind Map Book*, BBC Active, 2006.

180. Collins, J. and Porras, J.I., *Built to Last: Successful Habits of Visionary Companies*, Random House Business Books, 2005.

181. Covey, Stephen R., *The Seven Habits of Highly Effective People*, Simon & Schuster, 1989.

Index

Note: Page numbers in *italics* refer to figures and tables. The abbreviation PS-RO is used for Purposeful Self-Renewing Organisation.

'95' organisation 74, 287–9

'99' organisation 74, 289–92

adaptability of organisations 70–3

Africa 31, 32, 211

ageing population 29–31

Argyris, Chris 242–4

Asia 18, 26, 30, 32, 113–14

Korean innovation 85–6

see also China; India; Japan

assessing organisations, tools for 144–5, 177–8, 232–4

audits 117, 179, 193–202

banking sector

bailouts of banks 22–3, 43–4

role in financial crisis 18–23

scenarios for future crisis resolution 44–5, 51–3

behaviours

aligning values to 169, 171–2, 198–9

measuring 166–72

supporting a PS-RO 172–3

benign neglect 18

Berlin, Isaiah 9, 87

Best Buy, leadership 99

boom and bust 22–3

borrowing 20–1

and debt 23–8

Boston box 177–8

brainstorming 288–9, 294–5

brands 155, 251

Bryan, Lowell 232, 234

budgeting 219, 230–1

CEO, role of 97–8

Challenge Network forum website 41, 54, 145, 209, 303

change
    anticipating 139–40, 199–200
    in balance of power 45–6
    demographic 29–31
    technological and scientific
        39–40, 200
    see also organisational change
China 30–1, 32, 34, 140–1, 216
Christensen, Clayton M. 199–200
Christian Aid 135–6
Cisco 131–2
collateralised debt obligations
    (CDOs) 20–1, 22
'Commander's Intent' 152
commoditisation 4, 61, 67–9,
    88–9
    and renewal 77–9
communication
    and development of Narrative
        255–6
    methods & tools to encourage
        271–2, 278–83
    as a PS-RO process 273, 277–9
    role of Insight 206–8
    scenarios aiding dialogue
        209–11
competence(s) 5–6, 9, 101–2, 167,
    201–2
    assessing 168–71
    extraordinary 102–3, 162–6,
        222–3
    of people in a PS-RO 286
competition 2–4
    analysis of current position
        191–3

anticipating external change
    199–200
birth of new management style
    62
and commoditisation 67–9
comparison of core Values with
    155
consequences of outsourcing 65
as example of purpose-setting
    103–5
facilitation improving 292–4
use of mental models 208
complexity, managing 65–6, 73
consumer debt 23–6, 43–5
consumerism 17–18, 25–6
'Consumers' 47, 54
corporate social responsibility
    (CSR) 210–11
creativity *see* ideas; innovation
cultural differences
    functional 73, 100–1, 278
    societal 35–8, 165–6

D2D case study 115–16
Day, George 218
debt 2–3
    consumer 23–6, 43–5
    equities 26–7
    government role 27–8
decision making 117–19
    mind mapping, as aid to 288–9
    role of facilitation 292–3
    role of Values 151–2, 154
    by senior management and
        CEO 96–8

Delphi forecasting 182–3
demographic changes 29–31
deregulation 17, 19
'destinations'
  in five qualities of a PS-RO
    107–8
  in purpose-setting 103–5
diagnostic tools 144–5, 177–8,
    232–4
dialogue, enabling 271–2
disruptive innovation theory
    199–200
'domain spanners' 142–3, 179
double cone framework 4–5
  for Foxes and Hedgehogs of
    renewal 89–93
  incorporating the Three Ring
    Circus 7–8, 123–6
  linking with PS-RO qualities 7,
    117–19
  as part of planning cycle 133–5
  and processes 120–1, 264–5
Dow Corning 293
Dow Jones index 16

Eastern Europe 17–18
economic development 32–8
  effects of knowledge growth
    39–40
  predictions for the future
    43–57
  Western economies 17, 23–8,
    34
employment 17, 25
energy matrix 161–2

environmental issues 40–1, 210,
    281
equities 21, 26–7
experimental economics 37–8
extraordinary competence 102–3,
    162–6, 222–3

facilitation 292–4
financial crisis
  reasons for 2, 15–18
  role of banking sector 18–23
  role of debt 23–8
  scenarios for resolution of
    long term 51–6
    medium term 45–51
    short term 43–5
    value of 56–7
forecasting 182–5
Fox management type 9
  characteristics 86–9, 184–5
  in double cone framework
    89–93

Germany 81, 82
global issues
  changing balance of power 29,
    45–6
  economic growth 32–5
  emerging middle class values
    35–7
  population growth 29–31
  possible evolution of nations
    48–50
  systemic challenges 40–2, 50
Google, idea generation 79–80

government action, call for 27–8
groups
    competence within 5–6,
        101–2
    differences between 279
    elitism within 277
    and Insight 211–12
    large-group interventions
        289–91
    Machinery for effectiveness of
        292
        blocking influences, getting
            round 297–8
        brainstorming 294–5
        facilitation 292–4
        knowledge management 296
        leadership 296
        rapid prototyping 295–6
        social networking 276–7
        workshops 292
    and Narrative 255–6, 260
    and Values 163

Hedgehog management type 9
    characteristics 86–9, 184–5
    in double cone framework
        89–93
hedging risk 19–20
Hero's Journey, lifeline tool
    245–9
High Road scenario 3, *51*, 53, *54*,
    55–6
Horizon 2 projects 226–8
horizon scanning 32–3, 179–81
house prices 26

ICT *see* information technology
    (IT)
ideas
    brainstorming 288–9, 294–5
    case study, Google 79–80
    champions of 221–3
    external sources of 84–6,
        143–4, 209–10
    gap-filling 223
    and horizon scanning 181
    in a PS-RO 215–17, 219, 224
    tools 222, 223–5, 269–70
    see also innovation
India 30–1, 34, 81, *82*, 165–6,
    280
inflation 2, 16–17, 24, 26
information
    flows 126–8
    making sense of 240–1
information technology (IT)
    62–3
    role of ICT 275–7
    scenarios 115–16, 204–6
innovation
    case studies 85–6, 219
    disruptive 199–200
    effect of TQM 63–4
    in established organisations
        226–8
    hurdles to 82–6
    and Narrative 114, 240, 257
    and Options 213, 214, 218–28
    roadmaps as tool for 225
    role of leaders 101
    see also ideas

Insight 115, 175–6
    additional resources 302
    case studies 33, 115–16, 181–2,
        189, 196, 198, 204–7, 210,
        211
    in competitive environment
        analysis of current position
            190–3
        anticipating external change
            199–200
    costs of gaining 81–2
    deliverables from 208
    in double cone framework 116,
        119, 121, 175, 212
    gathering 202–8
    generators of 143
    and group reflection 211–12
    and growth 70
    identifying strengths &
        weaknesses 201–2
    internal and external 117
    methods for developing 178–9
        forecasting 182–5
        horizon scanning 33, 179–81,
            212, 291
        scenarios 176–7, 186–90,
            208–9
    relationship to other PS-RO
        qualities 6, 107–8, 109,
        177–8
    role in communication 206–8
    and the Three Ring Circus
        209–12, 267–70
    tools 177, 178, 180, 186–7, 196,
        197, 198–9

interest rates 2, 18, 23, 25
investment 27, 64, 79, 228–34

Japan
    Foresight projects 183
    product innovation 84
'journeys'
    Hero's Journey, lifeline tool
        245–9
    organisational 103–5

Kanter, Rosabeth Moss 102–3
knowledge
    continuum of 292
    effect on economic growth
        39–40
    filtering 240–1
    information flows 126–8
    tacit 139, 198
    transfer from outsiders
        143–4
knowledge management 198,
    284–5
    in '95'-type organisations
        287–8
    in '99'-type organisations
        291–2
    audit tool 198–9
    in groups 296
    and workers in a PS-RO
        142–4

ladder of inference 242–4
large-group interventions
    289–91

leadership 98–100
  development of 100–1
  in groups 296
  dispersed 98, 100, 102, 173
  and extraordinary competence
    102–3, 162–5
  'facilitative' 293
Low Road scenario 3, 51, 52, 53–4,
  55, 56

Machinery 4–5, 263–4
  and the '95' organisation 287–9
  and the '99' organisation 289–92
  additional resources 303
  case studies 293, 294
  and communications 273,
    277–83
  in double cone framework 118,
    119
  for group effectiveness 276–7,
    289–91, 292–8
  and ICT 275–7
  knowledge management 274,
    284–5, 287–8, 291–2, 296
  and PS-RO processes 119–21,
    274–5
  relationship to other PS-RO
    qualities 6, 107–8, 109,
    177–8
  role of Three Ring Circus
    265–71
    PS-RO added value 271–3
  tools 266–7, 269–70, 271–2,
    282–3, 288–9
  workforce 271, 285–6

Man Group plc 204–5
management see organisational
  management
manufacturing 17, 65, 81–2,
  115–16
Market Attractiveness/Capability
  matrix 232–4
McKinsey Company 81–2, 95–6,
  180
mental models 204–7, 208,
  242–4
  see also scenarios
mergers and acquisitions 18, 19,
  20
Metcalfe's law 275–6
middle class values 35–7
mind mapping 288–9, 295
mining company case studies 33,
  216
modelling 184, 268, 283
  mental models 204–7, 208,
    242–4
Moore, Geoffrey 226–8
moral dimensions of society
  36–8
My Road scenario 3, 51, 52, 54–6

Narrative 111–14, 237–8
  additional resources 303
  case studies 113–14, 135–6,
    244, 252, 260
  definitions of 111, 239–40
  individual narratives 245–9
  information processing 240–1
  and innovation 114, 240, 257

and language 241–2
and mental models 242–4
relationship to other PS-RO
    qualities 6, 107–8, *109*,
    177–8
tools 244, 245–7, 248–9, 253,
    256, 257–8
see also organisational narratives
natural resources, depletion of
    40–1
networking 140, 142, 217, 250,
    257, 287
and the Internet 223, 275–7
neural economics 37–8

Options 117–19, 213–14
additional resources 302
case studies 216, 219, 233–4
in double cone framework 90,
    121
innovation 213, 214, 218–28
iterative learning 216–17
portfolio management
    228–34
in a PS-RO 117–19, 123
relationship to other PS-RO
    qualities 6, 108, *109*
and the Three Ring Circus
    214
timescale by sector 217–18
tools 221, 222, 223–5, 226,
    232–3
organisational assessment, tools
    for 144–5, 177–8, 232–4
organisational audits 195–9

organisational change 270–1
anticipating 139–40, 172, 181
    external change 199–200
    in challenging environment
        69–70, 98–9
and exposure to risk 194–5
overcoming objections to
    138–9
and renewal 123–4
road maps as tools for 225
role of Narrative 240, 241,
    250–1
use of mental models 204–5
organisational management
    and commoditisation 67–9
previous environment
    information technology
        62–3
    outsourcing 64–6
    scientific management 61–2
    shareholder value movement
        64
    total quality management
        (TQM) 63–4
successful organisations 69–70
    archetypes of 70–3
    complexity and size of 73–4
organisational narratives
    249–50
architectural design 258–9
assumptions 254–5
brands 251
clashing 259–60
developing 255–8
emergence of 250–1

enquiry for uncovering 252–4,
    257–8
paradigms 254
scenarios 260
stories 251–2
see also Narrative
organisational renewal see renewal
outsiders, role of 84–6, 135–6,
    143–4, 209–10
outsourcing 64–6, 198, 201
own-account trading 20–1

paradigms 254
planning
    forecasting for short-term 182,
        185
    four types of 274–5
    planning cycles 125–7, 133–5,
        295–6
    role of the Three Ring Circus
        265–7
    strategic 98, 113, 134, 135–6
    timescale by sector 217–18
    see also scenarios
population growth 29–31
Porter's Five Forces 191–2
portfolio management
    case studies 233–4
    changing the portfolio 82
        active management 228–30
        assessing Options 231–4
        linking to budgets 230–1
    and destinations 105
    in double cone framework
        89–91

and innovation 226–8, 270
renewal of portfolio 126–7
    difficulty of 79–80
team work 268–9
in the Three Ring Circus
    124–9, 265–7
tools 232–3, 266–7
positive-sum games 102–3
poverty 31, 41
power, change in balance of 29,
    45–6
product innovation 83–6
productivity
    and commoditisation 67–9
    increase in 17, 62–3, 64–5
profitability 78–9
prototyping 295–6
public sector 193, 218–19, 270
purpose
    clarity of 95–6
    and competence 101–3, 162–3
    and leadership 98–101
    the purposeful organisation
        105–6
    and role of senior management
        96–8
    setting 103–5
    tools 163, 164
Purposeful Self-Renewing
    Organisation (PS-RO) 6,
        8–9, 105–6
    attributes 130
    behaviours for 172–3
    and communication 273,
        277–9

establishment of 133–5
  gaining legitimacy 137
  overcoming hurdles
    299–301
  overcoming objections 138
  staffing 135–6, 285–6
  use of workshops 138–9
five qualities
  in double cone framework 7,
    117–19
  Insight 115–17
  Machinery 119–21
  Narrative 111–14
  Options 117–19
  in planning cycle 133–5
  relationships between 6,
    107–8, *109*, 177–8
  Values 108–11
management of 139
  anticipating change 139–40
  diagnostic tool 144–5
  identifying emerging issues
    140–1
  knowledge management and
    transfer 142–4
  networks of competence 140
  processes for 79, 230–1
  staff participation and
    motivation 141–2
planning cycle 133–5
processes 129–30
  and double cone framework
    120–1, 264–5
  and the Three Ring Circus
    274–5

skills and competences 286
staffing 135–6, 285–6
Three Ring Circus added value
    271–3
see also renewal

questions for uncovering
    Narrative 252–3, 257–8

rapid prototyping 295–6
recruitment 152–4
regulation 19, 27–8, 194
Reich, Robert 28
relationships audit 197
renewal 77
  case studies 79–80, 131–2
  and clarity of purpose 95–6
  and commoditisation 77–9
  cost of specification 81–2
  and double cone framework
    89–93
  five qualities for 107–8, *109*,
    134
  Insight 115–17
  Machinery 119–21, 264–5
  Narrative 111–14
  Options 117–19
  Values 108–11
  Fox and Hedgehog roles 86–91
  and innovation 82–6
  measurement of 77–80
  organisational change 123–4
  organisational weaknesses
    80–1
  portfolio 82, *127*

PS-RO processes 120–1,
129–30, 264–5
and the Three Ring Circus
124–9
see also Purposeful Self-
Renewing Organisation
(PS-RO)
reputation audit 197
research management toolkit
223–5
resources
changes in 78–9
depletion of natural 40–1
respect 111, 171–2, 259
risk avoidance 115–16
risk exposure, use of audits
193–202
risk hedging 19–20
road maps, innovation 225–6

savings 18, 23, 26
Scenario Planning (Ringland) 51,
186, 190
scenarios
case studies 135–6, 189, 204–6,
210, 211, 233–4
communicating future 282–3
creation process 186–7, *188*
interviews & workshops 202
quantifying 208–9
role in generating Options
219–21
source of Insight 176–7
use of in organisations 186–90
visualisation methods 279–82
scientific advances 39–40

scientific management 61–2
'securitisation' 21
security issues 41, 52
senior management
competences 168–71, 293
management of people 224
role of 96–8
time spent on strategy 211
use of Insight 206–8
use of Narrative 244
shareholders 18, 19, 64
Shell 210, 232–3
skills 196, 271, 293–4
see also competence(s)
social networking 223, 276–7
society
cultural differences within 37–8
moral dimensions 36
value systems 35
specialisation 64–5, 285
specification of tasks, cost of 81–2
staffing a PS-RO 135–6, 285–6
stakeholders 155–6, 210–11, 297
StatoilHydro 230–1
SWOT and SOAR 177
'Systems Rationalists' 47–8, 54–6

tacit knowledge 139, 198
team working 64–5, 101–2, 268–9
see also groups
technological changes 39–40, 200
Three Ring Circus 7, *8*, *124*
and double cone framework
124–6
and Insight 209–12, 267–9
processes for connecting 274–5

role in planning
  inner ring (operations)
    125–6, 265
  middle ring (portfolio
    management) 125,
    265–7
  outer ring (Insight) 125,
    267–70
  value added by a PS-RO 271–3
total quality management (TQM)
  63–4
trading, own-account 20–1
'Traditionalists' 47–50, 52, 54–6

uncertainty 44–5, 232
unemployment 17, 25
United States of America (USA)
  consequences of outsourcing
    65–7
  economic performance 16, 17,
    20, 34
  possible evolution of 49–50, 52
  productivity growth and IT 63
  project costs in manufacturing
    81, 82
  role in financial crisis 15–16,
    18, 22–8
  senior managers 97, 211

value systems 35–8, 46–8
Values 108–11
  additional resources 302
  application of core 151–4

and behaviours 167–73, 198–9
case studies 153, 165–6, 168,
  171–2
core values 150–1
and decision making 151–2,
  154
generational differences in
  238
and leadership 161–2, 164–5,
  173
legacy of a PS-RO 173
managing clashes of 165–6
organisational 156–9, 163
origins of 155–7
personal 157–8, 160–2
relationship to other PS-RO
  qualities 6, 107–8, 109
and the Three Ring Circus 154
tools 158, 160–1, 163, 164
unlocking extraordinary
  competence 162–6

weaknesses of organisations
  identification of 144–5, 201–2
  self-perceived 80–1
WonderWeb of Possibility 288–9
workforce 141
  knowledge management 142–4
  multi-skilled 196, 271
  participation and motivation of
    141–2
  in a PS-RO 285–6
workshops 138–9, 190, 202–4, 292

Index compiled by Sophia Clapham